Beginning Helidon

Building Cloud-Native Microservices and Applications

Dmitry Kornilov
Daniel Kec
Dmitry Aleksandrov

Apress®

Beginning Helidon: Building Cloud-Native Microservices and Applications

Dmitry Kornilov
Praha, Czech Republic

Daniel Kec
Praha, Czech Republic

Dmitry Aleksandrov
Sofia, Bulgaria

ISBN-13 (pbk): 978-1-4842-9472-7
https://doi.org/10.1007/978-1-4842-9473-4

ISBN-13 (electronic): 978-1-4842-9473-4

Managing Director, Apress Media LLC: Welmoed Spahr
Acquisitions Editor: James Robinson-Prior
Development Editor: James Markham
Editorial Assistant: Gryffin Winkler
Copyeditor: Kim Burton

Cover designed by eStudioCalamar

Cover image designed by macrovector

Distributed to the book trade worldwide by Springer Science+Business Media New York, 1 New York Plaza, Suite 4600, New York, NY 10004-1562, USA. Phone 1-800-SPRINGER, fax (201) 348-4505, e-mail orders-ny@springer-sbm.com, or visit www.springeronline.com. Apress Media, LLC is a California LLC and the sole member (owner) is Springer Science + Business Media Finance Inc (SSBM Finance Inc). SSBM Finance Inc is a **Delaware** corporation.

For information on translations, please e-mail booktranslations@springernature.com; for reprint, paperback, or audio rights, please e-mail bookpermissions@springernature.com.

Apress titles may be purchased in bulk for academic, corporate, or promotional use. eBook versions and licenses are also available for most titles. For more information, reference our Print and eBook Bulk Sales web page at http://www.apress.com/bulk-sales.

Any source code or other supplementary material referenced by the author in this book is available to readers on the GitHub repository: https://github.com/Apress/Beginning-Helidon. For more detailed information, please visit http://www.apress.com/source-code.

Printed on acid-free paper

This is for my mother.

I miss you...

—Dmitry Kornilov

*To my extraordinary wife, who somehow managed
to put up with my endless late-night writing sessions.
I love you.*

—Daniel Kec

To my parents. They are the real heroes.

—Dmitry Aleksandrov

Table of Contents

About the Authors

Dmitry Kornilov is the Director of Software Development at Oracle. He leads the Helidon project and actively participates in Jakarta EE and MicroProfile communities. Dmitry is an open source enthusiast and speaker who has earned the Star Spec Lead and Outstanding Spec Lead awards.

Daniel Kec is a Java developer at Oracle working on the Helidon project. Daniel has been a Java developer for 15 years and is currently working at Oracle on the Helidon project, which enabled him to tinker with the coolest open source technologies. While working on reactive operators, reactive messaging, and Long Running Actions (LRA) for Helidon was fun, working with Loom features opens another chapter for an otherwise passionate reactive devotee.

ABOUT THE AUTHORS

 **Dmitry Aleksandrov** is a software developer at Oracle and a Java Champion and Oracle Groundbreaker. He is currently working on the Helidon project. He is a co-lead of the Bulgarian Java Users Group and co-organizer of the jPrime conference.

About the Technical Reviewers

 **Tomas Langer** is the architect of the Helidon project. He has been with the project since its inception. In his career, he has always been involved with service development, both hands-on and from an architectural point of view. He has also been in architecture and enterprise architecture roles, focusing on integration, security, and technology.

 **David Kral** is a Java software developer on the Helidon project at Oracle, with more than seven years of experience designing and developing Enterprise Java components and APIs. He is an active open source contributor, mainly to project Helidon, but also contributing to the various related Jakarta EE projects such as JSON-B, Yasson, and Jersey.

Introduction

Helidon is a Java framework for developing cloud-native microservices. Its performance, lightweight approach, and convenient APIs quickly became popular in the Java community. This book is all you need to get started with Helidon, and it will teach you how to use it effectively. It's written by the Helidon developers, who know best how the framework is designed to be used. A significant part of the book is dedicated to MicroProfile APIs and specifications which are explained in detail.

After reading this book, you will be able to do the following.

- Create and consume RESTful services

- Package and deploy your applications to Kubernetes

- Develop observable applications and utilize health checks, metrics, and tracing

- Secure your services using OpenID Connect

- Work with data

- Make your applications resilient

- Understand and use reactive messaging and reactive streams

Who This Book Is For

This book is for developers and architects who want to start developing cloud-native applications using Helidon, for developers interested in developing portable applications using MicroProfile and Jakarta EE, and those who are looking for preparation materials for Oracle Helidon Microservices Developer Professional certification.

Helidon Certification

Oracle announced the Helidon Microservices Developer Professional certification and the corresponding course to prove microservices development skills. The book authors participated in the exam and the course development. The book is designed as an additional preparation material for the certification test. Although the book covers Helidon version 3.x and the exam is created from the previous version of Helidon (2.x), it covers all certification topics, provides additional information, and explains technologies from a different angle.

You can find more information on the official page at `https://mylearn.oracle.com/ou/learning-path/become-a-helidon-microservices-developer-professional/114512`.

What This Book Covers

Chapter 1 introduces Helidon and explains its key advantages. It also discusses two Helidon flavors and explains the differences between them.

Chapter 2 introduces various tools for bootstrapping creating Helidon applications such as Helidon CLI, Project Starter, and Maven Archetypes; explains how to create your first application, build it using different profiles (executable jars, JLink images, and GraalVM native images), create a docker image and deploy it to Kubernetes.

Chapter 3 explains how to configure Helidon applications, introduces MicroProfile Config specification; explains concepts of config sources, defaults, and profiles; demonstrates integration with Kubernetes config maps.

Chapter 4 explains observability and why it's important for microservices, covers concepts of health checks, metrics, tracing, and logging, as well as the corresponding MicroProfile specifications.

Chapter 5 explains how to call other services in your Helidon application. It covers MicroProfile Rest Client and cross-origin resource sharing (CORS).

Chapter 6 explains how to work with databases, query, and update data using JDBC and Jakarta Persistence.

Chapter 7 discusses how to make your application resilient using MicroProfile Fault Tolerance APIs and explains timeout, retry, fallback, bulkhead, and circuit breaker concepts.

Chapter 8 explains how to secure your applications. It covers OpenID Connect and MicroProfile JWT RBAC specifications.

Chapter 9 explains how to document your APIs using OpenAPI and how to automatically generate clients based on it.

Chapter 10 explains how to test your applications using JUnit since Helidon integrates well with this framework.

Chapter 11 explains how you can schedule tasks in your Helidon applications.

Chapter 12 explains how well Helidon is integrated with other technologies like Neo4j, Verrazzano, Coherence CE, and the Kotlin programming language.

Chapter 13 explains how to use some reactive functionality in your Helidon applications. It covers MicroProfile Reactive Stream Operators, MicroProfile Reactive Messaging specifications and integration with Kafka.

Chapter 14 explains how to use distributed transactions in Helidon applications. It covers the Saga pattern and MicroProfile LRA specification.

Chapter 15 introduces Helidon SE - the reactive flavor of Helidon. It guides you through creating the first Helidon SE application, using different build profiles (executable jars, JLink images, GraalVM native images), and deploying it to Kubernetes.

Sample Code

You can access sources of all book samples in the book's official GitHub repository at https://github.com/Apress/Beginning-Helidon.

To compile samples, you need the following tools installed:

- Linux or macOS environment. On Windows we recommend using Windows Subsystem for Linux (WSL).

- JDK 17

- Maven 3.9.0

- Some samples rely on using utilities like cURL

If you found issues with the sample code, please file it in the issues tracker at https://github.com/Apress/Beginning-Helidon/issues.

Preface

About This Book

The cloud era we are living in dictates some requirements for applications. This book is about Helidon—a Java framework designed for developing cloud-native applications. Helidon collects all functionality you need to create cloud-native applications which start fast, has low disk image footprint, and low memory consumption. Helidon supports modern standards such as MicroProfile and partially Jakarta EE, which adds a portability aspect to your application, allowing it to be run on supported runtimes of different vendors.

After reading this book, you will know how to build Java cloud-native applications using Helidon, understand different options for packaging applications to a docker container, and deploy them to Kubernetes. You also learn how to use MicroProfile APIs and Helidon Reactive APIs.

The book contains many useful recipes, best practices, and methodologies around each covered topic. It comes with samples demonstrating the different functionality of Helidon and can be used as a hands-on reference. The information is given in increasing complexity order starting from creating a simple RESTful service and ending up in complicated scenarios with OpenID Connect and distributed transactions.

Prerequisites

You need to know Java language syntax, semantics, and the basics of Java functional programming, including lambda functions.

Some book chapters require some basic understanding of the dependency injection design pattern and Jakarta EE CDI specification.

Some book chapters require understanding reactive programming concepts, including backpressure, observers, and schedulers.

To run samples, you must have JDK 17 and Maven 3.8.4 installed. Samples should run fine with the newer versions of Maven, but we used this version to build them and can guarantee that everything works. The preferred environment is Linux or macOS with a bash shell. We recommend using Windows Subsystem for LInux (WSL) if you use Windows.

CHAPTER 1

Introduction

This chapter covers the following topics.

- Understanding cloud-native application
- Introducing Helidon
- Explaining Helidon flavors
- Discovering which flavor is suitable for your application

We live in a cloud computing era, and it dictates its application design requirements. This book is about building cloud-native applications.

Note   Applications designed to operate in a cloud environment utilizing all cloud benefits are called *cloud native*.

The main benefit of the cloud is the ability to scale applications quickly—something we didn't have when we hosted applications in data centers. For example, in the cloud, you can scale up your application during working hours when it's intensively used and then scale it down for the rest of the time. Another example is testing. You can deploy an extensive testing infrastructure quickly and dispose of it quickly when your testing is finished. In both instances, you are not paying extra for resources you don't need. This makes the cloud environment very cost-efficient when a good application design is used.

So, what makes good cloud-native application design? Well, it depends on what you want to achieve. The most common scenario is using microservices deployed on Kubernetes. Microservices architecture allows you to scale some parts of your application independently. Kubernetes is a de facto standard container management system. It can be deployed on-premises or in the cloud. All big clouds provide managed Kubernetes services. This book does not discuss Kubernetes setup and microservices architecture. Instead, it concentrates on the design of individual services.

And what's the right design for your service? Cloud-native applications have some specific requirements.

- Your application should be containerized. It's a requirement to make it run in a Kubernetes environment.

- Your application should be observable. It should provide some telemetry data to help identify and quickly fix problems. For example, you want to only redirect user requests to a node that has been fully initialized, or you may want to restart a node running out of memory. Or you may want to know which operations take more time to execute for optimization. Observability is not a requirement, but it makes your life much easier.

- Your application should start fast. The sooner you start your node, the sooner it will serve requests. Time is money.

- Your application should consume the least amount of memory possible. In a typical cloud environment, you pay for RAM. The less RAM used, the less you pay.

- Your application disk image footprint should be as small as possible. You pay for disk space. The less disk space used, the less you pay. You are also paying for traffic. The smaller your application, the less traffic is used.

Java EE was an excellent choice for building on-premises, back-end applications for years. While it can be used to build cloud-native applications, it could be better.

It's like using an LTE phone in a 5G network. Will it work? Yes. Will it work fast? Indeed. Will it use all the benefits of 5G? No. Will it work as fast as devices with native 5G support? Certainly not.

There was a need for a new Java framework for building cloud-native applications to compete with Spring Boot. This is why Oracle started working on the Helidon framework.

Introducing Helidon

A product name should reflect its purpose and trigger proper brain associations. "Bulldog" or "Elephant" would not be good names. We wanted a name that could convey something small, lightweight, and fast, like a bird. "Swallow" would be a perfect fit. Wikipedia says it has "a slender, streamlined body and long pointed wings, which allows for great maneuverability and... very efficient flight." Perfect for darting through the clouds. We wanted to know how *swallow* sounded in other languages. In Greek, for example, it's Χελιδόνι. We slightly changed it and proposed Helidon to the team. There were other options, but Helidon was the clear winner.

Here is a one-sentence description: Helidon is a set of Java libraries for developing cloud-native services. This definition is very general, and it is challenging to understand all its nuances. But if someone asks what Helidon is, it's a good answer. It's clear and doesn't include any confusing subatomic and supersonic concepts.

Helidon was designed to achieve the following high-level goals.

- Performance by design

- Cloud-native

- Embrace Java SE

- Compatibility with modern Enterprise Java standards

- Support GraalVM Native Image

The first goal is very clean. The whole Helidon design is done with performance in mind. The core of Helidon is the reactive web server built on top of Netty.

Note   Netty is an asynchronous event-driven network application framework for rapidly developing maintainable high-performance protocol servers and clients. (See more at `https://netty.io`.)

The reactive non-blocking implementation allows Helidon to achieve impressive performance numbers. Oracle's performance tuning team worked closely with us to tune Helidon's performance, and our users are happy with the results.

The cloud-native goal is listed second, but it's a primary goal. Helidon is created as a tool for developing cloud-native applications. It provides a fast start-up time, low memory consumption, a small disk footprint, and all other cloud-native application features listed in the previous section.

The third goal is embracing Java SE. *Embrace* in this context means several things. We are trying to quickly adopt the latest Java versions and use new Java features. For example, Helidon is fully modularized and leverages jlink advantages. We heavily use the Flow API and rely on `java.util.logging`. Another advantage is minimizing the number of third-party dependencies. We do not use third-party libraries if the same functionality is achievable using pure JDK. As a result, we only depend on half of the Internet, and the Helidon application footprint becomes reasonably tiny. Also, it saves time for our corporate customers who need legal approvals for all third-party dependencies used in their applications.

Note   Helidon keeps the number of third-party dependencies low by design.

And the fourth goal is compatibility with modern Enterprise Java standards. There are two standards in the Enterprise Java world now: Jakarta EE and MicroProfile. Helidon fully supports MicroProfile and partially Jakarta EE. Why? Because the standards are reducing entropy. Systems built on standards are portable and highly maintainable. Developers get APIs, and the development experience they are used to, and architects get confidence that the system will be upgradable and supportable. Jakarta EE is a successor of Java EE. It makes Helidon a good choice for migrating old Java EE-based applications to microservices. All supported specifications are covered later in the book.

GraalVM Native Image creates a native executable from your Java application. With GraalVM Native Image, you don't need JVM anymore. Your application will be compiled into one executable file. It starts in milliseconds and consumes less RAM, making it perfect for cloud-native applications, mainly functions. Supporting GraalVM Native Image became a standard feature for modern microservices frameworks like Quarkus and Micronaut. Even Spring, with its runtime nature, now supports it with Spring Native. Helidon is not an exception. It supports the native image in all flavors. Jumping ahead a bit, it's worth mentioning that Helidon makes it possible to use CDI (including portable extensions) with the native image. Other frameworks usually don't support it because of the runtime nature of CDI extensions.

The work that ultimately became Helidon started in 2017, but there were several prototypes before the main design concepts were shaped. The primary focus was made on reactive APIs. It was a popular concept allowing us to achieve excellent performance. It was inspired by Netflix—like most other reactive frameworks at the time. We wanted to create a lightweight set of libraries that didn't require any application server runtime, allowing your application to be a standard Java SE application. These libraries could be used separately from each other, but when used together, they would provide everything a developer needs to create a cloud-native service.

Note   Helidon is an open source product hosted on GitHub at https://github.com/helidon-io/helidon and licensed under the Apache 2.0 license.

The open source model is now the obvious choice for modern frameworks and libraries. It gives users transparency and the ability to check our progress and provide contributions.

Note   Oracle requires all external contributors to sign the Oracle Contributor Agreement (OCA) to get their contributions accepted. It's an easy process. You can find more details about it at https://oca.opensource.oracle.com/.

Helidon Flavors

Helidon *flavors* are different APIs providing different development experiences you can use to develop your application.

For example, imagine that you are playing a computer game. Your goal is to kill the last boss and save the planet. When you start playing, you must choose your character, and you have several options, like warrior or sorcerer. The gaming mechanics of these two are different. Warrior is a melee character with a sword, and a sorcerer uses magic and range attacks. Despite that, you can finish the game and kill the final boss using any of them.

In this example, the *game* is an application you are developing, and the *characters* you choose to play are the different programming approaches you can choose. Helidon offers two characters, called *flavors*.

Note   Helidon has two flavors: Helidon MP and Helidon SE.

To better understand the differences, let's look at two snippets of code. Both implement a simple RESTful service that returns "Hello World" when a Get request is sent to the /hello endpoint.

Listing 1-1 shows how it looks in Helidon MP.

Listing 1-1. Helidon MP Code-Style Sample

```
@Path("hello")
@ApplicationScoped
public class HelloWorld {
    @GET
    public String hello() {
        return "Hello World";
    }
}
```

Listing 1-2 shows how it can be done in Helidon SE.

Listing 1-2. Helidon SE Code-Style Sample

```
Routing routing = Routing.builder()
        .get("/hello", (req, res) -> res.send("Hello World"))
        .build();

WebServer.create(routing)
        .start();
```

The differences are collected in Table 1-1.

Table 1-1. *Helidon Flavors Comparison*

Helidon MP	Helidon SE
Declarative style APIs	Functional style APIs
Blocking, synchronous	Reactive, non-blocking
Small memory footprint	Tiny memory footprint
Annotations are heavily used	No annotations
Jakarta Contexts and Dependency Injection (CDI)	No dependency injection
Full support of MicroProfile and partial support of Jakarta EE	No Enterprise Java standards support

The flavors are a logical consequence of the Helidon design (see Figure 1-1).

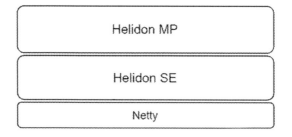

Figure 1-1. *Helidon architecture*

Helidon SE forms a high-performance lower level, and Helidon MP is built on top of it. It explains why both flavors pretty much provide the same functionality. A Helidon feature is implemented in Helidon SE, and a thin adapter layer is built in Helidon MP. It helps to achieve high performance.

Helidon MP

Helidon MP is a flavor that supports modern Enterprise Java standards. It's designed for ease of use and provides a Spring Boot-like development experience with heavy usage of dependency injection, annotations, and other magic. As a drawback, you have less control because the framework does many things automatically. This drawback should not be considered a showstopper. It's a relatively small limitation, but it's still worth mentioning to make this book fair.

Referring to the game sample, Helidon MP is a sorcerer. Magic makes him a powerful opponent. Magical attacks are solid and magical shields are effective. It's easy to play as a sorcerer, even without a complete understanding of the nature of magic.

MODERN ENTERPRISE JAVA STANDARDS

Jakarta EE is a new name for Java EE since it's been transferred to its new home at the Eclipse Foundation. As of this writing, it contained 40 individual and three platform specifications. There are specifications Enterprise Java developers use on almost every single project, such as CDI, JAX-RS, and JSON-P/B, as well as new specifications, such as Jakarta EE Core Profile and Jakarta Config. Jakarta EE is supported by major industry players such as Oracle, IBM, RedHat, Payara, and Tomitribe. Jakarta EE always cared about backward compatibility and stability, making it a perfect fit for enterprise applications. (See more at `https://jakarta.ee`.)

MicroProfile is a collection of open source community-driven specifications designed to help build cloud-native applications using Enterprise Java. It makes it an excellent extension to Jakarta EE. MicroProfile is an Eclipse Foundation project using a specification process derived from Eclipse Foundation Specification Process (EFSP). Unlike Jakarta EE, MicroProfile has a faster release cadence delivering three releases per year: one major and two minor. Fast innovations and staying at the edge of modern technologies often mean breaking backward compatibility. Although preserving backward compatibility is not a goal, MicroProfile tries to minimize the number of backward incompatible changes and follows the semantic versioning model to deliver breaking changes only in major releases. More information can be found on MicroProfile's official web page at `https://microprofile.io`.

As shown in Figure 1-2, Helidon MP supports the whole MicroProfile 5.0 platform, which includes ten specifications and eight Jakarta EE specifications which include Jakarta CDI and Jakarta RESTful Web Services (former JAX-RS). CORS and gRPC are two components not covered by any specifications; they are Helidon-specific.

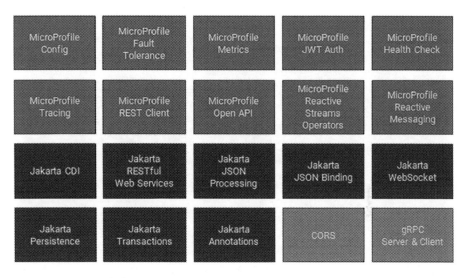

Figure 1-2. Helidon MP components

There are different opinions about what MP in Helidon MP means. Some people think that MP comes from MicroProfile. But there is also another opinion that MP means Magic Powered.

Helidon SE

I already said that Helidon is based on the reactive web server built on Netty. It forms a reactive, non-blocking flavor called *Helidon SE*. Reactive Programming is a big topic that deserves a whole book. It is discussed briefly in Chapter 15.

Helidon SE features APIs based on Java SE Flow API. It intensively uses the Builder pattern, fluent APIs, and lambdas. Neither annotations nor dependency injection is used. We say, "No magic involved." The produced code is very clean, and you have complete control over what the code is doing because the framework doesn't generate any code at a build or run time. It naturally makes Helidon SE a perfect fit for GraalVM Native Image. A drawback is that more coding is required. Also, reactive programming

11

is not easy to use. Is this drawback big? It depends on your programming experience. If you are familiar with reactive programming, it's small. If not, it's bigger.

The reactive web server APIs are inspired by Express. It makes Helidon SE a good choice for JavaScript developers who want to switch to Java.

Note   Express is a fast, unopinionated, minimalist web framework for Node.js. (See more at `https://expressjs.com`.)

Referring to our game example, Helidon SE is a warrior with fast dual-wield short swords and no armor. Light weight allows him to move fast and quickly dodge enemy attacks. With the dual-wield weapon, he can hit his enemy twice as fast. But to use it effectively, you as a player need to know how to play for this character. One wrong move, one slow reaction, and your warrior is dead.

Which Flavor Should You Use?

Note   Your application must be either a Helidon MP application or a Helidon SE application.

You can use Helidon SE functionality in your Helidon MP applications, but not vice versa. It's a consequence of Helidon's design. Helidon SE belongs to a lower layer and isn't aware of Helidon MP's existence. Also, most Helidon MP features require an initialized CDI container which doesn't exist in Helidon SE by design. Referring to my game example, you cannot play with two characters simultaneously. But your sorcerer can use a dagger sometimes when magic is not efficient enough.

A good example of using Helidon SE functionality in Helidon MP is reactive messaging (covered in Chapter 13).

So which flavor should you use in your application? When in doubt, use Helidon MP.

Tip   If you don't know which flavor to use, use Helidon MP.

Table 1-2 is a collection of recommendations.

Table 1-2. *Helidon Flavors Recommendations*

Use Helidon MP	Use Helidon SE
• You don't know what flavor to choose.	• Performance achieved by heavy usage of concurrency is your primary goal.
• You want to use CDI and other MicroProfile or Jakarta EE APIs.	• You want to have complete control of your application.
• You are migrating from the existing Java EE/Jakarta EE application.	• You have experience with reactive programming.
• You are a Spring Boot or Java EE developer and want a similar development experience.	• Your application deals with uploading files.
	• Your application is not CDI based, and you are not planning to use any MicroProfile and Jakarta EE APIs.

This book is mainly about Helidon MP, but Helidon SE is briefly covered in Chapter 15.

Summary

- Applications designed to operate in a cloud environment utilizing all cloud benefits are called *cloud native*.

- Helidon is a set of Java libraries for developing cloud-native services.

- Helidon comes in two flavors: Helidon MP (declarative style APIs implementing MicroProfile and some Jakarta EE specifications) and Helidon SE (reactive, non-blocking APIs).

  If you don't know which flavor to use, use Helidon MP.

CHAPTER 2

Your First Application

This chapter covers the following topics.

- Creating a Helidon application using Project Starter, a command-line interface (CLI), or Maven archetypes

- Building an executable JAR, jlink-optimized JVM, and GraalVM Native Image

- Making a Docker image and deploying it to Kubernetes

This is the first practical chapter offering hands-on coding. It's interesting how book-writing methods have evolved. In the early 1990s, technical books were quite boring to read. The authors didn't care much about making the book entertaining. Studying is work, and work is challenging. Reading books requires thinking about every sentence and understanding the author's words. It was difficult, but it forced your brain to work. Now it's changed. Technical books try to be easy and fun to read while delivering the same amount of pure knowledge. These books are also easier and more fun to write. We want to make our book easy to read; this short introduction is part of "making it fun."

Generating Your First Application

What's the first thing a developer starting with Helidon should do? Create a project and start coding, of course. Let's do that now.

© Dmitry Kornilov, Daniel Kec, Dmitry Aleksandrov 2023
D. Kornilov et al., *Beginning Helidon*, https://doi.org/10.1007/978-1-4842-9473-4_2

Tip   There are three ways to create a new Helidon project: a command-line interface (CLI), Project Starter, or Maven archetypes.

Helidon CLI

Helidon CLI is a command-line utility that simplifies your work with Helidon. Using CLI, you can create a project based on provided templates. It also has a feature called developer loop. When a source code change is detected, it automatically recompiles and restarts your application. We'll take a deeper look at it later. Now, let's install CLI and generate our first project.

First, you must ensure that JDK 17 and the latest version of Maven are installed. To check it, type **java -version** and **mvn -version** in your terminal. You should have an output similar to the following.

```
$ java -version
java version "17.0.2" 2022-01-18 LTS
Java(TM) SE Runtime Environment (build 17.0.2+8-LTS-86)
Java HotSpot(TM) 64-Bit Server VM (build 17.0.2+8-LTS-86, mixed
mode, sharing)
```

```
$ mvn -version
Apache Maven 3.8.6 (84538c9988a25aec085021c365c560670ad80f63)
Maven home: /usr/local/Cellar/maven/3.8.6/libexec
Java version: 18.0.1.1, vendor: Homebrew, runtime: /usr/local/
Cellar/openjdk/18.0.1.1/libexec/openjdk.jdk/Contents/Home
Default locale: en_RU, platform encoding: UTF-8
OS name: "mac os x", version: "12.5", arch: "x86_64",
family: "mac"
```

If not, please install JDK and Maven. Detailed instructions on how to do this can be found on the Internet.

Now, let's install CLI. Installation commands depend on the operating system you are using.

Use the following if you are on macOS.

```
curl -O https://helidon.io/cli/latest/darwin/helidon
chmod +x ./helidon
sudo mv ./helidon /usr/local/bin/
```

Use the following if you are on Linux.

```
curl -O https://helidon.io/cli/latest/linux/helidon
chmod +x ./helidon
sudo mv ./helidon /usr/local/bin/
```

If you are on Windows, you must run PowerShell as administrator and execute the following command.

```
PowerShell -Command Invoke-WebRequest -Uri "https://helidon.io/
cli/latest/windows/helidon.exe" -OutFile "C:\Windows\system32\
helidon.exe"
```

Type **helidon** in your command prompt to test that CLI has been installed. A screen with short instructions should confirm the successful CLI setup.

```
$ helidon

Helidon command line tool

Usage: helidon [OPTIONS] COMMAND

Options

  -D<name>=<value>     Define a system property
  --verbose            Produce verbose output
```

```
  --debug                 Produce debug output
  --plain                 Do not use color or styles in output

Commands

  build                   Build the application
  dev                     Continuous application development
  info                    Print project information
  init                    Generate a new project
  version                 Print version information

Run helidon COMMAND --help for more information on a command.
```

When CLI is installed, it's time to generate your first project and see what's been generated. Use the init command to initiate the process.

```
$ helidon init
```

You are asked questions about a project you want to generate. The first question is about a Helidon flavor to use in your project.

```
| Helidon Flavor

Select a Flavor
  (1) se | Helidon SE
  (2) mp | Helidon MP
Enter selection (default: 1):2
```

You want to use the MP flavor, so type **2** in the command prompt.

The next question is about the type of project to generate.

```
| Application Type

Select an Application Type
  (1) quickstart | Quickstart
  (2) database   | Database
  (3) custom     | Custom
Enter selection (default: 1):1
```

There are three options.

- **Quickstart** generates a Maven project with all dependencies, Dockerfiles, Kubernetes application descriptors, and a simple greeting service application containing a sample of a RESTful service and all needed bootstrap code. If you plan to develop a RESTful service, it's a good option.

- **Database** is the best option if your application works with databases. The generated project contains all needed third-party dependencies, configuration files, and bootstrap code.

- **Custom** offers more choices and allows fine-grained customization of your project. It asks about the media support you want and whether you want to enable metrics, health checks, and tracing. Also, it asks about database support and allows you to choose between Hibernate and EclipseLink.

Let's use the Quickstart template. Type **2** in the command prompt. The next question concerns a JSON library you want to use in your project. There are two options.

- Jackson is a popular library for binding Java classes to JSON objects. It's the default choice.

- JSON-B is Jakarta JSON Binding specification implementation. To be more specific, Yasson is used. Choose this option if you want to be fully standards-compliant.

Let's use JSON-B for this sample application.

```
Select a JSON library
(1) jackson | Jackson
(2) jsonb   | JSON-B
Enter selection (default: 1): 2
```

And the last series of questions is about the Maven coordinates and Java package names to use. Feel free to use defaults for this sample. You should change it to a real application.

```
Project groupId (default: me.dmitry-helidon):
Project artifactId (default: quickstart-mp):
Project version (default: 1.0-SNAPSHOT):
Java package name (default: me.dmitry.mp.quickstart):

Switch directory to /Users/dmitry/quickstart-mp to use CLI

Start development loop? (default: n):
```

Tip   Development Loop is a CLI mode that keeps your application running and observes its source code for changes. When changes are detected, your application is automatically recompiled and restarted.

Use the CLI `helidon dev` command to start the development loop.

You can use batch mode if you want one command to generate your project. In batch mode, you answer all questions in the `init` command parameters.

You can use the following command to generate the same project.

```
helidon init --batch --flavor MP --archetype quickstart
```

A complete list of parameters can be found on the help page for the helidon init command.

helidon init --help

Project Starter

Project Starter is a web application allowing the generation of Helidon projects (see Figure 2-1). It has the same features as the CLI described in the previous section.

To open the Project Starter, open https://helidon.io/starter in your browser or press the Starter button at the top of the Helidon home page at https://helidon.io.

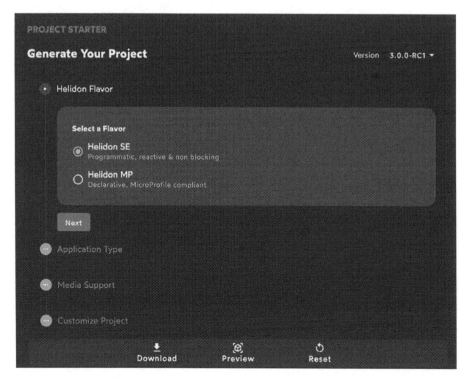

Figure 2-1. *Project Starter*

Project Starter guides you through multiple steps where you should select an option/feature you want to include in your project. The number of steps can vary depending on your previous choices. Still, you can click Download at any stage to fill all unvisited pages with defaults and download a zip file containing the generated project.

Helidon Maven Archetypes

Another method of generating a Helidon project is using Maven archetypes. Helidon provides Maven archetypes for all options offered by CLI.

The following shows how to generate the same Quickstart application using CLI.

```
mvn -U archetype:generate -DinteractiveMode=false \
    -DarchetypeGroupId=io.helidon.archetypes \
    -DarchetypeArtifactId=helidon-quickstart-mp \
    -DarchetypeVersion=3.0.0 \
    -DgroupId=me.dmitry-helidon \
    -DartifactId=quickstart-mp \
    -Dpackage=me.dmitry.mp.quickstart
```

A complete list of Maven archetypes and corresponding CLI options are in Table 2-1.

Table 2-1. *Helidon Maven Archetypes and Corresponding CLI Options*

Maven Archetype	CLI Option	Description
helidon-bare-mp	`--flavor MP` `--archetype bare`	Helidon MP application with minimum dependencies
helidon-quickstart-mp	`--flavor MP` `--archetype quickstart`	Sample Helidon MP project that includes multiple REST operations (greeting service) (It is analyzed later in this chapter.)
helidon-database-mp	`--flavor MP` `--archetype database`	Helidon MP application that uses JPA with in-memory H2 database
helidon-bare-se	`--flavor SE` `--archetype bare`	Minimal Helidon SE project suitable to start from scratch
helidon-quickstart-se	`--flavor SE` `--archetype quickstart`	Sample Helidon SE project that includes multiple REST operations (greeting service)
helidon-database-se	`--flavor SE` `--archetype database`	Helidon SE application that uses Helidon DBClient with in-memory H2 database

Analyzing Generated Project

Quickstart Application

Congratulations! You just created your first Helidon application. This simple but fully functional greeting service can greet the world and a given user. It allows you to customize the greeting, fully supports health checks, metrics, and tracing, uses externalized configuration, and contains a Docker build file and Kubernetes deployment descriptor. It's a great candidate to bootstrap your bigger service.

You can see a full REST API description with invocation samples in Table 2-2.

Table 2-2. *Quickstart Application REST API*

Endpoint	Description and Sample

GET /greet	Greets the world
	`curl -X GET http://localhost:8080/greet`
	`{"message":"Hello World!"}`

GET /greet/{user}	Greets the specified user
	`curl -X GET http://localhost:8080/greet/`
	`Dmitry`
	`{"message":"Hello Dmitry!"}`

PUT /greet/
greeting
	Changes the greeting
	`curl -X PUT -H "Content-Type: application/`
	`json" -d '{"greeting" : "Hola"}' http://`
	`localhost:8080/greet/greeting`
	
	`curl -X GET http://localhost:8080/greet/`
	`Dmitry`
	`{"message":"Hola Dmitry!"}`

GET /health	Health check `curl -s -X GET http://localhost:8080/health`

GET /metrics	Metrics in Prometheus format
	`curl -s -X GET http://localhost:8080/`
	`metrics`
	
	Metrics in JSON format
	`curl -H 'Accept: application/json' -X GET`
	`http://localhost:8080/metrics`

Listing 2-1 shows what's been generated.

Listing 2-1. Generated Quickstart Application Source Code

```
$ tree quickstart-mp/
quickstart-mp
      app.yaml                                              ①
      Dockerfile                                            ②
      Dockerfile.jlink                                      ③
      Dockerfile.native                                     ④
      pom.xml                                               ⑤
      README.md
      src
          main
              java
                  me
                      dmitry
                          mp
                              quickstart
                                  GreetingProvider.java     ⑥
                                  GreetResource.java        ⑦
                                  Message.java
                                  SimpleGreetResource.java
                                  package-info.java
                  resources
                      META-INF
                          beans.xml                         ⑧
                          microprofile-config.properties    ⑨
                          native-image
                              reflect-config.json           ⑩
                      application.yaml
                      logging.properties
```

```
test
    java
        me
            dmitry
                mp
                    quickstart
                        MainTest.java            ⑪
        resources
            application.yaml
```

① Kubernetes deployment descriptor

② Dockerfile to build a Docker image with your application running on standard Java runtime

③ Dockerfile to build a Docker image with your application running on custom Java runtime (jlink image)

④ Dockerfile to build a Docker image with your application's native image

⑤ Maven project

⑥ Application scoped Jakarta Enterprise bean

⑦ JAX-RS resource serving REST requests

⑧ CDI bean archive descriptor

⑨ Configuration properties of the Quickstart project

⑩ Configuration file for fine-tuning GraalVM native image build

⑪ Example JUnit test

This small application includes everything you need to build a fully functional RESTful web service, test it, package it as a Docker image, and deploy it to Kubernetes. This chapter explains how to do it, starting with analyzing the `GreetingResource` class representing a RESTful web service.

Maven Project

The Maven `pom.xml` is created automatically as part of Quickstart application generation. It's clean and straightforward. It can be opened with all IDEs supporting Maven projects. As heavy IntelliJ Idea users (this book is written in IntelliJ!), we can confirm that it opens without problems.

There is only one dependency required to build a MicroProfile application.

```
<dependency>
    <groupId>io.helidon.microprofile.bundles</groupId>
    <artifactId>helidon-microprofile</artifactId>
</dependency>
```

It's a bundle containing all dependencies required by the MicroProfile platform. It makes sense to use it during your application development phase.

If you don't use all MicroProfile features, you can minimize the dependencies, decreasing your application footprint. In this case, you can use the helidon-microprofile-core bundle, which contains only a minimal set of dependencies, and add all other dependencies manually.

```
<dependency>
    <groupId>io.helidon.microprofile.bundles</groupId>
    <artifactId>helidon-microprofile-core</artifactId>
</dependency>
```

CDI

Jakarta Contexts and Dependency Injection (CDI) is a key part of all MicroProfile applications. It wires all components altogether and enables injection in users' applications. Helidon MP is a big CDI container that starts automatically when your application starts.

JAKARTA CONTEXTS AND DEPENDENCY INJECTION (CDI)

CDI is a dependency injection (DI) specification. It's a part of Jakarta EE and used to be a part of Java EE earlier. CDI is heavily annotation based. It allows users to define beans, manage their life cycle using contexts, and inject them to other managed beans using constructor injection, field injection, or setter injection. In addition to that, CDI offers other valuable features such as interceptors, decorators, and event notifications. It's highly customizable and integration-friendly. CDI provides functionality similar to what Spring Dependency Injection (Spring DI) does. There are several CDI implementations on the market. Helidon MP is using Weld (https://weld.cdi-spec.org).

The best way to learn about CDI is to read the specification itself. You can find it here: https://jakarta.ee/specifications/cdi/3.0/jakarta-cdi-spec-3.0.html.

The injection works only with CDI-managed beans. If CDI does not manage your class, you won't be able to inject it.

The easiest way to make your class a CDI-managed bean is to assign it a scope by annotating it with @RequestScoped, @ApplicationScoped, or @Dependent.

A @RequestScoped bean's life cycle is tied to an HTTP request life cycle. It's a singleton per request. A new object is created for each HTTP request and shared with other objects within this request life cycle.

@ApplicationScoped beans are singletons. They are created once and shared with other objects in your application.

A @Dependent bean's life cycle is tied to the bean it is injected into. These beans are not singletons. A new instance is created for every injection point and never shared.

Listing 2-2 shows how the injection is used in our Quickstart application.

Listing 2-2. CDI Usage in GreetingProvider.java

```java
@ApplicationScoped                    ①
public class GreetingProvider {
    ...
    @Inject                           ②
    public GreetingProvider(
      @ConfigProperty(name = "app.greeting") String message) {
        ...
    }
    ...
}
```

① It makes this class a singleton. It's created only once, and this instance gets injected into other objects.

② It's an example of *constructor injection*. A configuration property gets injected into the constructor. The configuration is discussed in Chapter 3.

Listing 2-3. CDI usage in GreetingResource.java

```
@RequestScoped                          ①
public class GreetResource {
    ...
    @Inject                             ②
    public GreetResource(GreetingProvider greetingConfig) {
        ...
    }
    ...
}
```

① This class is instantiated on every HTTP request (different requests == different instances).

② It is another example of *constructor injection.* An instance of GreetingProvider is injected as a constructor parameter. Remember that GreetingProvider is an application scoped, so the same instance is injected when a new instance of GreetResource is created.

Tip   If you need to run some code when your application starts, you can create an observer in one of your managed beans that observes the initialization of the application scope. Initialization of the application scope is exactly when your application starts.

```
void onAppStart(@Observes @Initialized(ApplicationScoped.
class) Object ignoredEvent) {
    ...
}
```

RESTful Web Service

The greeting service is a RESTful web service. Helidon MP is a MicroProfile implementation, and MicroProfile relies on the Jakarta RESTful Web Services specification for creating RESTful services.

JAKARTA RESTFUL WEB SERVICES (JAX-RS)

JAX-RS is a Jakarta EE specification defining APIs to work with web services using the Representational State Transfer (REST) architectural pattern. It's heavily annotation based and well-integrated with CDI. There are many JAX-RS implementations currently on the market. The top three of them are Jersey, RESTeasy, and Apache CXF. Helidon MP is using Jersey.

To learn more about JAX-RS, visit `https://jakarta.ee/specifications/restful-ws`. You can find links to the specification documents there.

JAX-RS uses annotations to configure the request's path (@Path) and HTTP method (@GET, @POST, @PUT, etc.). If the incoming request is matched, the annotated method is executed. There are many possible variations and combinations, so you have a lot of flexibility.

Listing 2-4. JAX-RS Usage in GreetingResource.java

```
@Path("/greet")
@RequestScoped
public class GreetResource {                              ①

    ...
    @GET
    @Produces(MediaType.APPLICATION_JSON)
    public Message getDefaultMessage() {                  ②

        ...
    }
```

31

```
@Path("/{name}")
@GET
@Produces(MediaType.APPLICATION_JSON)                          ③
public Message getMessage(@PathParam("name") String name) {

    ...

}

@Path("/greeting")
@PUT
@Consumes(MediaType.APPLICATION_JSON)
@Produces(MediaType.APPLICATION_JSON)
@RequestBody(...)
@APIResponses(...)
public Response updateGreeting(Message jsonObject) {  ④

    ...

}
...
}
```

① This is the request scoped CDI bean serving
   requests on the /greet URI.

② This method is invoked on the GET /greet
   endpoint and returns JSON.

③ This method is invoked on the GET /greet/
   {name} endpoints and returns JSON. Valid URIs
   include /greet/Dmitry, /greet/Daniel.

④ This method is invoked on the PUT /greet/
   greeting endpoint. It returns and consumes
   JSON. It also contains two OpenAPI annotations
   for REST API documentation: @RequestBody and
   @APIResponses. OpenAPI is covered in Chapter 9.

Build and Run

To build the project, you must change the directory to where your pom.xml is located and run this command.

mvn package

Tip   You can also build your project with the CLI helidon build command.

Helidon builds an *executable JAR* by default. The different packaging options are discussed later on in this chapter. For now, it's important to know that the JAR is located at target/quickstart-mp.jar and it's executable. Let's run it.

```
$ java -jar target/quickstart-mp.jar
```

When the server starts, you can find interesting information in the output, like which port it runs on or which features are active.

```
... Server started on http://localhost:8080 (and all other host
addresses) in 1742 milliseconds (since JVM startup).
... Helidon MP 3.0.0 features: [CDI, Config, Health, JAX-RS,
Metrics, Open API, Server]
```

Now let's trigger some greeting application endpoints to see that the application is appropriately functioning. You need to keep the server running, so you must open another terminal window or tab.

Let's test the default greeting first.

```
$ curl -X GET localhost:8080/greet
{"message":"Hello World!"}
```

The following is the personalized greeting.

```
$ curl -X GET localhost:8080/greet/Reader
{"message":"Hello Reader!"}
```

You also try to change the greeting. The curl command is listed in Table 2-2.

Packaging

A Helidon application has three package options.

- An **executable JAR** is the default packaging for Java applications, optimized for Docker layers.

- A **jlink image** is a custom Java Runtime Environment (JRE) with just the modules the application requires.

- A **native image** is a binary natively compiled executable for lightning-quick startup.

Executable JAR

An executable JAR file is the default packaging when building a project using Maven. It's activated if no additional profiles are specified.

```
mvn package
```

Tip   You can also build your project with the CLI helidon build command.

We use the *Hollow JAR* approach. It means that the JAR file contains only your application code. All third-party runtime dependencies are collected in the lib subdirectory of the directory where the application JAR is produced.

In our Quickstart application, the JAR is built in the target directory, and all third-party dependencies are collected in target/libs.

The Hollow JAR approach works very well with Docker layering. A Dockerfile (automatically generated as part of the project creation) creates a separate layer for the application JAR, and all application dependencies are stored in the libs directory. Despite the application, dependencies are not changing often, allowing the layer to build once and not rebuild every time a Docker image is created. Also, a layer with the application becomes very small, which helps reduce network traffic and the application deployment time.

To build the Docker image, run the following command.

```
docker build -t quickstart-mp .
```

It creates a quickstart-mp Docker image. To run it, use the following command.

```
docker run --rm -p 8080:8080 quickstart-mp:latest
```

jlink Image

JRE distribution is quite big. Your application most probably is not using all Java features. There is a way to create a custom (smaller) Java runtime image that includes only your application's functionality. It can be done using the jlink utility, which is included in JDK.

Warning   Not all Java distributions provide JDK modules needed for custom JRE generation. Before using the Helidon JLink profile, ensure these modules are present by running `ls $JAVA_HOME/jmods`. If nothing is listed, you don't have it installed. RPM-based distributions provide `*.jmod` files in separate `java-*-openjdk-jmods` packages. Debian-based distributions only provide `*.jmod` files in the `openjdk-*-jdk-headless` packages.

Helidon provides a special build profile to simplify working with it. It uses Java Platform Module System (JPMS) and some advanced analysis to make it work even with automatic modules, which is not the case by default. You can invoke it using the following command.

```
mvn package -Pjlink-image
```

Tip   You can also build a jlink image using CLI: `helidon build --mode JLINK`.

The result of executing this command is the `target/quickstart-mp-jri` directory. It contains a self-contained custom image of your application, including your application itself, its runtime dependencies, and the JDK modules it depends on. You can start it using the following command.

```
./target/quickstart-mp-jri/bin/start
```

The image also includes a class data sharing (CDS) archive, which improves startup performance and in-memory footprint but doesn't improve the disk footprint. It increases it to get these performance optimizations. The increase can be significant—many megabytes. The size of the CDS archive is always reported at the end of the build output.

Helidon provides an option to disable CDS archive creation. It makes sense if your goal is to keep the disk footprint as small as possible.

```
mvn package -Pjlink-image -Djlink.image.addClassDataSharingArc
hive=false
```

To build a Docker image containing your custom JRE, use the Dockerfile.jlink included with the Quickstart.

```
docker build -t quickstart-mp-jri -f Dockerfile.jlink .
```

This does a full build inside the Docker container. It might take time to download some Maven dependencies. When finished, you will have a quickstart-mp-jri Docker image in your local Docker repository.

The following starts the application.

```
docker run --rm -p 8080:8080 quickstart-mp-jri:latest
```

Native Image

When you run your Java application, you must install the Java Runtime Environment (JRE). Your application is compiled to a byte code which is executable by JRE. JRE is a native application on a platform you are using. There are versions for Linux, Windows, macOS, and other operating systems.

GraalVM is a Java runtime that comes with many additional features. One of these features is the ability to compile Java byte code into a native executable. This feature is called Native Image.

There are several advantages users get when they use native images.

- Native applications start almost instantly.

- Disk footprint is smaller than JRE plus your compiled application. Also, it's just one file that is simple to transfer.

- Memory footprint is also lower as much metadata is not needed at runtime for fully native code.

37

These advantages don't come for free. There are also some limitations.

- GraalVM native compiler must know about all invocations of functionality allowing you to read or modify class information at run time. It includes all usages of Reflection API, byte code manipulations, and usages of `sun.misc.Unsafe`, and so on. It can complicate your work, especially if this functionality is used in third-party dependencies needed by your application.

- It takes significant time to build.

- Native image is compiled statically and doesn't use any runtime optimizations. For long-running services, it may make more sense to use HotSpot VM, which optimizes your application at run time. With these optimizations, your application will eventually overperform the same application running as a native image.

Helidon supports two approaches to building a native image.

- Local build using locally installed GraalVM

- Using Docker

Local Native Image Build

This approach uses locally installed GraalVM. Before building, you need to ensure that GraalVM and native image components are installed and the `GRAALVM_HOME` variable points to the `Contents/Home/` directory inside your GraalVM installation. It should be something like the following.

```
export GRAALVM_HOME=/opt/graalvm-ce-21.3.0/Contents/Home/
```

To verify that GraalVM is installed correctly, run the following command.

```
$GRAALVM_HOME/bin/native-image --version
```

It should display the GraalVM version. If it doesn't, you must play more with your GraalVM installation.

Now let's build a native image.

```
mvn package -Pnative-image
```

Tip   You can also build a native image using CLI: `helidon build --mode NATIVE`.

The build may take several minutes. When finished, you can find your native executable in the `target` directory and run it as you usually run native applications.

```
./target/quickstart-mp
```

Docker Native Image Build

This method builds a native image inside a Docker container. The result is a Docker image based on *scratch* with just the native binary. You don't need to install GraalVM locally, but you need to have Docker installed.

To build it, run the following command.

```
docker build -t quickstart-mp-native -f Dockerfile.native .
```

The first time you run it, it takes a while because it downloads all the Maven dependencies and caches them in a Docker layer. Subsequent builds are much faster.

The build result is the `quickstart-mp-native` Docker image. You can verify it using the `docker images` command.

```
$ sudo docker images
REPOSITORY              TAG       IMAGE ID        CREATED         SIZE
quickstart-mp-native    latest    18a7c74dd257    47 seconds ago  95.6MB
```

Start your native application in Docker using the following command.

```
docker run --rm -p 8080:8080 quickstart-mp-native:latest
```

Deploying to Kubernetes

Now let's look at deploying your application to Kubernetes. If you don't have a cloud Kubernetes cluster, you can install minikube or Docker Desktop on your local computer. It would be enough for deploying our Quickstart application.

Kubernetes deployment descriptor `app.yaml` was generated as part of the project creation. So now, all you have to do is deploy your application.

First, let's make sure that your cluster is up and running.

```
kubectl cluster-info
kubectl get nodes
```

If you see any errors on the screen, your cluster is not functional. You need to spend some time fixing it.

Now let's ensure you've built a Docker image containing your application.

```
docker images
```

Make sure that `quickstart-mp` exists in the command output. If not, you should build your Docker image as described in the "Executable JAR" section.

Tip   If you want to deploy jlink or native image containers, change the `image` property in `app.yaml` to `quickstart-mp-jri` or `quickstart-mp-native` accordingly.

Run the following to deploy your application.

```
kubectl create -f app.yaml
```

Deployment may take some time, but it shouldn't take much. Keep executing `kubectl get pods` until you see the `quickstart-mp` pod status as RUNNING.

You need to find the port it's running on to test that the application is functional. Look at the result of the following command; note the PORT(S). The second port number is what you need to use.

```
kubectl get service quickstart-mp
NAME            TYPE       CLUSTER-IP      EXTERNAL-IP  PORT(S)          AGE
quickstart-mp NodePort 10.108.202.98 <none>          8080:30324/TCP  3m50s
```

For example, if the port is 30324, run the following command.

```
curl -X GET http://localhost:30324/greet
```

To remove your application from Kubernetes, run the following command.

```
kubectl delete -f app.yaml
```

Summary

- Helidon provides a convenient way to bootstrap your application using Project Starter, CLI, and Maven Archetypes.

- You can build an executable JAR, custom jlink image, and GraalVM Native Image.

- Helidon MP application is CDI-ready.

- Building a Docker image containing your application is easy, thanks to the provided Dockerfiles.

- Kubernetes deployment descriptor is generated automatically on project creation.

CHAPTER 3

Configuration

This chapter covers the following topics.

- Using MicroProfile Config in Helidon-based microservices
- Understanding the concept of config sources
- Integrating with Kubernetes config maps
- Configuring arrays or collections
- Using defaults, profiles, and expressions

Your microservice needs to be configurable. Why? Because any deployment depending on hard-coded values makes your service non-portable. Imagine a character from the sorcerer game. When you want to send him for a quest, you equip him with various potions and weapons most suitable for the quest he is being sent for. But if you couldn't? If the sorcerer has hard-coded inventory, he is probably only good for some quests. It's the same with a well configurable service; you can deploy it anywhere without rebuilding and repackaging it just because the name of the database differs. And what would you do when moving your service from the test environment to production? You would not want to rebuild the application just to change connection credentials, right? Java has its own tooling for configuration. You know about `System.getProperties()` and `System.getenv()`. These properties are a great way for providing configuration over the command line.

© Dmitry Kornilov, Daniel Kec, Dmitry Aleksandrov 2023
D. Kornilov et al., *Beginning Helidon*, https://doi.org/10.1007/978-1-4842-9473-4_3

By invoking the Java application with `java -DorcSlayingPotions=5 -jar mySorcerer.jar`, you can set the property and retrieve the value inside the application with the simple call `System.getProperty("orc SlayingPotions")`. It works great until you want it to do more, such as overriding the default values, resolving placeholders, or switching quickly, based on the environment profile. But what if there is a tool to do that, which can map your properties to the right type and inject them where you need them the most? Let's introduce you to the Helidon MicroProfile configuration implementation. Let's call it "Config" from now on. It's used by many other Helidon features and is mentioned quite often later in this book.

As Helidon MP provides CDI, you can effortlessly inject the config properties directly into your beans; no special setup is required.

Listing 3-1. Default Value Definition with the @ConfigProperty Annotation

```
@ApplicationScoped
public class SorcererBean {
    @Inject
    public SorcererBean(
        @ConfigProperty(name="sorcerer.orcSlayingPotions",
                        defaultValue = "0")    ①
        Integer orcSlayingPotions){            ②
```

① The default values are always defined as strings. The converter used for values coming from a config source is also applied to defaults.

② This injects the config property to the bean constructor with CDI.

If you inject the property without providing a default value and if the property is not found in any of the available config sources, the NoSuchElementException error is thrown during deployment. But don't worry, for optional properties, you can use one of the following nullable data types.

- org.eclipse.microprofile.config.ConfigValue
- Optional<TheType>

Expressions

Sometimes, the same value needs to be used by several configuration properties or compiled from several others. In such cases, expressions become helpful for composing property values from other property values. Expressions help you avoid duplicities in the configuration and define context related defaults.

Listing 3-2. Expression with a Default Value in a Properties File

```
sorcerer.level=30
sorcerer.name=Merlin
sorcerer.title=${sorcerer.name}_${sorcerer.level:15}    ①
```

① Notice the default value of 15 for the sorcerer.
level expression.

In Listing 3-2, the sorcerer's title is Merlin_30. However, if the sorcerer.level property is missing, the default expression value is used, and the title becomes Merlin_15. Expressions are extremely handy for composing database connection strings or JAAS configs directly in a config file.

Programmatic API

When CDI injection is not available, programmatic API saves the day. All the goodness works the same way as with the injected config properties. You can access `org.eclipse.microprofile.config.Config` as a singleton.

Listing 3-3. Obtaining a Configuration Property over the Programmatic API

```
Integer orcSlayingPotions =
   ConfigProvider.getConfig()
      .getValue("sorcerer.orcSlayingPotions", Integer.class);
```

Or, simply inject the config to your bean with `@Inject Config`. This method allows you to manually access the available properties from all config sources. And what is that Config source? That is the place where property values come from!

Config Sources

The first thing MicroProfile Config does is it looks for the available config sources. Config sources provide properties that are retrievable in your application. Each config source has a special ordinal number that defines the order in which a property is resolved. If the config sources contain the same property, the one with the higher ordinal number is used. This feature provides an elegant way to override the properties when required. The following three default config sources are defined by the specification.

- All `META-INF/microprofile-config.properties` files on the classpath with the default priority ordinal number 100.

- Environment variables with the default priority ordinal number 300 override the same properties in the property files. The environment variable key names are not case-sensitive, non-alphanumeric, and interchangeable with underscores. For example, the SORCERER_ORCSLAYINGPOTIONS key is resolved when sorcerer.orcSlayingPotions has no candidate in environment variables.

- System properties (our -Dsorcerer. orcSlayingPotions=5 also works here and has a default priority ordinal number 400). So, it overrides the same properties from all the other default config sources.

Figure 3-1 shows that multiple default config sources supply the sorcerer.orcSlayingPotions property with different values. You already know that the property from the config source with the highest ordinal is injected. In our example, SorcererBean gets five orcSlayingPotions, no invisibility cloak, and as weapons—an axe and a sword. Properties from all the config sources are merged, and duplicities are resolved according to the source ordinal.

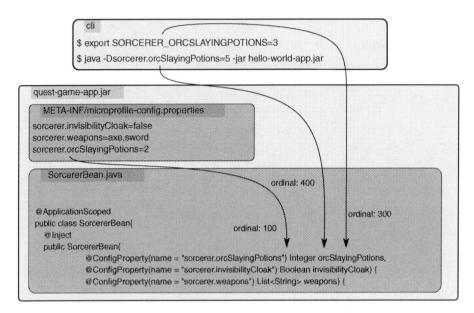

Figure 3-1. *Injecting config properties from various config sources with priority expressed by ordinals. The property with the same key from the config source with the highest ordinal is injected*

Priorities of the default config sources aren't set in stone. You can change the priority from within with a special config key `config_ordinal`. For example, if you need to add another JAR on the classpath with the properties file overriding the one in the main JAR, you can make the file's priority higher with the help of this special key, like this: `config_ordinal=105`.

Looking at the weapons configuration in Figure 3-1, you quickly recognize an array. By default, arrays are delimited with commas. A config array can be injected as a list, set, or an array of the desired type.

Listing 3-4. Configuration Properties Injected into a Bean
Constructor

```
@Inject
public SorcererBean(
        @ConfigProperty(name="sorcerer.weapons")
        String[] weaponsArray,    ①
        @ConfigProperty(name="sorcerer.weapons")
        List<String> weaponsList,    ②
        @ConfigProperty(name="sorcerer.weapons")
        Set<String> weaponsSet{    ③
```

① Weapons injected as an array

② A list of strings

③ A set of strings

Converters

Every config value is treated as plain text and converted to the desired type
by a set of built-in and custom converters, no matter from which config
source the value is loaded. The converter is selected according to the target
property type, as shown in Figure 3-2.

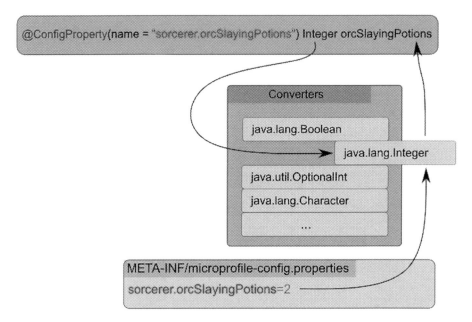

Figure 3-2. *The converter for parsing the text value of a given property is selected by the type of the injection point*

The built-in converters cover all the basic types you can think of—numbers, boolean values, characters, class references, dates, and patterns.

- Boolean: `true`, `1`, `YES`, `Y`, and `ON` are converted as `true`; all other values as `false`.

- Numbers: Basically, all primitive and boxed Java types that represent numbers are supported; a dot is parsed as a decimal separator.

- Date and Time: `LocalDate`, `Duration`, `Period`, `Instant`, and many other types are supported.

- Others: `Path`, `File`, `URL`, `URI`, `Charset`, `Pattern`, and many other types are supported.

Is that enough? Because you have just started!

Automatic Converter

Any custom type can be automatically converted with the automatic converter, if the custom type provides one of the following:

- Has the method `public static T of(String val)`

- Has the method `public static T valueOf(String val)`

- Has the method `public static T parse(CharSequence val)`

- Has a public constructor with a single `String` parameter

An automatic converter is applied if no custom converter is registered for the custom type.

Aggregated Properties

You can group properties logically. It is easier to understand and work with such a configuration. In the case of config files with a flat structure, such as the properties file, you can achieve grouping based on a common prefix.

Listing 3-5. Properties with a Common Prefix

```
sorcerer.orcSlayingPotions=68
sorcerer.invisibilityCloak=false
sorcerer.weapons=axe,sword
```

Grouping is much easier in tree-structured formats such as YAML. Let's use the word *readable* but stay neutral in the never-ending YAML flame war.

Listing 3-6. YAML Properties with a Common Prefix

```
sorcerer:
  orcSlayingPotions: 68
  invisibilityCloak: false
  weapons: axe,sword
```

Injecting such grouped properties one by one adds quite a clutter to our Orc slaying business code.

Listing 3-7. Injection of Each Separate Property To a Bean Constructor

```
@Inject
public SorcererBean(
    @ConfigProperty(name="sorcerer.orcSlayingPotions")
    int potions,
    @ConfigProperty(name="sorcerer.invisibilityCloak")
    boolean cloak,
    @ConfigProperty(name="sorcerer.weapons")
    List<String> weapons)
```

In this code, you would group such properties under the same Java object anyway; something such as SorcererProperties sounds nice. You can leave the work of filling the properties in the object to the config.

Listing 3-8. Properties with a Common Prefix Grouped to a Common Bean

```
@ConfigProperties(prefix="sorcerer")
public class SorcererProperties {
 @ConfigProperty(name="orcSlayingPotions") int potions;
 boolean cloak;
 List<String> weapons;
}
```

Notice the CDI config bean; the property names are derived from the field names unless overridden with annotations. Our `SorcererProperties` can be injected as if it was a standard CDI bean, so you can inject it wherever you want and access all the grouped properties inside.

Listing 3-9. Properties Bean Injected to a Bean Constructor

```
@Inject
public SorcererBean(@ConfigProperties SorcererProperties
  sorcererProperties)
```

Custom Converter

If all the converters mentioned until now don't solve your use case, you can still create your own custom Config converter and register it over the service locator.

You can create a converter to convert JSON, which is saved as a property value. Let's say that in our example, Orcs are configured in such a way.

Listing 3-10. Property with a Raw JSON Value

```
app.jsonOrc={"orcName":"Scullcrack", "level":"34"}
```

But you would like to inject the property value as `jakarta.json.JsonObject` directly, so our business code doesn't get cluttered with all the JSON parsing. Let's create a custom converter for this purpose; it's just a class implementing `org.eclipse.microprofile.config.spi.Converter`.

Listing 3-11. Custom JSON Converter for Parsing Properties with JSON as the Value

```
@Priority(101)    ①
public class JsonConverter implements Converter<JsonObject>{

    private static final JsonReaderFactory JSON =
            Json.createReaderFactory(Collections.emptyMap());

    @Override
    public JsonObject convert(String value) {
        return JSON.createReader(new StringReader(value))
                .readObject();
    }
}
```

    ① If multiple converters for the same type are
       available, the one with the highest priority is used;
       100 is the default priority.

Note   A converter gets registered as a service provider. If you are working on a classpath-based project, create a provider-configuration file with `my.package.JsonConverter` as its content.

`META-INF/services/org.eclipse.microprofile.config.spi.Converter`

Config runtime finds your converter over the service loader facility.

Don't forget to use `module-info.java` when registering a service provider in a JPMS module-based project. Just add the `provides org.eclipse.microprofile.config.spi.Converter` with `my.package.JsonConverter;` clause to `module-info.java`.

You can test our brand-new custom converter directly within the JAX-RS resource. You can see how easy it is to inject our converted value directly where needed.

Listing 3-12. JAX-RS Resource with the Directly Injected Converted Property

```
@Path("/jsonOrc")
public class OrcResource {

    private JsonObject jsonOrc;

    @Inject
    public OrcResource(@ConfigProperty(name = "app.jsonOrc")
                       JsonObject jsonOrc) {
        this.jsonOrc=jsonOrc;
    }

    @GET
    @Produces(MediaType.APPLICATION_JSON)
    public JsonObject getJsonOrc() {
        return jsonOrc;
    }
}
```

Configuration converters are powerful tools for keeping the boilerplate configuration code cleanly separated from the sorcerer business.

Profiles

Production or not that is the question! It's quite a typical situation when you have the test environment and production one.

Do you remember the Dieselgate emissions scandal? It's a good example of a configuration profile. The car control units have been programmed to operate the engines with lower emissions when tested in the laboratory. For the control units, a whole set of parameters had to change depending on whether the car was in the laboratory or on the highway. Let's try to achieve that with Helidon Config.

The first thing is setting the profile itself with the `mp.config.profile` property. You can set the property over any of the used config sources. For example, as an environment variable `export MP_CONFIG_PROFILE=TEST` or use the `-Dmp.config.profile=TEST` property.

Listing 3-13. Running Helidon with Profile TEST

```
java -Dmp.config.profile=TEST -jar myCarControlUnit.jar
```

Config profiles can be used at the Config source level by switching whole configuration files or at the property level using prefixed properties.

Property Level

At the property level, the property prefixed with % followed by the profile name gets precedence over the other properties with the same key.

Listing 3-14. Properties Specific for a Given Profile

```
%PROD.engine.emission.control=false     ①
%TEST.engine.emission.control=true      ②
engine.emission.control=false           ③
```

① `false` wins if the `PROD` profile is active

② `true` wins if the `TEST` profile is active

③ `false` wins if there is no active profile

Config Source Level

At the Config source level, whole config files are included if the file name matches the selected profile. If the config file `microprofile-config-<PROFILE NAME>.properties` exists on the classpath in the `META-INF` folder and the proper profile is active, the properties are merged. When the same properties are present in both files, values from the file with an active profile in its name take precedence.

Listing 3-15. Property file specific for a given profile

```
META-INF/
        microprofile-config.properties
        microprofile-config-TEST.properties
```

But let's get back to our example of the Orc hunting adventure. You may decide to deploy our already built game artifact with a different config source setup. For that, you need something more powerful: meta configuration.

Meta Configuration

Configuration files packed inside your JAR file are practically immutable. All your settings in those config sources are written in stone. You can override its values with system properties or environment variables, but you must rely on the priorities already defined somewhere deep in your JAR package. Helidon has an extra feature for redefining configuration

outside the artifact, called the meta configuration. It's one place to
configure the config sources in the way you want, which overrides
any existing implicit or explicit setting except the one created with the
programmatic API.

Note   This is a Helidon-specific feature.

After the mp-meta-config.yaml or the mp-meta-config.properties
file is found on the classpath, in the current directory, or discovered in
an externally specified location, configuration sources are organized
according to it. You can specify the location of the meta config file either
with the io.helidon.config.mp.meta-config property or the HELIDON_
MP_META_CONFIG environment variable.

Meta configuration supports YAML and the properties file formats.
Let's take a look at the YAML example mp-meta-config.yaml.

Listing 3-16. Meta Configuration

```
add-discovered-sources: true    ①
add-discovered-converters: true
add-default-sources: true

sources:
  - type: "environment-variables"
  - type: "system-properties"
  - type: "properties"             ②
    classpath: "weapons.properties"
    ordinal: 50                    ③
    optional: true
  - type: "yaml"
    path: "/config/orc-army.yaml"
```

① Include or exclude implicit sources or converters.

② Explicitly define the sources.

③ Define the config source priority.

You can change the priority ordinals and choose to use the default sources or the custom sources. Even excluding custom converters or adding some optional config sources is possible.

YAML Config Source

On top of the built-in config sources mandated by the MP specification, Helidon provides other convenient config sources. For example, loved by many and cursed by many others: the YAML configuration.

Note   This is a Helidon-specific feature.

Unlike with the MP default property file, Helidon looks for files named `application.yaml` in the root of the classpath. The default priority 200 overrides the properties in the MP default property file but gets overridden by the system properties and the environment variables.

Listing 3-17. YAML Configuration File

```
sorcerer:
  invisibilityCloak: false
  orcSlayingPotions: 2
  weapons:
    - "axe"
    - "sword"
```

The *sequences* feature is the most notable in the YAML format when you compare it with properties. You can express sequences in YAML either in the flow style or the block style.

Listing 3-18. Sequence Styles in YAML Files

```
amulets: ["Hearth of Zeard", "Spider's eye"]    ①
weapons:      ②
  - "axe"
  - "sword"
```

① Flow style sequence

② Block style sequence

The Helidon YAML config source maps sequences as a config array. Even though all config sources can also declare arrays with comma-separated values, you can still declare an array with a simple text value: weapons: "axe,sword".

The YAML null value is converted as a missing property. The NoSuchElementException is thrown when such a property is injected directly. This feature aligns nicely with the default properties config source, which can define a null value only with a missing property or an empty value.

Listing 3-19. Empty Property in YAML File

```
sorcerer.invisibilityCloak=    ①
#sorcerer.invisibilityCloak=2
```

① There is no null in the properties file. An empty value or a missing property behaves like a null value.

Listing 3-20. Null Property in YAML File

```
sorcerer:
  invisibilityCloak: null    ①
  orcSlayingPotions:
  #ghoulSlayingPotions: 2
```

① YAML has a special `null` value

But remember, you can always specify the default value or inject optional `@ConfigProperty(name = "sorcerer.invisibilityCloak")` `Optional<Boolean> cloak`, and then decide what to do with the null during runtime.

To use the YAML config source, you need the following dependency, which is already part of the Helidon MicroProfile bundle.

Listing 3-21. Maven Dependency for the YAML Configuration Support

```
<depencency>
  <groupId>io.helidon.config</groupId>
  <artifactId>helidon-config-yaml-mp</artifactId>
</depencency>
```

Custom Config Source

There is always a use case when YAML or properties are just not enough. Whether you need to get your configuration from some exotic database, a super secure binary file, or a very complicated XML document, you can always create your own config source. This new config source only needs to provide the property values based on the key, a list of available keys, an ordinal number for priority resolution, and the config source name. All the logic can fit in one class implementing a single interface `org.eclipse.microprofile.config.spi.ConfigSource`.

61

Let's try it with a simple config source providing entries of the hard-coded map as configuration properties. To make it more interesting, set one of the properties as a JSON value, so let's try our config source with the custom JsonConverter created earlier in this chapter.

Listing 3-22. Custom Config Source

```java
public class CustomConfigSource implements ConfigSource {
    private static final Map<String, String> props = Map.of(
            "sorcerer.orcSlayingPotions", "55",
            "app.jsonOrc",
            """
            {"orcName":"Bonecrash", "level":"28"}
            """
    );
    @Override
    public int getOrdinal() {return 105;}    ①
    @Override
    public Set<String> getPropertyNames() {
        return props.keySet();
    }
    @Override
    public String getValue(String key) {
        return props.get(key);
    }
    @Override
    public String getName() {
        return "custom-sorcerer-map";    ②
    }
}
```

① Priority of the new custom config source.

② Source name used by the ordering logic.

The process of registration is very similar to that used for custom converters. You need to register our implementation as a service provider.

Note   If you are working on a classpath-based project, create the provider-configuration file with `my.package.CustomConfigSource` as its content.

`META-INF/services/org.eclipse.microprofile.config.spi.ConfigSource`

The config runtime finds your converter over the service loader facility.

Don't forget to use `module-info.java` when registering a service provider in a JPMS module-based project. Just add the `provides` clause to `module-info.java`.

`provides org.eclipse.microprofile.config.spi.ConfigSource with my.package.CustomConfigSource;`

Dynamic Config Source

So far, you have looked at configuration as it is an immutable data source. The only way to re-inject your config property with a new value would be to restart the Helidon application. But config sources can provide mutable properties. Most of the built-in file-based config sources support mutability. With the file-based config sources, you can use a built-in change watcher or polling with custom intervals.

You can try out the dynamic config source with the custom `JsonConverter` created earlier so you know for sure it all works together nicely. First, let's create a configuration file on the file system.

Listing 3-23. Dynamically Loaded Configuration

```
helidon.config.watcher.enabled: true    ①
app.jsonOrc: '{"orcName":"Scullcrack", "level":"37"}'    ②
```

> ① The dynamic source needs to register a watcher or
> use polling. When it is first loaded, use a change
> watcher.

> ② The `app.jsonOrc` property requires a conversion
> with the custom converter.

As the dynamic config file is somewhere on the file system, you must register it with meta config, so Helidon knows where to look for it. Let's create the `mp-meta-config.yaml` file in the working directory.

Listing 3-24. Meta Configuration for the Dynamic Config Source

```
add-discovered-converters: true    ①
sources:
- type: "yaml"
  path: "./dynamic-config.yaml"    ②
  optional: false
```

> ① Uses the custom JsonConverter

> ② The path to the dynamically changing config file

Now, you just need to inject the config value. However, injection is done only once in a singleton bean, right? It's not very practical for a dynamically changing configuration. You have to inject `java.util.function.Supplier` instead of the actual value.

Listing 3-25. Injecting a Dynamically Loaded Configuration Property

```
@ConfigProperty(name = "app.jsonOrc")
Supplier<JsonObject> jsonOrc
```

This way, you can get the actual value each time you call `jsonOrc.get()`. The change watcher reloads the config source each time it changes, and new values are cached. There is no need to worry about supplier invocation reading the file each time. The second possibility is polling. You can just configure the interval you want the config source to reload.

Listing 3-26. Dynamically Polled Configuration

```
helidon.config.polling.enabled: true     ①
helidon.config.polling.duration: PT5S     ②
app.jsonOrc: '{"orcName":"Scullcrack", "level":"37"}'
```

① Use polling for dynamic source reloading.

② Poll every five seconds. The duration is expressed in the ISO-8601 format.

The properties used for enabling change watching or polling are not dynamically interpreted, despite being a part of the dynamically reloaded config. You can't change the polling interval dynamically.

Note   While the dynamic config sources are part of the MicroProfile specification, polling and change watching are Helidon features.

Kubernetes ConfigMap

Kubernetes ConfigMap is a convenient tool for distributing configuration in the Kubernetes cluster. Properties from the ConfigMap can be made accessible from the pod by mapping them to the container environment variables or mounting them as configuration files directly to the file system.

Environment Variables

The easiest way to propagate Kubernetes ConfigMap to your application is over environment variables. As Helidon Config uses these variables as a default config source, you do practically nothing from the application side. Kubernetes maps to the pod's OS level, and Helidon Config takes over from there.

Listing 3-27. K8s ConfigMap Propagated to Helidon As Environment Variables

```
apiVersion: v1
kind: ConfigMap
metadata:
  name: my-sorcerer-config
data:
  SORCERER_ORCSLAYINGPOTIONS: 68    ①
  APP_JSONORC: '{"orcName":"Sharpteeth","level":"22"}'    ②
---
apiVersion: v1
kind: Pod
metadata:
  name: my-sorcerer-pod
spec:
```

```
containers:
  - name: my-sorcerer-container
    image: my-sorcerer-app
    envFrom:
    - configMapRef:
        name: my-sorcerer-config    ③
```

① The SORCERER_ORCSLAYINGPOTIONS environment variable is propagated to the my-sorcerer-app config as the sorcerer.orcSlayingPotions config property.

② The environment variable APP_JSONORC is propagated to the my-sorcerer-app config as app.jsonOrc.

③ This is a reference to ConfigMap as the environment variables source.

Mounted Volume

Sometimes the flat structure of the environment variables is just not enough. Kubernetes ConfigMap can specify the configuration that should be mounted to the container's file system as a config file. You can mount your favorite configuration format, whether it's a properties file, YAML, or JSON, to the folder of your choice.

Listing 3-28. K8s ConfigMap Propagated to Helidon over the Configuration File on the Mounted Volume

```
apiVersion: v1
kind: ConfigMap
metadata:
  name: my-sorcerer-config
```

```
data:
  my-sorcerer-app-config.yaml: |    ①
    app.jsonOrc: '{"orcName":"Sharpteeth", "level":"22"}'
    sorcerer:
      orcSlayingPotions: 68
      invisibilityCloak: false
      weapons: axe,sword
---
apiVersion: v1
kind: Pod
metadata:
  name: my-sorcerer-pod
spec:
  containers:
    - name: my-sorcerer-container
      image: my-sorcerer-app
      volumeMounts:
        - mountPath: /config    ②
          name: config-volume
  volumes:
    - name: config-volume
      configMap:
        name: my-sorcerer-config
```

① The name of the resulting config file

② The path of the mounted folder containing the
   resulting my-sorcerer-app-config.yaml file

In my-sorcerer-app, you need to set up the meta config mp-meta-config.yaml file to specify the location of the mounted configuration file.

Listing 3-29. Mounted Configuration File Usage with Meta Config

```
sources:
  - type: "yaml"
    path: "/config/my-sorcerer-app-config.yaml"   ①
    ordinal: 250   ②
    optional: true   ③
```

       ① The path to the mounted config file.

       ② The priority over the default config file on the classpath.

       ③ This value is optional, so you can run the application without the mounted file when required.

From the start, the Helidon config is designed for use in the microservice environment. You can see how every feature converges to the same goal of minimizing the needed boilerplate code related to the configuration in your microservice application.

Summary

- Microservices need to be configurable.

- Config sources are available for every occasion.

- Use ordinals in the config sources to make overriding possible.

- No need to stick with YAML; create your own config source.

- Converters solve parsing or deserializing.

- Work with dynamically changing configuration without restarting your service.

- Integration with Kubernetes ConfigMap makes your application truly cloud-native.

CHAPTER 4

Observability

This chapter covers the following topics.

- Understanding observability

- Understanding health checks

- Adding metrics support to Helidon applications

- Using tracing in Helidon applications

- Configuring logging in Helidon

You've possibly heard this word many times and already know it has some importance for microservices. You also understand that it's somehow related to monitoring or telemetry. This chapter explains what observability means, how it differs from monitoring and telemetry, which observability features are included in Helidon, and how to use them.

What Is Observability?

The term *observability* comes from control theory. Control theory deals with algorithms driving a dynamic system to a desired state optimally using sensor data. A dynamic system is observable if its state at every moment in time can be determined by analyzing the outputs of external sensors. The system is not observable if data collection from external

© Dmitry Kornilov, Daniel Kec, Dmitry Aleksandrov 2023
D. Kornilov et al., *Beginning Helidon*, https://doi.org/10.1007/978-1-4842-9473-4_4

sensors doesn't give a complete picture of the state or if this data is ambiguous. The anti-lock braking system (ABS) is a good sample. It detects a wheel lock using a sensor, and a special algorithm unlocks the wheel repeatedly to provide the most efficient brake.

For computer systems, this definition is as follows: "Observability is the ability of a service to expose data externally that reflects its internal behavior."

It means that the service provides enough data for admins to understand what's happening. One may say that it's precisely what *monitoring* does. It's considered that the difference is that, unlike observability which provides data for all possible use cases, monitoring operates with only a predefined set of data and monitors only known use cases. It places observability at a level higher than monitoring.

Telemetry is all remotely collected data from the system for monitoring. The word combines two Greek roots: *tele*, meaning "remote," and *metron*, meaning "measure." So, it's a remote measurement. For example, Formula 1 teams are collecting telemetry data from the cars in the race to detect some engine failures. Technically, telemetry assumes only gathering and transferring the data. Monitoring tools do data analysis. One can say that monitoring tools in the past were also doing some remote data collection, and telemetry word was never used. Yes, that's right. Telemetry became a buzzword thanks to the OpenTelemetry project, which standardizes collecting metrics from cloud-based systems. OpenTelemetry aims to provide the full cross-platform, cloud-native observability stack. And here comes the confusion. The OpenTelemetry project is about *observability,* and *telemetry* only collects remote data.

There are four main areas of observability.

- **Health** determines that the service is on, ready to serve requests, and reacting as expected using simple requests returning true or false.

- **Metrics** collects data for monitoring, such as the number of times a method is called, average execution time, and so forth.

- **Tracing** collects the steps of each request processing with additional details such as call durations.

- **Logging** stores important information about internal service machinery.

Health

The primary purpose of health checks is to provide an API allowing external automated management systems to check if your application is available and ready to serve requests. Based on returned data, the management system decides whether it should forward requests to this node or decommission and replace it with another node.

Health checking is essential to guarantee that your whole system operates smoothly. Requests should not be forwarded to nodes that cannot process them; otherwise, your users could see failing or hanging requests.

Note   Health checks are designed to be used by automated systems. Human operators could use it, but it's not the typical use.

Kubernetes Probes

To get the application status, the Kubernetes node agent sends *probes* to some defined application endpoints, which return UP (status 2xx) or DOWN (status 5xx). It may also optionally return some additional information to help identify the issue.

The application may perform multiple checks to define its state. Each check returns UP or DOWN, and the final response is determined by combining all checks results with a logical AND operator. Meaning that the response is DOWN if at least one check returns DOWN.

Table 4-1. *Kubernetes Probes*

Probe	Description
Startup	Determines whether your application has started. If configured, the node agent only triggers other probes once the *startup* probe succeeds.
Readiness	Determines whether your application is ready to serve requests. Requests are only forwarded to your application if the *readiness* check succeeds.
Liveness	Determines whether your application faced some critical issue like out of memory or threads deadlock and must be restarted or decommissioned.

MicroProfile Health

Helidon implements MicroProfile Health specification, which defines APIs and REST endpoints to work with health checks in Java applications. The spec version implemented by Helidon may vary depending on the Helidon version. Helidon 3.x supports MicroProfile Health 3.1.

MICROPROFILE HEALTH

MicroProfile Health is an open-source specification developed by the MicroProfile working group. Its goal is to standardize how microservices report their health status using REST endpoints. You can get more information from the spec document or the spec API sources.

The spec defines four REST endpoints (see Table 4-2).

Table 4-2. *MicroProfile Health REST API*

Probe(s)	URI	Method	Status
Startup	/health/started	GET	200 - UP
			503 - DOWN
			500 - ERROR
Readiness	/health/ready	GET	200 - UP
			503 - DOWN
			500 - ERROR
Liveness	/health/live	GET	200 - UP
			503 - DOWN
			500 - ERROR
Startup + Readiness + Liveness	/health	GET	200 - UP
			503 - DOWN
			500 - ERROR

The probe URLs must be configured in the *container* section in your application Kubernetes deployment descriptor *app.yaml* (see Listing 4-1).

Listing 4-1. Configuring Health Probes in app.yaml

```
livenessProbe:              ①
  httpGet:
    path: /health/live      ②
    port: 8080
  periodSeconds: 3

readinessProbe:             ③
  httpGet:
    path: /health/ready     ④
    port: 8080
  periodSeconds: 3

startupProbe:               ⑤
  httpGet:
    path: /health/started   ⑥
    port: 8080
  periodSeconds: 3
```

  ① Liveness probe configuration

  ② Liveness probe URL

  ③ Readiness probe configuration

  ④ Readiness probe URL

  ⑤ Startup probe configuration

  ⑥ Startup probe URL

Now let's look at what MicroProfile Health REST API endpoints return. They return your application health status in JSON format. It has the same schema for all types of probes. For example, Listing 4-2 depicts a JSON entity returned by a liveness check, returning status 200 (UP).

Listing 4-2. A Sample Health Check Status

```
{
  "status": "UP",                ①
  "checks": [                    ②
    {
      "name": "firstCheck",      ③
      "status": "UP",            ④
      "data": {                  ⑤
        "key": "foo",
        "foo": "bar"
      }
    },
    {
      "name": "secondCheck",     ⑥
      "status": "UP"             ⑦
    }
  ]
}
```

① Probe status. UP if all checks return UP or no checks defined, DOWN otherwise

② An array with all checks for this probe (It can be empty)

③ Name of the first check

④ Status of the first health check. It can be
UP or DOWN

⑤ Optional object containing additional data for
this check

⑥ Name of the second health check

⑦ Status of the second health check status

MicroProfile specification also defines an API for adding custom health checks to your application, which is explained later in this chapter. Now, let's look at how to enable MicroProfile Health support in your Helidon application.

Adding Health Checks to Your Helidon Application

If you want to add health checks support to your existing project, manually add dependencies to your Maven project.

Using Project Starter

The easiest way is to use Project Starter to generate a project with health support.

The following explains what you need to do.

1. Open Project Starter at `https://helidon.io/
   starter`.

2. Select Helidon MP on the Helidon Flavor screen and
   click Next.

3. On the Application Type screen, select Custom and
   click Next.

4. On the Media Support screen, keep Jackson selected or select JSON-B if you want to comply with the MicroProfile platform. Click Next.

5. On the Observability screen, select Health Checks. You may also select other offered options like Metrics and Tracing.

6. Click Download to generate your project, or go through the rest of the steps to continue configuration.

Using CLI

You need to have Helidon CLI installed, as explained in Chapter 2.

Start new project generation using the `helidon init` command. CLI and Project Starter use the same configuration wizard. Answer questions as explained earlier. Once you finish the configuration wizard, and you get a project with health check support generated.

Adding Dependencies Manually

If you want to add health checks support to your existing project, manually add dependencies to your Maven project.

The easiest option is using the `helidon-microprofile` bundle, which contains `helidon-microprofile-health` as a transitive dependency.

```
<dependency>
    <groupId>io.helidon.microprofile.bundles</groupId>
    <artifactId>helidon-microprofile</artifactId>
</dependency>
```

If you don't want to depend on the bigger `helidon-microprofile` bundle, you can add Health support manually by adding the following dependencies to your `pom.xml`.

```
<dependency>
    <groupId>io.helidon.microprofile.bundles</groupId>
    <artifactId>helidon-microprofile-core</artifactId>     ①
</dependency>
<dependency>
    <groupId>io.helidon.microprofile.health</groupId>
    <artifactId>helidon-microprofile-health</artifactId> ②
</dependency>
<dependency>
    <groupId>io.helidon.health</groupId>
    <artifactId>helidon-health-checks</artifactId>         ③
</dependency>
```

    ① MicroProfile Core dependency

    ② MicroProfile Health

    ③ Optional built-in checks

Built-in Checks

Helidon comes with built-in health checks that help determine general issues each application can face.

Table 4-3. *Built-in Checks*

Built-in Check	Description
Deadlock	Liveness check which looks for thread deadlocks with the help of `ThreadMXBean`. Returns DOWN if a deadlock is detected.
Disk space	Liveness check returning DOWN if used disk space exceeds the threshold. The threshold is configured by the `helidon.health.diskSpace.thresholdPercent` configuration property and has a value of 99.99 by default. Users can also configure a file system path to check available space using the `helidon.health.diskSpace.path` configuration property. Returned JSON entity contains additional disk space information, such as total volume size, and available space.
Heap memory	Liveness check returning DOWN if used heap memory goes beyond the threshold. The threshold is configured by the `helidon.health.heapMemory.thresholdPercent` configuration property and has a value of 98 by default. Returned JSON entity contains additional information, such as total memory size, and available memory.

Listing 4-3 demonstrates the response of Helidon liveness health check (`/health/live`) if no custom checks are configured.

Listing 4-3. Built-in Health Checks

```
{
    "status" : "UP",                          ①
    "checks" : [
        {
            "name" : "deadlock",              ②
            "status" : "UP"
        },
```

```
    {
        "name" : "diskSpace",                    ③
        "status" : "UP",
        "data" : {
            "free" : "428.01 GB",
            ...
        }
    },
    {
        "name" : "heapMemory",                   ④
        "status" : "UP"
    }
  ]
}
```

① Overall status

② Deadlock check

③ Disk space check

④ Heap memory check

Custom Checks

Although built-in health checks provide a basis suitable for all applications, you may want to extend its coverage by adding application-specific health checks. For example, add database connectivity checks if you are dealing with databases or third-party systems checks if you use third-party systems.

To create your custom health check, add a CDI bean implementing the org.eclipse.microprofile.health.HealthCheck interface and annotate it with one of the following annotations defining the check type.

- @Liveness for a liveness check

- @Readiness for a readiness check

- @Startup for a startup check

Listing 4-4 is a simple liveness check that returns UP only if invoked during working hours.

Listing 4-4. Working Hours Liveness Custom Check

```
@Liveness                                              ①
@ApplicationScoped                                     ②
public class WorkingHoursCheck implements HealthCheck { ③
    @Override
    public HealthCheckResponse call() {
        return HealthCheckResponse.builder()
                .name("working-hours-check")
                .withData("time", LocalDateTime.now()
                    .toString())
                .status(getStatus())                   ④
                .build();
    }

    private boolean getStatus() {
        int hour = LocalDateTime.now().getHour();
        return hour >= 9 && hour <= 17;
    }
}
```

① Marks this bean as a liveness health check

② Makes this class an application-scoped CDI bean

③ Interface defining call() method invoked every time a health check is probed

④ Status computation

Note   You can find sample application sources in the GitHub repository at: `https://github.com/apress/beginning-helidon`.

When running between 9:00 and 18:00 your local time, you see an output like the one listed in Listing 4-5.

Listing 4-5. Working Hours Health Check Output

```
{
  "status": "UP",
  "checks": [
    ...
    {
      "name": "working-hours-check",
      "status": "UP",
      "data": {
        "time": "2022-05-29T14:00:09.119199400"
      }
    }
  ]
}
```

Metrics

If the health metric provides information about the current state of the service, Metrics gives some aggregated statistics about how your service is performing over time. It can be the number of requests an endpoint gets, the average request processing time, and so on. Service administrators can use this information to improve service performance, tune upscaling strategies, optimize business logic, and collect some data for reporting. Health and metrics are designed to work with monitoring systems. The monitoring stack consists of a database collecting and storing data and a UI system displaying the data as graphics and diagrams.

Prometheus and Grafana are popular systems for collecting and displaying metrics data.

Note   Prometheus is an open-source system to collect and store metrics data from different applications. It's not used to view the data. You can think about it as a single-purpose database for storing metrics data. Prometheus provides client libraries for many programming languages, including Java.

Grafana is a visualization tool for presenting metrics data to users. It shows a dashboard with nice graphs and updates them in real-time. It also allows defining alerts to notify administrators in case something goes wrong. It's integrated with metrics storing systems like Prometheus, where it gets the data.

Your Helidon application provides a set of metrics the user wants to track. Prometheus polls your application, collects metrics data, and stores them internally. Grafana is querying Prometheus for a specific subset of data and displaying them on a web page using graphs and diagrams. A user loads Grafana UI and views the Helidon application metrics in his browser. Figure 4-1 illustrates these concepts.

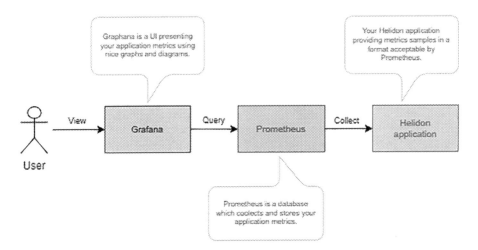

Figure 4-1. *Metrics stack operation and components*

The next question is how Helidon gathers and provides metrics data to Prometheus. And the answer is that Helidon implements the MicroProfile Metrics specification. To be more specific, Helidon 3.0 implements MicroProfile Metrics 4.0.

MICROPROFILE METRICS

MicroProfile Metrics is an open-source specification developed by the MicroProfile working group. Its goal is to standardize the way microservices define and expose metrics data. You can get more information from the specification document at `https://download.eclipse.org/ microprofile/microprofile-metrics-4.0/microprofile- metrics-spec-4.0.pdf`.

MicroProfile Metrics specification defines RESTful API allowing systems like Prometheus collecting metrics data (see the "MicroProfile Metrics REST API" section). The entry point is `/metrics`.

Let's look at how the Helidon application processes metrics requests. It's illustrated in Figure 4-2.

1. Request comes to the /metrics endpoint or any other endpoint defined in MicroProfile Metrics REST API.

2. Helidon gathers data for *base* and *vendor* metrics. Its metrics are defined by the MicroProfile specification and provided by Helidon out of the box (see the "Metric Scopes" section).

3. Helidon processes all metrics defined in the Helidon application by developers. To define metrics, developers can use annotations or programmatic APIs.

4. Helidon aggregates metrics data from 2 and 3 and produces a response in Prometheus or JSON format.

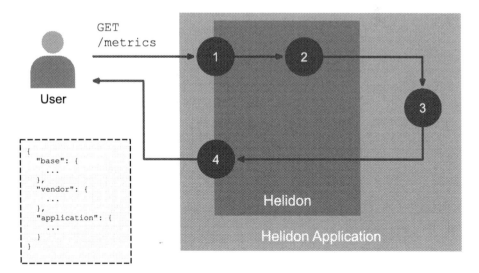

Figure 4-2. *Metrics requests processing by Helidon application*

Now you are familiar with the metrics stack architecture and metrics request workflow inside the Helidon application. So, it's a good time to explain what metrics are, how they're represented, and how to add custom metrics to your application. But before jumping to a theory, let's discuss how to add MicroProfile metrics support to your Helidon application. After you understand that (don't worry, it's easy), let's use a simple Helidon application for metrics demonstration. It's easier to learn by example.

Adding MicroProfile Metrics Support to Your Helidon Application

Using Project Starter

The easiest way is to use Project Starter to generate a project with metrics support.

The following explains what you need to do.

1. Open Project Starter at `https://helidon.io/starter`.

2. Select Helidon MP on the Helidon Flavor screen and click Next.

3. On the Application Type screen, select Custom and click Next.

4. On the Media Support screen, keep Jackson selected or select JSON-B if you want to comply with the MicroProfile platform. Click Next.

5. On the Observability screen, check Metrics and
    choose MicroProfile as Metrics Provider. You may
    also select other offered options, like Health Checks
    and Tracing.

6. Click Download to generate your project, or
    go through the rest of the steps to continue
    configuration.

Using CLI

You need Helidon CLI installed, as explained in Chapter 2.

Start new project generation using the `helidon init` command.
CLI and Project Starter are using the same configuration wizard. Answer
questions as explained earlier. Finish the configuration wizard, and you get
a project with metrics support generated.

Adding Dependencies Manually

The easiest way is using the `helidon-microprofile` bundle, which
contains `helidon-microprofile-metrics` as a transitive dependency.

```
<dependency>
    <groupId>io.helidon.microprofile.bundles</groupId>
    <artifactId>helidon-microprofile</artifactId>
</dependency>
```

If you don't want to depend on the bigger `helidon-microprofile`, you
can add Metrics support manually by adding the following dependencies
to your `pom.xml` file.

```
<dependency>
    <groupId>io.helidon.microprofile.bundles</groupId>
    <artifactId>helidon-microprofile-core</artifactId>    ①
</dependency>
```

```
<dependency>
    <groupId>io.helidon.microprofile.metrics</groupId>
    <artifactId>helidon-microprofile-metrics</artifactId>②
</dependency>
```

① MicroProfile Core dependency

② MicroProfile Metrics

Sample Application

Let's create a sample application demonstrating the usage of MicroProfile metrics annotations and programmatic APIs. It uses the generated Project Starter Quickstart application as the base and added JAX-RS resources for all metric types supported by the specification. Snippets from these resources are used later when discussing MicroProfile APIs.

The sample application is called *ch04-metrics* and is available in the book GitHub repository at `https://github.com/apress/beginning-helidon`.

The README.md file in the project's root directory contains instructions for building and running the project. These commands are provided in the book for the sake of space. Also, we don't want to drag your attention to the sample-related bash commands; we want you to concentrate on the metrics topic.

MicroProfile Metrics REST API

MicroProfile specification defines REST API for accessing metrics data. It's the first step in Figure 4-2. This API allows users and systems like Prometheus to get metrics data and metadata from your application.

Table 4-4. *MicroProfile Metrics REST API*

URL	Request Type	Description
/metrics	GET	Returns all registered metrics in JSON or OpenMetrics formats.
/metrics/<scope>	GET	Returns all metrics registered for the given scope (see the "Metric Scopes" section) in JSON or OpenMetrics formats.
/metrics/<scope>/ <metric_name>	GET	Returns the metric that matches the metric name for the given scope (see the "Metric Scopes" section) in JSON or OpenMetrics formats.
/metrics	OPTIONS	Returns all registered metrics' metadata.
/metrics/<scope>	OPTIONS	Returns metrics' metadata registered for the given scope (see the "Metric Scopes" section).
/metrics/<scope>/ <metric_name>	OPTIONS	Returns the metric's metadata that matches the metric name for the given scope (see the "Metric Scopes" section).

OPENMETRICS

OpenMetrics is a specification built upon and carefully extends the Prometheus exposition format in almost 100% backward-compatible ways. It defines a protocol and a file format containing metrics data accepted by systems like Prometheus. The file is text by nature.

MicroProfile Metrics supports JSON and OpenMetrics data formats. By default, it uses OpenMetrics simply because it's the format Prometheus accepts. Use the following command to get metrics data in OpenMetrics format.

```
curl http://localhost:8080/metrics
```

The result is the full metrics data produced in OpenMetrics format.

```
# TYPE base_classloader_loadedClasses_count gauge
# HELP base_classloader_loadedClasses_count Displays the number
of classes that are currently loaded in the Java virtual
machine.
base_classloader_loadedClasses_count 8008
# TYPE base_gc_total counter
# HELP base_gc_total Displays the total number of collections
that have occurred. This attribute lists -1 if the collection
count is undefined for this collector.
base_gc_total{name="G1 Old Generation"} 0
base_gc_total{name="G1 Young Generation"} 7
...
```

OpenMetrics is a text format containing both metrics data and metadata. You see metadata in lines starting with #. Metrics data is in lines which are not start with #. These lines contain metric names (e.g., base_classloader_loadedClasses_count) and values (e.g., 8008).

To switch to JSON format, specify the Accept: application/json header to your REST request.

```
curl -H 'Accept: application/json' http://localhost:8080/
metrics
```

The result is full metrics data in JSON format.

```
{
  "base": {
    "classloader.loadedClasses.count": 8008,
    "classloader.loadedClasses.total": 8008,
    ...
  },
  ...
}
```

It's just a fragment. The actual output is much lengthy. JSON format includes only metrics data (no metadata). To get metadata, you should use the OPTIONS request type.

```
curl -X OPTIONS http://localhost:8080/metrics
```

Metrics Model

Each metric has a unique ID, scope, and one of the seven types supported by the MicroProfile Metrics specification and metadata. Let's take a closer look at these characteristics.

Metric Identity

The metric's *name* should reflect what's measured (like http_requests_total) and an optional collection of key-value pairs called *tags*. Tags are used to build a *dimensional data model* which allows querying and aggregating data. These two (name + tags) form the unique metric identity. Think of it as a primary key in a database table.

```
<metric name>{<tag name>=<tag value>, ...}
```

One of the earlier samples showed a response of calling the /metrics endpoint in OpenMetrics format. It contains metrics with two tags.

```
# TYPE base_gc_total counter
# HELP base_gc_total Displays the total number of collections
that have occurred. This attribute lists -1 if the collection
count is undefined for this collector.
base_gc_total{name="G1 Old Generation"} 0
base_gc_total{name="G1 Young Generation"} 7
```

You see a tag 'name' specifying which garbage collector was used in this metric. So, "G1 Young Generation" was used seven times, and "G1 Old Generation" was never used.

Metric Scopes

Think about scopes as categories logically separating your metrics catalog. MicroProfile Metrics specification defines three metrics scopes: *base, vendor* and *application* (see Table 4-5).

Table 4-5. *MicroProfile Metrics Scopes*

Scope	Description	URL
Base	A set of metrics each MicroProfile Metrics compliant implementation must provide.	/metrics/base
Vendor	Helidon-specific metrics that are provided out of the box.	/metrics/vendor
Application	Your application-specific metrics.	/metrics/application

Let's take a closer look at each of them.

Base Scope

The base set of metrics each MicroProfile Metrics compliant implementation must provide. There are about 18 base metrics defined by the spec, and five are optional. It includes data about memory consumption, garbage collection, and class loading. Helidon implements only the required base metrics.

Note   You can find a complete list of base metrics in the specification document at `https://download.eclipse.org/microprofile/microprofile-metrics-4.0/microprofile-metrics-spec-4.0.pdf`.

Use this command to retrieve base metrics in OpenMetrics format.

```
curl http://localhost:8080/metrics/base
```

Use this command to retrieve base metrics in JSON format.

```
curl -H 'Accept: application/json' http://localhost:8080/metrics/base
```

Vendor Scope

Vendor scope is a set of metrics provided by MicroProfile Metrics implementation out of the box. Different implementations offer different sets of metrics. Helidon provides thread pool executor metrics and the total count and rate of received requests.

Use this command to retrieve vendor metrics in OpenMetrics format.

```
curl http://localhost:8080/metrics/vendor
```

Use this command to retrieve vendor metrics in JSON format.

```
curl -H 'Accept: application/json' http://localhost:8080/
metrics/vendor
```

Application Scope

Application Scope is a scope that contains metrics specific to your application. It's empty unless you add metrics in your application source code (see the "Using MicroProfile Metrics API" section).

You can list all application scope metrics registered using the following command.

```
curl -H 'Accept: application/json' http://localhost:8080/
metrics/application
```

Metric Metadata

Metric metadata is where all information about the metric is collected. All metadata fields are listed in Table 4-6. Although *description* and *display name* are optional, providing them is a good practice. It helps to get a context and an explanation of the metric. Multiple metric instances can share the same metadata.

Table 4-6. *MicroProfile Metrics Metadata*

Metadata Field	Required	Description
name	Yes	Metric name
type	Yes	One of the seven metrics types ((see the "Metric Types" section)
description	No	Human-readable description of what the metric does
display name	No	Human-readable name of the metric
units	Yes	Measurement units (milliseconds, minutes, etc.)

Metrics Types

MicroProfile Metrics specification defines seven metric types (see Table 4-7).

Table 4-7. *MicroProfile Metric Types*

Metric Type	Description
Counter	A simple monotonically increasing counter (e.g., number of HTTP requests processed over time; see the "Counter" section for more information)
Gauge	A simple numeric value that can increase or decrease (e.g., number of concurrent processes, available RAM; see the "Gauge" section for more information)
ConcurrentGauge	The number of concurrent invocations over time plus min/max over the previous completed minute (see the "Concurrent Gauge" section for more information).
Meter	Throughput with rates (see the "Meter" section for more information)
Histogram	Distribution of long values (see the "Histogram" section for more information)
SimpleTimer	Total elapsed time and a count of samples (see the "Simple Timer" section for more information)
Timer	Meter plus histogram of sample times (see the "Timer" section for more information)

Using MicroProfile Metrics API

MicroProfile metrics provides APIs allowing you to quickly add metrics support to your application. It includes *annotations* and *programmatic APIs*. You can use either or both. These are different tools with different purposes. The programmatic APIs are more powerful. You can do more things with it than with the annotations. But the annotations are easier to use and provide enough functionality for most cases.

Counter

The counter is a simple, monotonically increasing value. Its name is self-explanatory. Use it to count something and see how this number grows over time. Important to understand that the counter cannot decrease.

On a plane preparing to take off, flight attendants go across the plane and count passengers. They are using counting machines to simplify counting. Pressing a button on this machine increases the counter by one. Click, click, click, and the total number of passengers is displayed. This counting machine is an excellent real-life sample of the counter.

Another sample is an electronic steps counter. You move; it counts your steps. This number cannot decrease.

The most common use case in programming is to count how often your method was called. If this method is a JAX-RS handler, you count how many requests were made to this endpoint. You can also calculate how many times your business method was called.

Using Annotations

The MicroProfile Metrics API defines @Counted annotation, which introduces a counter counting how many times the annotated method has been called. It can be placed on a method, a constructor, or a class. While seated on a class, it affects all its constructors and non-private methods.

The `@Counted` annotation can be used without any arguments. The simplest use case looks as follows.

```
@GET
@Counted
public void counter() {
    // Some logic is here
}
```

The `@GET` annotation in the snippet is not required and only indicates that the method is a JAX-RS resource handler. You can put `@Counted` and other MicroProfile Metrics annotations on non-private methods. The only requirement is that your class must be a CDI bean, and you invoke this method via its CDI proxy.

Optionally, users can specify metric metadata such as *name, tags, displayName, description*, and *unit* in the annotation parameters.

To demonstrate it let's create a slightly more complicated example: a method that returns the number of times it's been called. A complication is that we must access our counter inside a method annotated with `@Counted`.

A solution is to inject the same counter into a class field and use it to get the number of calls. There are many ways to get access to all registered metrics. Many are covered in this chapter. The next example uses the `@Metric` annotation. It injects a metric from the MetricRegistry application with a type of annotated field that matches the `@Metric` annotation parameters. If such a metric is not found, it gets registered.

Note   The `@Metric` annotation can be used on type Meter, Timer, SimpleTimer, Counter, and Histogram fields.

To inject the same metric as used in @Counted, Listing 4-6 provides the same parameters to @Metric annotations.

Listing 4-6. Creating a Counter Using Annotations

```
@Inject
@Metric(name="cntr1", absolute=true)
Counter counter;

@GET
@Counted(name="cntr1", absolute=true,
  description = "Simple annotation-based counter")
public Long count() {
    return counter.getCount();
}
```

After running the sample application and triggering its endpoint several times, the metric data in OpenMetrics format looks as follows.

```
# TYPE application_cntr1_total counter
# HELP application_cntr1_total Simple annotation-based counter
application_cntr1_total 5
```

Using Programmatic API

MicroProfile Metrics has a rich programmatic API that can be used stand-alone or in combination with annotations. The Counter class was used in the previous example. Listing 4-7 demonstrates how to reproduce the same functionality using pure programmatic API.

The key class in the programmatic API is MetricRegistry. It belongs to a metric scope and holds all metrics of this scope. There are three MetricRegistry objects: for base, vendor, and application scopes. You'll use the application scope MetricRegistry the most. MetricRegistry is used to register and retrieve metrics. It has a variety of double-purpose methods for it. For example, overloaded `counter(...)` methods retrieve or register a counter if it doesn't exist in the registry.

The only way to obtain `MetricRegistry` is by injecting it. By default, the application registry is injected. If you want to inject a registry of another scope, use the `@RegistryType` annotation specifying a desired scope.

```
@Inject
@RegistryType(type = Type.VENDOR)
MetricRegistry metricRegistry;
```

Let's come back to our sample. The logic is as follows.

1. Use constructor injection to inject `MetricRegistry`.

2. Pass injected registry to the `createCounter` method, which creates a counter and registers it in the metric registry.

3. The `GET` handler increases the counter using `counter.inc()` and returns its current value using `counter.getCount()`.

Listing 4-7. Creating a Counter Using Programmatic API

```
private Counter counter;                                    ①

@Inject                                                     ②
public CounterProgrammaticResource(MetricRegistry
  metricRegistry) {
    createCounter(metricRegistry);
}

private void createCounter(MetricRegistry
  metricRegistry) {
    Tag tag = new Tag("method", "programmatic");            ③
```

```
    Metadata metadata = Metadata.builder()                    ④
      .withName("cntr2")
      .build();

    counter = metricRegistry.counter(metadata, tag);          ⑤
}

@GET
public Long counterProgrammatic() {
    counter.inc();                                            ⑥
    return counter.getCount();                                ⑦
}
```

① Class field holding the counter

② Using constructor injection to inject
   MetricRegistry

③ Creating a tag

④ Creating metadata

⑤ Registering the counter and assigning it to a
   class field

⑥ Increasing the counter

⑦ Returning the current counter value

Gauge

Gauge is a simple numeric value that can increase or decrease. It's different
from the counter, which can only increase. A good sample of the gauge
is the temperature in the room. It changes up and down during the day.
A more technical example is available RAM or the number of concurrent
processes.

Gauge is the only metric type that doesn't store, aggregate, or process the measurement. It only takes a value available in your application and passes it to Prometheus or any other external metrics processing system.

Using Annotations

MicroProfile Metrics API defines @Gauge annotation. It can be placed only on methods. It defines a gauge based on the value this method returns. The value can be any type, but Prometheus accepts only numeric values for gauges, so you must use numeric types if you plan to use Prometheus for data collection.

@Gauge annotation doesn't provide the default value for *unit*. Users are required to specify it explicitly.

Technically, the @Gauge annotation only tells the system that the gauge value is obtained as a return value of the annotated method.

Listing 4-8 is a method returning some measurements. In this case, it's just a random number between 0 and 100, but it can be something more meaningful. This method is annotated with @Gauge with the name gauge1. When you obtain metrics, the gauge returns a new random number.

Listing 4-8. Creating a Gauge Using Annotations

```
@Gauge(name = "gauge1",
        absolute = true,
        description = "Simple annotation-based gauge",
        unit = MetricUnits.NONE)
public Integer measurement() {
    return random.nextInt(100);
}
```

103

Using Programmatic APIs

There are similar steps for working with gauge metric programmatically, as described earlier on how it works with counters. There is one difference, though. When registering a gauge in your metric registry, you must specify a lambda reference, Supplier, or Function responsible for providing the gauge value.

Here is an implementation of a random gauge using programmatic API.

Listing 4-9. Creating a Gauge Using Programmatic API

```
private Random random = new Random();

@Inject                                                    ①
public GaugeProgrammaticResource(
        MetricRegistry metricRegistry) {
    metricRegistry.gauge("gauge2", this::measurement);    ②
}

public Integer measurement() {                             ③
    return random.nextInt(100);
}
```

  ① Injecting `MetricRegistry` using constructor injection

  ② Creating a gauge

  ③ Method returning the measurement

Concurrent Gauge

The concurrent gauge metric is used to count parallel invocations of methods. It means how many concurrent threads are executing this method at a single moment. It's the first multi-value metric from what we've studied so far. Besides the current number of concurrent invocations, it also contains its highest and lowest values from the previous full completed minute.

Note   The previous full completed minute is different from the last 60 seconds. It's better to explain it by example. If the sample time is 8:32:36 (8 a.m., 32 minutes, 36 seconds), the last full completed minute is an interval from 8:31:00 until (but not including) 8:32:00.

Table 4-8. *Concurrent Gauge Metric Data*

Description	OpenMetrics Suffix	JSON Format Field	ConcurrentGauge Class Method
Number of concurrent invocations	current	current	getCount( )
Highest concurrent invocations number for the last complete full minute	max	max	getMax( )
Lowest concurrent invocations number for the last complete full minute	min	min	getMin( )

Using Annotations

MicroProfile Metrics API defines the @ConcurrentGauge annotation. It can be placed on a method, constructor, and class. While placed on a class, it affects all its constructors and non-private methods.

@ConcurrentGauge annotations don't have any required parameters. Listing 4-10 adds some metadata to make it more readable in the output file.

It creates a method that does nothing but sleeps for 20 seconds. To get some results, you must call its REST endpoint within 20 seconds using different instances of *curl*. You can do it by opening new tabs in your terminal application.

Listing 4-10. Creating a Concurrent Gauge Using Annotations

```
@GET
@ConcurrentGauge(name="cgauge1",
        absolute=true,
        description = "Simple annotation-based
        concurrent gauge")
public void concurrentGauge() throws InterruptedException {
    Thread.sleep(20 * 1000);
}
```

In OpenMetrics format, the output for cgauge1 looks as follows.

```
# TYPE application_cgauge1_current gauge
# HELP application_cgauge1_current Simple annotation-based
concurrent gauge
application_cgauge1_current 1
# TYPE application_cgauge1_min gauge
application_cgauge1_min 0
# TYPE application_cgauge1_max gauge
application_cgauge1_max 2
```

Using Programmatic API

Now let's learn how to use the concurrent gauge using programmatic APIs. MicroProfile Metrics has a class ConcurrentGauge, which is used to work with concurrent gauges. It holds a count of concurrent invocation internally and has methods inc() and dec() to increase and decrease it. It also has methods to retrieve all concurrent gauge metrics data.

Listing 4-11. Creating a Concurrent Gauge Using Programmatic API

```
@ApplicationScoped
@Path("/concurrentgauge/programmatic")
public class CGaugeProgrammaticResource {
    ConcurrentGauge concurrentGauge;

    @Inject
    public CGaugeProgrammaticResource(MetricRegistry registry)
    {                                                            ①
        concurrentGauge = registry
            .concurrentGauge("cgauge", new Tag("method",
            "programmatic"));                                    ②
    }

    @GET
    public void concurrentGauge() {
        concurrentGauge.inc();                                   ③
        try {
            Thread.sleep(20 * 1000);                             ④
        } catch (InterruptedException e) {
            throw new RuntimeException(e);
        } finally {
            concurrentGauge.dec();                               ⑤
        }
    }
}
```

① Constructor injection of `MetricRegistry`

② Creating concurrent gauge

③ Increasing the gauge before starting the operation to measure

④ Measured business logic (sleeping in our case)

⑤ Decreasing the gauge value when the measured operation is completed (It is done in the final block, so the gauge is decreased regardless of the operation's success.)

Histogram

Histogram is a complex metric showing how measurements are distributed across specific ranges, often called buckets. The key word here is *distribution*. The use case for the histogram is when you only care a little about the absolute values but want to see how these values are distributed.

Graphically histogram looks like a bar chart. Each bar represents a bucket. The higher the bar, the more measurements fall into this range.

Figure 4-3 is a sample of a histogram demonstrating the age distribution of people participating in a conference.

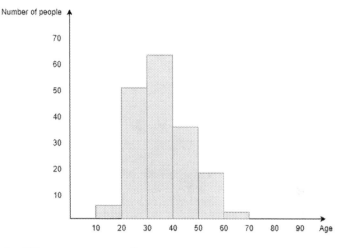

Figure 4-3. *Histogram sample*

Another sample is photography. Histograms are used directly in cameras to show the brightness of your picture. Each tone is presented as a bar. The higher the bar, the more frequently this tone is in your image. It's a perfect tool to see how your picture is exposed.

In our area, the use cases for the histogram are, for example, request duration or response size distributions.

Histogram metric contains 12 fields, including the lowest, highest, and median values in the distribution, the standard deviation of the values, and the sum of all values and values of the 50th, 75th, 95th, 98th, 99th, and 99.9th percentile (see Table 4-9).

Table 4-9. *Histogram Metric Data*

Description	OpenMetrics Suffix	JSON Format Field	Histogram Class Method
The lowest value in the distribution	min_\<units>	min	getSnapshot( ). getMin( )
The highest value in the distribution	max_\<units>	max	getSnapshot( ). getMax( )
The median value in the distribution	mean_\<units>	mean	getSnapshot( ). getMean( )
The standard deviation of the values	stddev_\<units>	stddev	getSnapshot( ). getStdDev( )
The number of values in the distribution	\<units>_count	count	getCount( )
The sum of all values	\<units>_sum	sum	getSum( )
The value at the 50th percentile in the distribution	\<units>{quantile="0.5"}	p50	getSnapshot( ). getMedian( )
The value at the 75th percentile in the distribution	\<units>{quantile="0.75"}	p75	getSnapshot( ). get75thPercentile( )
The value at the 95th percentile in the distribution	\<units>{quantile="0.95"}	p95	getSnapshot( ). get95thPercentile( )

(continued)

Table 4-9. (*continued*)

Description	OpenMetrics Suffix	JSON Format Field	Histogram Class Method
The value at the 98th percentile in the distribution	\<units\>{quantile="0.98"}	p98	getSnapshot( ). get98thPercentile( )
The value at the 99th percentile in the distribution	\<units\>{quantile="0.99"}	p99	getSnapshot( ). get99thPercentile( )
The value at the 99,9th percentile in the distribution	\<units\> {quantile="0.999"}	p999	getSnapshot( ). get999thPercentile( )

Note   A percentile is a value below which a given percentage of observations in a group of observations falls. For example, the 70th percentile is the value below which 70% of the observations may be found.

MicroProfile Metrics provides only programmatic APIs to work with the histogram.

Using Programmatic API

MicroProfile Metrics API has a Histogram class, which is used to work with histograms. It can be obtained the same way as other metric classes using one of the overloaded histogram methods of the MetricRegistry class.

To demonstrate a histogram, Listing 4-12 is a simple service that registers a passed value in the histogram.

Listing 4-12. Creating a Histogram Using Programmatic API

```
@ApplicationScoped
@Path("/histogram")
public class HistogramProgrammaticResource {
    private Histogram histogram;

    @Inject
    public HistogramProgrammaticResource(MetricRegistry
    metricRegistry) {
        createHistogram(metricRegistry);
    }

    @GET
    @Path("/{value}")
    public void histogram(@PathParam("value") Long value) {
        histogram.update(value);
    }

    private void createHistogram(MetricRegistry
    metricRegistry) {
        Metadata metadata = Metadata.builder()
                .withName("histogram")
                .withDescription("Histogram programmatic")
                .withType(MetricType.HISTOGRAM)
                .build();

        histogram = metricRegistry.histogram(metadata);
    }
}
```

The sample output in OpenMetrics format looks like Listing 4-13.

Listing 4-13. Histogram Metric Output in OpenMetrics Format

```
# TYPE application_histogram_mean gauge
application_histogram_programmatic_mean 3.0688587149767783
# TYPE application_histogram_max gauge
application_histogram_programmatic_max 5
# TYPE application_histogram_min gauge
application_histogram_programmatic_min 1
# TYPE application_histogram_stddev gauge
application_histogram_programmatic_stddev 1.4120173733941095
# TYPE application_histogram summary
# HELP application_histogram Histogram programmatic
application_histogram_programmatic_count 5
application_histogram_programmatic_sum 15
application_histogram_programmatic{quantile="0.5"} 3
application_histogram_programmatic{quantile="0.75"} 4
application_histogram_programmatic{quantile="0.95"} 5
application_histogram_programmatic{quantile="0.98"} 5
application_histogram_programmatic{quantile="0.99"} 5
application_histogram_programmatic{quantile="0.999"} 5
```

Meter

The specification defines *meter* as a metric that tracks mean throughput and one-, five-, and fifteen-minute exponentially-weighted moving average throughput measured in hits per second. All data provided by the meter is listed in Table 4-10.

The *exponentially-weighted moving average* is a statistical measure widely used in finance for stock technical analysis and volatility modeling. It calculates a weighted average on a subset of the full data set and is designed the way that older observations are given lower weights. The weight for older observations is decreasing exponentially.

113

The primary purpose of the meter is to monitor the traffic on a RESTful service endpoint or a data access component. Helidon provides a vendor metric for monitoring the total throughput of your service, which is a meter.

Table 4-10. *Meter Metric Data*

Description	OpenMetrics Suffix	JSON Format Field	Meter Class Method
The total number of observations	total	count	getCount( )
The average rate per second	rate_per_second	meanRate	getMeanRate( )
The exponentially-weighted moving average for the last minute	one_min_rate_per_second	oneMinRate	getOneMinuteRate( )
The exponentially-weighted moving average for the last five minutes	five_min_rate_per_second	fiveMinRate	getFiveMinuteRate( )
The exponentially-weighted moving average for the last fifteen minutes	fifteen_min_rate_per_second	fifteenMinRate	getFifteenMinuteRate( )

MicroProfile Metrics specification allows users to work with meters using annotations and programmatic APIs.

Using Annotations

MicroProfile Metrics API defines @Metered annotation to work with meters. It can be placed on a method, constructor, and class. While placed on a class, it affects all its constructors and non-private methods.

For each method/constructor annotated with @Metered, a metric is created and registered in the application metric registry. Each time the method is invoked, the meter is marked.

Listing 4-14 is a simple sample that returns a random number. It's annotated with @Metered, so the mtr1 metric collects this method throughput.

Listing 4-14. Creating a Meter Using Annotations

```
@GET
@Metered(name = "mtr1",
        absolute = true,
        description = "Simple annotation-based meter")
public String meteredMethod() {
  ...
}
```

After triggering the metered method several times, the mtr1 metric produces an output similar to the following.

```
# TYPE application_mtr1_total counter
# HELP application_mtr1_total Simple annotation-based meter
application_mtr1_total 15
# TYPE application_mtr1_rate_per_second gauge
application_mtr1_rate_per_second 0.13889050670608735
# TYPE application_mtr1_one_min_rate_per_second gauge
application_mtr1_one_min_rate_per_second 0.22974035264337553
# TYPE application_mtr1_five_min_rate_per_second gauge
application_mtr1_five_min_rate_per_second 0.049149433089204296
```

```
# TYPE application_mtr1_fifteen_min_rate_per_second gauge
application_mtr1_fifteen_min_rate_per_second
0.016571380739795517
```

Using Programmatic APIs

MicroProfile Metrics API contains the Meter class, which is used to work with meters. It has methods mark() and mark(long), which increase the number of hits by one and by a specified value accordingly. It also contains methods to retrieve all calculated rates.

The MetricRegistry class contains methods meter(String) and meter(Metadata), which are used to register and retrieve meters.

Listing 4-15 demonstrates creating a meter named mtr2 and a method that marks a hit and returns the meter's mean rate.

Listing 4-15. Creating a Meter Using Programmatic API

```
@ApplicationScoped
@Path("/meter/programmatic")
public class MeterProgrammaticResource {
    private Meter meter;

    @Inject
    public MeterProgrammaticResource(MetricRegistry
    metricRegistry) {
        meter = metricRegistry.meter("mtr2");
    }

    @GET
    public double meterProgrammatic() {
        meter.mark();
        return meter.getMeanRate();
    }
}
```

Simple Timer

The simple timer is a metric recording method execution times. It's a complex metric that includes the total number of executions, elapsed time, and highest and lowest time for the last complete full minute.

Table 4-11. *Simple Timer Metric Data*

Description	OpenMetrics Suffix	JSON Format Field	SimpleTimer Class Method
Number of executions	total	count	getCount( )
Elapsed time	elapsedTime_ seconds	elapsedTime	getElapsedTime( )
Highest time for the last complete full minute	maxTimeDuration_ seconds	maxTimeDuration	getMaxTimeDuration( )
Lowest time for the last complete full minute	minTimeDuration_ seconds	minTimeDuration	getMinTimeDuration( )

Note   In OpenMetrics format, *elapsedTime*, *maxTimeDuration*, and *minTimeDuration* metrics are produced in seconds and JSON format in nanoseconds.

MicroProfile Metric provides annotations and programmatic APIs to work with simple timer metrics.

Using Annotations

MicroProfile Metrics API defines the @SimplyTimed annotation. It can be placed on a method, constructor, and class. While placed on a class, it affects all its constructors and non-private methods. The @SimplyTimed annotation doesn't have any required parameters.

Listing 4-16 is a method that sleeps a random time between 0 and 5 seconds and uses the @SimplyTimed annotation.

Listing 4-16. Creating a Simple Timer Using Annotations

```
@GET
@SimplyTimed(name="stmr1",
        absolute=true,
        description = "Simple timer using annotations")
public void simpleTimer() throws InterruptedException {
    Thread.sleep(random.nextInt(5000));
}
```

The output in OpenMetrics format looks similar to the following.

```
# TYPE application_stmr1_total counter
# HELP application_stmr1_total Simple timer using annotations
application_stmr1_total 4
# TYPE application_stmr1_elapsedTime_seconds gauge
application_stmr1_elapsedTime_seconds 5.011884846
# TYPE application_stmr1_maxTimeDuration_seconds gauge
application_stmr1_maxTimeDuration_seconds 2
# TYPE application_stmr1_minTimeDuration_seconds gauge
application_stmr1_minTimeDuration_seconds 0
```

Using Programmatic API

MicroProfile Metrics API has a class SimpleTimer, which is used to work with simple timers. It can be obtained the same way as other metric classes using one of the overloaded simpleTimer methods of the MetricRegistry class.

There are several ways how to use simple timer metric programmatically.

- Make the method you want to time Callable and use SimpleTimer.time(Callable) to run and time it.

- Make the method you want to time Runnable and use SimpleTimer.time(Runnable) to run and time it.

- Time your method manually and update your simple timer using SimpleTimer.update(Duration).

- Use Context context = SimpleTimer.time() to start timing your method, execute all logic that needs to be timed and call context.close() when it's finished to update your metric.

Listing 4-17 demonstrates using a Runnable object with a simple timer.

Listing 4-17. Using Programmatic API to Create a Simple Timer

```
@ApplicationScoped
@Path("/simpletimer/programmatic")
public class SimpleTimerProgrammaticResource {
    private Random random = new Random();
    private SimpleTimer simpleTimer;

    @Inject
    public SimpleTimerProgrammaticResource(MetricRegistry
    metricRegistry) {
        createSimpleTimer(metricRegistry);
    }
```

119

```
    @GET
    public void simpleTimer() {
        Runnable runnable = () -> {
            try {
                Thread.sleep(random.nextInt(5000));
            } catch (InterruptedException e) {
                throw new RuntimeException(e);
            }
        };

        simpleTimer.time(runnable);
    }

    private void createSimpleTimer(MetricRegistry
    metricRegistry) {
        Metadata metadata = Metadata.builder()
                .withName("stmr2")
                .withDescription("Simple timer programmatic")
                .withType(MetricType.SIMPLE_TIMER)
                .build();

        simpleTimer = metricRegistry.simpleTimer(metadata);
    }
}
```

Timer

The timer metric is a big brother of the simple timer, covered in the previous section. In addition to tracking a method execution time, it contains a meter tracking throughput rate and a histogram with the statistical distribution of recorded times. Table 4-12 contains all timer metric data, access methods, and the corresponding field in OpenMetrics and JSON formats.

It makes sense to use a timer if you need this additional data. If you need to track only elapsed time, use a simple timer.

Table 4-12. Timer Metric Data

Description	OpenMetrics Suffix	JSON Format Field	Timer Class Method
The average rate per second	rate_per_second	meanRate	getMeanRate( )
The exponentially-weighted moving average for the last minute	one_min_rate_per_second	oneMinRate	getOneMinuteRate( )
The exponentially-weighted moving average for the last five minutes	five_min_rate_per_second	fiveMinRate	getFiveMinuteRate( )
The exponentially-weighted moving average for the last fifteen minutes	fifteen_min_rate_per_second	fifteenMinRate	getFifteenMinuteRate( )
The minimum duration	min_seconds	min	getSnapshot( ).getMin( )
The maximum duration	max_seconds	max	getSnapshot( ).getMax( )
The mean duration	mean_seconds	mean	getSnapshot( ). getMean( )

(continued)

121

Table 4-12. (*continued*)

Description	OpenMetrics Suffix	JSON Format Field	Timer Class Method
The standard deviation of duration	stddev_seconds	stddev	getSnapshot().getStdDev()
Number of hits	seconds_count	count	getCount()
Elapsed time	seconds_sum	elapsedTime	getElapsedTime()
The value at the 50th percentile	seconds{quantile="0.5"}	p50	getSnapshot().getMedian()
The value at the 75th percentile	seconds{quantile="0.75"}	p75	getSnapshot().get75thPercentile()
The value at the 95th percentile	seconds{quantile="0.95"}	p95	getSnapshot().get95thPercentile()
The value at the 98th percentile	seconds{quantile="0.98"}	p98	getSnapshot().get98thPercentile()
The value at the 99th percentile	seconds{quantile="0.99"}	p99	getSnapshot().get99thPercentile()
The value at the 99,9th percentile	seconds{quantile="0.999"}	p999	getSnapshot().get999thPercentile()

To work with timers, MicroProfile Metrics provides annotations and programmatic APIs.

Using Annotations

MicroProfile Metrics API defines the @Timed annotation. It can be placed on a method, constructor, and class. While placed on a class, it affects all its constructors and non-private methods.

Although the @Timed annotation doesn't have any required parameters, it makes sense to add some metadata for clarity. Listing 4-18 demonstrates a timed method, which blocks for some random time not longer than five seconds.

Listing 4-18. Creating a Timer Using Annotations

```
@GET
@Timed(name="tmr1",
        absolute=true,
        description = "Timer using annotations")
public void timer() throws InterruptedException {
    Thread.sleep(random.nextInt(5000));
}
```

Listing 4-19 shows a sample output in OpenMetrics format produced after triggering the timed method several times.

Listing 4-19. Timer Metric Data in OpenMetrics Format

```
# TYPE application_tmr1_rate_per_second gauge
application_tmr1_rate_per_second 0.14116614752306147
# TYPE application_tmr1_one_min_rate_per_second gauge
application_tmr1_one_min_rate_per_second 0.07122550418795522
# TYPE application_tmr1_five_min_rate_per_second gauge
application_tmr1_five_min_rate_per_second 0.018664201095054796
```

```
# TYPE application_tmr1_fifteen_min_rate_per_second gauge
application_tmr1_fifteen_min_rate_per_second
0.00651434969860056
# TYPE application_tmr1_mean_seconds gauge
application_tmr1_mean_seconds 3.2017328639808618
# TYPE application_tmr1_max_seconds gauge
application_tmr1_max_seconds 4.0069105
# TYPE application_tmr1_min_seconds gauge
application_tmr1_min_seconds 2.0115542
# TYPE application_tmr1_stddev_seconds gauge
application_tmr1_stddev_seconds 0.6872868729178253
# TYPE application_tmr1_seconds summary
# HELP application_tmr1_seconds Timer using annotations
application_tmr1_seconds_count 6
application_tmr1_seconds_sum 19
application_tmr1_seconds{quantile="0.5"} 3.0055081
application_tmr1_seconds{quantile="0.75"} 4.0027326
application_tmr1_seconds{quantile="0.95"} 4.0069105
application_tmr1_seconds{quantile="0.98"} 4.0069105
application_tmr1_seconds{quantile="0.99"} 4.0069105
application_tmr1_seconds{quantile="0.999"} 4.0069105
```

Using Programmatic API

MicroProfile Metrics API has a Timer class that works with timers. It can be obtained the same way as other metric classes using one of the overloaded timer methods of the MetricRegistry class. Timer contains getters for all timer metric fields (see Table 4-12).

It operates similarly to the SimpleTimer, as demonstrated using Runnable with a simple timer. Listing 4-20 demonstrates this using Callable as a contrast.

Listing 4-20. Creating a Timer Using Programmatic API

```java
@ApplicationScoped
@Path("/timer/programmatic")
public class TimerProgrammaticResource {
    private Random random = new Random();

    private Timer timer;

    @Inject
    public TimerProgrammaticResource(MetricRegistry
    metricRegistry) {
        timer = metricRegistry.timer("tmr2");
    }

    @GET
    public Integer timer() throws Exception {
        Callable<Integer> callable = () -> {
            int sleepSec = random.nextInt(5000);
            Thread.sleep(sleepSec);
            return sleepSec;
        };

        return timer.time(callable);
    }
}
```

Tracing

Troubleshooting microservices is a complicated task. Each request may travel through different instances of microservices working on different hosts in different locations and environments.

What if your service is handling requests too slowly? It shouldn't be, but it is. You need to find out what's going on. You know that it goes through multiple services depending on some business conditions. You don't have access to these services and don't know where they are hosted, so you cannot simply run your debugger and see what's happening. It's a use case where distributed tracing helps you.

Distributed Tracing

Note   Distributed tracing is a method to track a request journey as it travels across components of a distributed system.

This chapter uses the word *tracing* instead of *distributed tracking* because it's shorter.

Trace is a full route of a request as it goes through components in a distributed system. Trace includes a tree of spans.

Span is a unit of work representing a piece of the workflow like a method call. The first span in the tree is called the *root span*. It may include *child spans* representing sub-operations. Each span has a name and records the starting time of the operation, its duration, and, optionally, some more data.

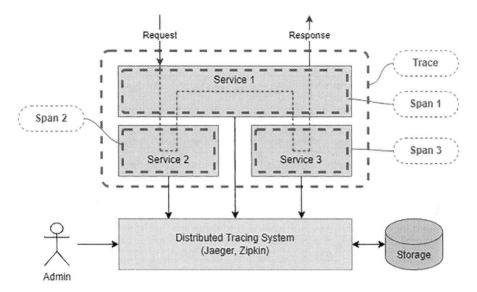

Figure 4-4. *Distributed tracing*

Helidon implements MicroProfile OpenTracing APIs.

MICROPROFILE OPENTRACING

MicroProfile OpenTracing is an open specification based on the OpenTracing standard. It provides a neutral tracing API that smoothly integrates with tracing systems like Zipkin and Jaeger.

MicroProfile OpenTracing enables completely automatic tracing without any actions needed from the developer. Developer chooses the integration he wants to use and adds the corresponding library to the project dependencies.

On each step of the request processing, Helidon invokes the tracing API to mark key points of Helidon's processing in the span. The developer can (but does not have to) invoke the same neutral API at key points in the application's processing. The tracing implementation library collects and transmits tracing information to the corresponding distributed tracing system, which accepts it and saves it to its storage. Distributed tracing systems usually provide a web UI to view application traces. Traces are usually visualized using waterfall diagrams (see Figure 4-5).

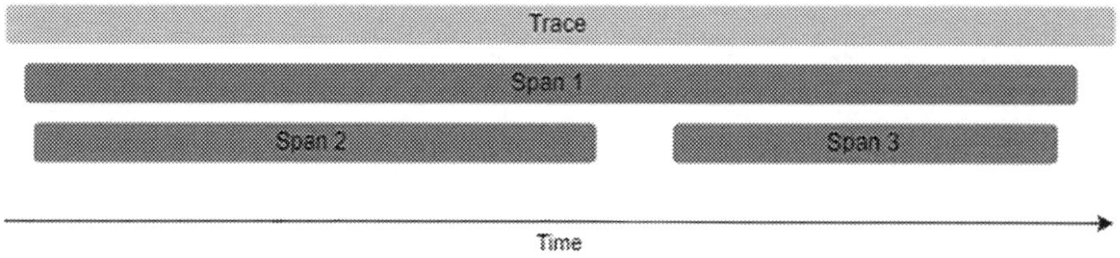

Figure 4-5. *Trace diagram*

Adding Tracing to Your Helidon Application

Using Project Starter

The easiest way is to use Project Starter to generate a project with tracing support.

The following explains what you need to do.

1. Open Project Starter at `https://helidon.io/starter`.

2. Select Helidon MP on the Helidon Flavor screen and click Next.

3. On the Application Type screen, select Custom and click Next.

4. On the Media Support screen, keep Jackson selected or select JSON-B if you want to be compliant with the MicroProfile platform. Click Next.

5. On the Observability screen, check Tracing and choose Tracing Providers you want to use. You may also select Health Checks and Metrics if you want to use them in your application.

6. Click Download to generate your project, or go through the rest of the steps to continue configuration.

Using CLI

You need to have Helidon CLI installed, as explained in Chapter 2.

Start new project generation using the `helidon init` command. CLI and Project Starter are using the same configuration wizard. Answer questions as explained in the preceding section. Finish the configuration wizard, and you get a project with tracing support generated.

Adding Dependencies Manually

You need to add a dependency to vendor-neutral MicroProfile OpenTracing API as well as a dependency on a distributed tracing system you would like to use.

The first option uses the `helidon-microprofile` bundle, which contains `helidon-microprofile-tracing` as a transitive dependency.

```
<dependency>
    <groupId>io.helidon.microprofile.bundles</groupId>
    <artifactId>helidon-microprofile</artifactId>
</dependency>
```

If you don't want to use all the MicroProfile dependencies that the `helidon-microprofile` bundle brings, you can use a more fine-grained configuration using the `helidon-microprofile-core`, which brings only required dependencies plus the `helidon-microprofile-tracing` artifact to enable MicroProfile OpenTracing.

```
<dependency>
    <groupId>io.helidon.microprofile.bundles</groupId>
    <artifactId>helidon-microprofile-core</artifactId>
</dependency>
<dependency>
    <groupId>io.helidon.microprofile.tracing</groupId>
    <artifactId>helidon-microprofile-tracing</artifactId>
</dependency>
```

In addition to that, you must add a dependency to a tracing provider you want to use. Helidon supports Jaeger and Zipkin out of the box.

For Jaeger, add this dependency.

```
<dependency>
    <groupId>io.helidon.tracing</groupId>
    <artifactId>helidon-tracing-jaeger</artifactId>
    <scope>runtime</scope>
</dependency>
```

For Zipkin, add the following.

```
<dependency>
    <groupId>io.helidon.tracing</groupId>
    <artifactId>helidon-tracing-zipkin</artifactId>
    <scope>runtime</scope>
</dependency>
```

Helidon Tracing Implementation

Helidon, as a compliant implementation of MicroProfile OpenTracing, provides automatic ("code-free") tracing. It works the following way.

- For each incoming JAX-RS request to a service endpoint

- Extracts parent span information from the request

- Starts a span or a child span (see the full list of spans in Table 4-13)

- Ends the span when the request completes

- For each outgoing JAX-RS request to another service

  - Injects current span information into the request

  - Starts a span or a child span when the request is sent (see the full list of spans in Table 4-13)

  - Ends the span when the request completes

- When some internal Helidon component is called, such as *security*

  - Adds a span or a child span (see the full list of spans in Table 4-13)

  - Optionally logs some useful information to the span

- Implements a vendor-neutral tracing API which developers can invoke to work with spans explicitly

Helidon Built-in Spans

When Helidon adds a span, it's one of the spans listed in Table 4-13. Each span belongs to a web server, security, or JAX-RS component. The component name is in the description column to save space. The spans are highly customizable. You can change their names and enable/disable them. Read more about it in the tracing configuration section.

Each span optionally contains *logs* and *tags*. *Logs* are key-value pairs that contain some additional span-specific information. *Tags* are key-value pairs used for labeling, querying, and filtering data. Table 4-13 only lists some of the logs and tags. Refer to Helidon's documentation for the detailed descriptions.

Table 4-13. Helidon Built-In Spans

Span Name	Description	Span Logging	Tags
HTTP Request	Overall span covering from request arrival to response transmission. Component: *web-server*	handler.class	component, http. method, http.status_ code, http.url, error
content-read	Reading the request entity. Component: *web-server*	N/A	requested.type
content-write	Writing the response entity. Component: *web-server*	N/A	response.type
security	Overall span covering security processing. Component: *security*	status	security.id
security:atn	Authenticating the client. Component: *security*	security.user, security. service, status	N/A
security:atz	Authorizing the client. Component: *security*	status	N/A
security:response	Security processing of the response. Component: *security*	N/A	N/A
security:outbound	Security processing of an outbound request. Component: *security*	status	N/A
generated name	Endpoint method invocation: name = HTTP method + class name + method name. Component: *jax-rs*	N/A	N/A
jersey-client-call	Outbound request. Component: *jax-rs*	N/A	http.method, http. status_code, http.url

MicroProfile OpenTracing API

MicroProfile OpenTracing works "code free." But it also contains APIs if developers want to work with spans explicitly. This API is very simple. It consists of the @Traced annotation and Tracer class.

@Traced annotation can be placed on a method or a class. While placed in a class, it affects all its public methods. The annotation creates a new child span covering each invocation of the method.

@Traced annotation uses interceptors, so the class must be a CDI bean, and the method must be invoked via CDI. Simple Java method invocations on instances created with new do not trigger tracing! Also, method calls within a type do not work. Any annotations on the target method are ignored if you call a method on a JAX-RS resource from another resource method.

The @Traced annotation has two optional arguments.

- **value=[true|false]**

  The default value is true. Enables or disables tracing of the corresponding methods (all public methods if placed on a class).

- **operationName=<span name>**

  The default value is "". If an empty string is specified, the name is automatically generated based on the class name and method name.

Listing 4-21. Using the @Traced Annotation

```
@Traced          ①
public String getMessage() {
    return message.get();
}
```

```
@Traced(false)  ②
public String getMessageWithNoTraces() {
    return message.get();
}
```

① Traced method

② Not traced method

The OpenTracing Tracer object provides more precise control over spans. It allows you to build spans, set tags, log events, and so on. Helidon automatically creates and initializes an OpenTracing Tracer object. The developer only needs to inject it into a bean class and invoke its methods.

Listing 4-22. Using the Tracer Object

```
@Inject
io.opentracing.Tracer tracer;

public void importantWork() {
    Span span = tracer.buildSpan("important-work").start();
    span.setTag(...);
    span.log(...);

    // Do some important work

    ...

    span.finish();
}
```

Configuration

Helidon allows users to configure its internal tracing components, enable and disable tracing completely for specified components or endpoints, and rename built-in spans.

Enabling/Disabling Tracing

MicroProfile OpenTracing specification allows disabling tracing for JAX-RS resources using configuration. You should specify a regular expression matching resources URIs in the `mp.opentracing.server.skip-pattern` configuration property, which usually sits in `/META-INF/microprofile-config.properties` file (see how to use configuration properties in Chapter 3).

Note   The endpoints defined in MicroProfile Health, MicroProfile Metrics, and OpenAPI specifications are always excluded from tracing.

The following disables all tracing.

```
mp.opentracing.server.skip-pattern=.*
```

Disabling tracing for the `/foo` endpoint and any endpoint starting with `/bar`.

```
mp.opentracing.server.skip-pattern=/foo|/bar.*
```

Helidon provides its own way of configuring tracing. Configuration can be defined in *application.yaml*. In addition to enabling/disabling tracing for some endpoints, you can enable/disable Helidon built-in spans.

Listing 4-23. Example of Tracing Configuration in application.yaml

```
tracing:
  paths:
    - path: "/favicon.ico"          ①
      enabled: false                ②
    - path: "/somepath"
      enabled: false
```

```
components:
  web-server:                           ③
    spans:
      - name: "HTTP Request"            ④
        enabled: true                   ⑤
        logs:
          - name: "content-write"       ⑥
            enabled: false              ⑦
```

① Path to configure (It uses a special format for pattern matching. You can read more about it in the Helidon documentation.)

② *true* to enable tracing and *false* to disable

③ Name of the configured component (one of *web-server, security, jax-rs*)

④ Name of a span (see Table 4-13 for all available span names)

⑤ Enables or disables the span

⑥ Log name (see options for the specified span in Table 4-13)

⑦ Enables or disables the log

If you don't like YAML, its content can be flattened into properties format and placed into `META-INF/microprofile-config.properties`.

Listing 4-24. Example of Tracing Configuration in microprofile-config.properties

```
tracing.paths.0.path="/favicon.ico"
tracing.paths.0.enabled=false
tracing.paths.1.path="/somepath"
```

```
tracing.paths.1.enabled=false
components.web-server.spans.0.name="HTTP Request"
components.web-server.spans.0.enabled=true
components.web-server.spans.0.logs.0.name="content-write"
components.web-server.spans.0.logs.0.enabled=false
```

Renaming a Top-Level Span

In some situations, renaming the top-level HTTP request span makes sense to better suit users' needs. Helidon provides this ability.

Note   This is supported only for the HTTP request span of the web server component. It's not supported for other spans.

Provide a new name in the new-name configuration property, as shown in the following sample.

```
tracing.components.web-server.spans.0.name="HTTP Request"
tracing.components.web-server.spans.0.new-name: "HTTP
%1$s %2$s"
```

You can use the following parameters.

- A **method** is an HTTP method.
- A **path** is a path of the request (such as /greet).
- A **query** is the request (may be null).

Logging

Logging is the final (and shortest) section of this chapter. Logging is what developers use the most compared to health checks, metrics, and tracing. Most of you are familiar with logging and know what it is and why it should be used, but if you are not, we'll try to explain it.

Logging tells you what is happening inside individual software components within a service.

The information answering this question gets written in a log.

Note   A *log* is a sequence of timestamped records (messages) describing what the components of a service are doing and, in some cases, why.

Most often, logs are written to log files. Log files are normal text files with the *.log* extension. But sometimes logs are written to databases or even special logs collecting systems.

Logs are very useful for debugging and detecting problems in your application. Developers are manually adding logging code to their sources to log records which would help track code execution and warn about situations that are not supposed to happen.

Each record in the log has a *logging level*.

Note   A *logging level* measures the logging record importance (higher = more important).

Standard Java logging (`java.util.logging`) has seven logging levels.

- SEVERE (highest value)
- WARNING
- INFO
- CONFIG
- FINE
- FINER
- FINEST (lowest value)

It's a developer's responsibility to choose the appropriate logging level for his logging record. A minimum logging level is configured for the application, so records with a lower logging level are not written to the log. Enabling all logging levels (FINEST level) makes logs too big and verbose. It makes it difficult to find needed information. On the other hand, enabling lower logging levels may help find problems.

Listing 4-25 demonstrates creating a logger and using different logging levels.

Listing 4-25. Using Different Logging Levels

```
private static final Logger LOGGER =
    Logger.getLogger(Main.class.getName());           ①

public void loggingDemo() {
    LOGGER.severe("Severe message");                  ②
    LOGGER.log(Level.SEVERE,
        "Another severe message");                    ③

    LOGGER.warning("Warning message");                ④
    LOGGER.log(Level.WARNING,
        "Another warning message");                   ⑤

    LOGGER.info("Info message");                      ⑥
    LOGGER.log(Level.INFO,
        "Another info message");                      ⑦
}
```

① Logger initialization

② Logging a severe message

③ Another way of logging a severe message

④ Logging a warning message

⑤ Another way of logging a warning message

⑥ Logging an info message

⑦ Another way of logging an info message

Logging in Helidon

Helidon components contain extensive logging using the `java.util.logging` (JUL) API. To use it in your applications, you don't need any extra third-party dependencies.

Developers are not limited to JUL. Helidon also supports other popular logging frameworks such as Log4j and SLF4J (Simple Logging Facade for Java). In this case, extra third-party dependencies are needed.

The following is for Log4j.

```
<dependency>
    <groupId>io.helidon.logging</groupId>
    <artifactId>helidon-logging-log4j</artifactId>
</dependency>
<dependency>
    <groupId>org.apache.logging.log4j</groupId>
    <artifactId>log4j-api</artifactId>
</dependency>
<dependency>
    <groupId>org.apache.logging.log4j</groupId>
    <artifactId>log4j-core</artifactId>
</dependency>
<dependency>
    <groupId>org.apache.logging.log4j</groupId>
    <artifactId>log4j-jul</artifactId>
</dependency>
```

For SLF4J.

```
<dependency>
    <groupId>org.slf4j</groupId>
    <artifactId>slf4j-api</artifactId>
</dependency>
<dependency>
    <groupId>io.helidon.logging</groupId>
    <artifactId>helidon-logging-slf4j</artifactId>
</dependency>
<dependency>
    <groupId>org.slf4j</groupId>
    <artifactId>jul-to-slf4j</artifactId>
</dependency>
<dependency>
    <groupId>ch.qos.logback</groupId>
    <artifactId>logback-classic</artifactId>
</dependency>
```

Mapped Diagnostic Context (MDC)

Mapped Diagnostic Context (MDC) is a feature of modern logging framework allowing registering and using in your logging messages information that is not available in the current logging scope. Good samples are an ID of the currently logged-in user, tracing id, transaction id, or any other context-related information.

If you want to use this feature, some additional configuration is required in addition to adding third-party dependencies.

MDC with JUL

For JUL, you need to add a dependency to a Helidon module that enables MDC for JUL.

```
<dependency>
    <groupId>io.helidon.logging</groupId>
    <artifactId>helidon-logging-jul</artifactId>
</dependency>
```

And configure handlers in your `logging.properties` file this way or similar.

```
# Send messages to the console
handlers=io.helidon.logging.jul.HelidonConsoleHandler

# !thread! is replaced by Helidon with the thread name
# any %X{...} is replaced by a value from MDC
java.util.logging.SimpleFormatter.format=%1$tY.%1$tm.%1$td
%1$tH:%1$tM:%1$tS %4$s %3$s !thread!: %5$s%6$s "%X{name}"%n

# Global logging level. Can be overridden by specific loggers
.level=INFO
```

It's important to use `HelidonConsoleHandler`. `%X{name}` prints the name property from MDC.

Now let's take a look at how MDC can be used in your application. In one part of your application, you need to set an MDC property you want to be printed out in all your log messages as follows.

```
import io.helidon.logging.common.HelidonMdc;

public class Foo {
    ...
    public SetupMdcLogging() {
        HelidonMdc.set("name", "Falco");
    }
}
```

In another class, you initialize your logger and log some messages.

```
import java.util.logging.Logger;

private static final Logger LOGGER = Logger.getLogger(Main.
class.getName());

public class Bar {
    ...
    public TestLogging() {
        LOGGER.info("It comes from MDC:");
    }
}
```

Here is what's going to be logged.

```
2022.11.01 2:00:00 INFO Main Thread[main,5,main]: It comes
from MDC: "Falco"
```

MDC with Log4j

Log4j allows you to use file-based configuration or programmatic configuration. File-based configuration is not friendly with GraalVM native-image. Samples are provided for both, but you choose which to use based on your setup.

Listing 4-26 shows how to configure MDC `log4j2.xml` standard Log4j 2.x configuration file.

Listing 4-26. Example of MDC Configuration in log4j2.xml

```
<Configuration status="INFO">
    <Appenders>
        <Console name="stdout" target="SYSTEM_OUT">
            <PatternLayout
              pattern="%d{HH:mm:ss.SSS} %-5level [%t]
              %logger{36} - %msg %X{name}%n" />
        </Console>
    </Appenders>
    <Loggers>
        <Root level="INFO">
            <AppenderRef ref="stdout" />
        </Root>
    </Loggers>
</Configuration>
```

Listing 4-27 provides the same configuration but in a programmatic way.

Listing 4-27. Example of Programmatic MDC Configuration in Log4j

```
import org.apache.logging.log4j.core.appender.ConsoleAppender;
import org.apache.logging.log4j.core.config.Configurator;
import org.apache.logging.log4j.core.config.builder.api.
ConfigurationBuilderFactory;
...
private static void configureLog4J() {
```

```
var builder = ConfigurationBuilderFactory.
newConfigurationBuilder();
builder.setStatusLevel(Level.INFO);

var appenderComponentBuilder = builder.
newAppender("stdout", "CONSOLE")
        .addAttribute("target", ConsoleAppender.Target.
        SYSTEM_OUT);

appenderComponentBuilder.add(builder.
newLayout("PatternLayout")
        .addAttribute("pattern", "%d{HH:mm:ss.SSS}
        %-5level [%t] %logger{36} - %msg %X{name}%n"));

builder.add(appenderComponentBuilder);
builder.add(builder.newRootLogger(Level.INFO)
                    .add(builder.
                    newAppenderRef("stdout")));

Configurator.initialize(builder.build());
}
```

Again, the important MDC-related configuration part is %X{name}, which prints the name property from your MDC context, which can be set as follows.

```
import org.apache.logging.log4j.ThreadContext;
...
ThreadContext.put("name", "Cassidy");
```

You can find the full sample as part of this chapter sample code.

MDC with SLF4J

To configure MDC with SLF4J, add the following or a similar configuration to your logback.xml file.

Listing 4-28. Example of MDC Configuration in SLF4J

```
<configuration>
    <appender name="STDOUT" class="ch.qos.logback.core.
    ConsoleAppender">
        <encoder>
            <pattern>
                %d{HH:mm:ss.SSS} %-5level [%thread]
                %logger{36} - %msg %X{name}%n
            </pattern>
        </encoder>
    </appender>
    <root level="INFO">
        <appender-ref ref="STDOUT" />
    </root>
</configuration>
```

As with JUL and Log4j, the %X{name} prints the name property from your MDC context.

Now you can set your MDC property as follows.

```
import org.slf4j.MDC;
...
MDC.put("name", "Jaspis");
```

Its value is printed in each log message.

Summary

- Observability is the ability of a service to expose data externally that reflects its internal behavior.

- There are four main areas of observability: health, metrics, tracing, and logging.

- Helidon implements MicroProfile Health, MicroProfile Metrics, and MicroProfile OpenTracing specifications.

- Health checking is essential for guaranteeing your whole system's smooth operation. Health checks allow external automated management systems to check if your application is available and ready to serve requests.

- Helidon comes with built-in health checks, which help in determining general issues each application can face, as well as an ability to create custom health checks.

- MicroProfile Metrics gives aggregated statistics about how your service is performing over time. It can be used to improve service performance, tune upscaling strategies, optimize business logic, and collect data for reporting.

- Distributed systems like microservices are difficult to debug because of their distributed nature. Distributed tracing is a method to track a request journey as it travels across components of a distributed system. It helps in debugging and performance tuning your distributed system.

- Helidon provides automatic "code-free" distributed tracing support and an ability to explicitly work with tracing spans.

- Logging tells you what is happening inside individual software components within a service.

- Helidon supports MDC (Mapped Diagnostic Context), allowing registering and using in your logging messages information that is not available in the current logging scope.

CHAPTER 5

Communicating with Other Services

This chapter covers the following topics.

- Understanding MicroProfile Rest Client APIs

- Exception handling and filters in MicroProfile Rest Client

- Calling RESTful services using the JAX-RS Client API

- Providers and asynchronous calls using the JAX-RS Client API

- Adding CORS support to Helidon applications

Microservices not only provide data but also consume it. Sometimes one business action can contain multiple REST calls, which can even form a distributed transaction.

Note Services call other services!

And these *service call hierarchies* can be widely spread across many services.

© Dmitry Kornilov, Daniel Kec, Dmitry Aleksandrov 2023
D. Kornilov et al., *Beginning Helidon*, https://doi.org/10.1007/978-1-4842-9473-4_5

There are multiple ways to call a RESTful service in Helidon. Imagine a "sorcery ministry" that manages all wizards and their licenses to do magic. This ministry retrieves this information from two services: a wizard service for wizards and a licensing service for the licenses. Both these services provide data using their REST endpoints. Thus, the sorcery ministry is a client for those services.

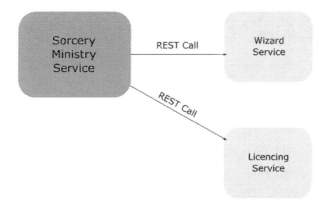

Figure 5-1. *Services calling other services Different microservice client options*

- **MicroProfile Rest Client** is a standard REST client in MicroProfile Ecosystem.

- **JAX-RS Client** API is a popular REST client following the builder pattern model.

Let's get acquainted with each of them.

Note   In Helidon SE, there is a specially designed reactive Helidon WebClient. It is described in Chapter 15.

MicroProfile Rest Client

The MicroProfile Rest Client provides a type-safe approach to invoke RESTful services over HTTP. It is designed to extend the Jakarta REST (JAX-RS) specification. MicroProfile Rest Client is a specification under the MicroProfile umbrella, and Helidon MP implements it.

Let's directly jump into the real code and create a small REST client, which consumes data from our wizard service—a repository of all wizards.

The wizard service is straightforward. Just three endpoints for providing a wizard by name and getting the mightiest wizard.

Listing 5-1. Wizard Resource

```
@Path("/wizard")
@RequestScoped
public class WizardResource {
    private final WizardProvider wizardProvider;

    @Inject
    public WizardResource(WizardProvider wizardProvider) {      ①
        this.wizardProvider = wizardProvider;
    }

    @GET
    @Produces(MediaType.APPLICATION_JSON)
    public Wizard getMostMightyWizard() {                       ②
        return wizardProvider.getWizard();
    }

    @Path("/{name}")
    @GET
    @Produces(MediaType.APPLICATION_JSON)
    public Wizard getWizard(@PathParam("name") String
    name) {    ③
```

```
        return wizardProvider.getWizardByName(name);
    }

    @Path("/add")
    @POST
    @Produces(MediaType.APPLICATION_JSON)
    @Consumes(MediaType.APPLICATION_JSON)
    public Response addWizard(JsonObject jsonObject) {              ④
        if (!jsonObject.containsKey("name")) {
            JsonObject entity = JSON.createObjectBuilder()
                    .add("error", "No name provided")
                    .build();
            return Response.status(Response
            .Status.BAD_REQUEST).entity(entity).build();
        }

        String name = jsonObject.getString("name");
        Wizard wizard = new Wizard();
        wizard.setName(name);
        wizardProvider.addWizard(wizard);
        return Response.noContent().build();
    }
}
```

① A class that holds and provides wizards

② An endpoint that provides the mightiest wizard in
    JSON format

③ An endpoint that provides a wizard by name in
    JSON format

④ A POST endpoint to add a new wizard, which
    consumes in JSON format

Note   The wizard service MicroProfile Rest example can be found in the Book Samples repository.

This resource is a reference for what is happening on the server side. It runs on localhost port 8080.

Now let's look at the client side.

MicroProfile Rest Client is already included in the full helidon-microprofile bundle. To use a REST client with all other MicroProfile options, include Listing 5-2 in the pom.xml file.

Listing 5-2. MicroProfile Full Bundle

```
<dependency>
    <groupId>io.helidon.microprofile</groupId>
    <artifactId>helidon-microprofile</artifactId>
</dependency>
```

If more fine-grained control is required, and helidon-microprofile-core is used, add the dependency in Listing 5-3 to our project's pom.xml file.

Listing 5-3. MicroProfile Core Bundle

```
<dependency>
    <groupId>io.helidon.microprofile.bundles</groupId>
    <artifactId>helidon-microprofile-core</artifactId>        ①
</dependency>
<dependency>
    <groupId>io.helidon.microprofile.rest-client</groupId>
    <artifactId>helidon-microprofile-rest-client</artifactId>  ②
</dependency>
```

① MicroProfile Core dependency

② MicroProfile Rest Client dependency

Let's now create the client interface for the wizard service used by the sorcery ministry.

Since it is in a *managed environment,* let CDI take care of the REST client creation. A REST client interface must be annotated with `@RegisterRestClient` to automatically register it with CDI.

You must create an interface with the desired methods and properly annotate them. Let's use `@RegisterRestClient` with `baseUrl` to declare that our client should connect to a specific endpoint. Then add the `getMostMightyWizard()` method and annotate it with `@GET`, which means the client performs a `GET` request to the base URI and map the result to the wizard. To get a wizard by name, add another method and annotate it with `@GET` and `@Path("/{name})`. The method has a parameter annotated with `@PathParam("name")` which means the name is provided from the parameter and the endpoint is invoked with the resulting path.

Listing 5-4. REST Client Interface

```
@RegisterRestClient(baseUri="http://localhost:8080/wizard")  ①
interface WizardRestClient {

    @GET                                                      ②
    Wizard getMostMightyWizard();

    @Path("/{name}")                                          ③
    @GET
    Wizard getWizardByName(@PathParam("name") String name);
}
```

① This registers the REST client with a `http://localhost:8080/wizard` base URI.

② This method declares a client to perform a GET
request to the *base URI* and map the result to
the wizard.

③ This method performs a GET request to the base
URI with a path parameter name.

You can see that familiar annotations like @GET and @Path are used.
This unification makes it easy to get used to it.

Let's use the WizardRestClient in our class, as shown in Listing 5-5.

Listing 5-5. Resource with REST Endpoints

```
@ApplicationScoped                                          ①
@Path("/wizardClient")
public class SorceryMinistryResource {

    @Inject
    @RestClient                                             ②
    private WizardRestClient restClient;

    @GET
    @Produces(MediaType.APPLICATION_JSON)
    public Wizard getMostMightyWizard() {
        return restClient.getMostMightyWizard();           ③
    }

    @GET
    @Path("/{name}")
    @Produces(MediaType.APPLICATION_JSON)
    public Wizard getWizardByName
                    (@PathParam("name")String name) {
        return restClient.getWizardByName(name);           ④
    }
}
```

① It must be a CDI bean.

② The @RestClient annotation injects an automatic proxy implementing a REST client.

③ This is a simple use of the MicroProfile Rest Client without any parameters.

④ This shows using the MicroProfile Rest Client with the name parameter.

Calling client.getWizardByName(name) reaches the endpoint of the Helidon wizard service. You may notice there is no implementation of the WizardRestClient interface. A proxy is created and injected automatically.

Note   A REST client implementation allows us to configure its parameters using a programmatic API based on the builder pattern, annotations, and configuration. All the configuration parameters are standard and portable in MicroProfile and can be found in the official documentation.

Integration with MicroProfile Config

It is also possible to use MicroProfile Config properties to override values specified in the @RegisterRestClient annotation of the REST interface.

Listing 5-6 overrides baseUri in *microprofile-config.properties*.

Listing 5-6. URI Properties

```
io.helidon.book.ch05.WizardRestClient/mp-rest/uri=http://
someotheruri:8080/wizard
```

baseUri annotation property (or specified as */mp-rest/uri in external configuration) is required by the REST client. However, implementations may have other ways to define these URLs/URIs. If specified in *microprofile-config.properties*, it overrides any baseUri value for the interface annotated with @RegisterRestClient.

Other properties such as scope, providers, connectTimeout, readTimeout, followRedirects, and proxyAddress can also be specified following the *<class>/mp-rest/<property>* pattern.

If the client works behind a proxy and has to follow redirects, Listing 5-7 shows how to specify it this way.

Listing 5-7. Proxy and Redirect Properties

```
io.helidon.book.ch05.WizardRestClient/mp-rest/
proxyAddress="http://someobscureproxy.com:9999"   ①
io.helidon.book.ch05.WizardRestClient/mp-rest/follow
Redirects=true                                     ②
```

① Sets MicroProfile Rest Client to use a proxy

② Sets MicroProfile Rest Client to follow redirects

As MicroProfile Rest Client supports SSL, the trust store setup in the CDI environment is easily done using properties.

- io.helidon.book.ch05.WizardRestClient/mp-rest/
  trustStore sets the trust store location. Can point to a classpath resource or a file.

- io.helidon.book.ch05.WizardRestClient/mp-rest/
  trustStorePassword specifies the keystore password.

- io.helidon.book.ch05.WizardRestClient/mp-rest/
  trustStoreType is the trust store type. The default is "JKS".

The same is achieved for the key store.

- `io.helidon.book.ch05.WizardRestClient/mp-rest/keyStore` is the key store location. It can point to a classpath resource or a file.

- `io.helidon.book.ch05.WizardRestClient/mp-rest/keyStorePassword` specifies the keystore password.

- `io.helidon.book.ch05.WizardRestClient/mp-rest/keyStoreType` is the key store type. The default is `"JKS"`.

Exception Handling

In a perfect world, all the servers are always up and running, and the line is always free with zero latency, but it is typical that a server is down or disconnected. The data may be somehow jammed or incorrectly marshaled/unmarshaled. You must be prepared for that, and our Helidon app should handle these situations gracefully. MicroProfile Rest Client provides a solution for that: `ResponseExceptionMapper`. This mapper takes a `Response` object retrieved via an invocation of a client, checks its status, and converts it to an exception according to our needs.

Let's create a simple exception mapper for our wizard client. First, create a class that implements `ResponseExceptionMapper<T>` with the corresponding exception as a template parameter. Then override `public T toThrowable(Response response) {}` function where you can define different behavior on different responses. In this case, return `RuntimeException` with another description depending on the `Response` status code.

Listing 5-8. Exception Mapping

```
public class WizardExceptionMapper
        implements ResponseExceptionMapper<RuntimeException>
        {                                                           ①
```

```java
@Override
public RuntimeException toThrowable(Response response) {
    if (response.getStatus() ==
                Response.Status.NOT_FOUND.getStatusCode())
                {                                          ②
        return new RuntimeException("Resource not found");
    } else if (response.getStatus() ==
                Response.Status.INTERNAL_SERVER_ERROR.
                getStatusCode()) {                         ③
        return new RuntimeException("Server bad response");
    } else {
        return new RuntimeException("Something went
        terribly wrong: " + response);                     ④
    }
}
}
}
```

① This class implements ResponseExceptionMapper
   <RuntimeException>.

② If the Response has 404 status, a
   RuntimeException with a "Resource not found"
   message is returned.

③ If the Response has 500 status, a
   RuntimeException with a "Server bad response"
   message is returned.

④ Otherwise, a RuntimeException with a
   "Something went terribly wrong" message is
   returned.

Since this exception mapper is ready, all you need to do is to register it to the REST client interface. Otherwise, it is registered using the @RegisterProvider annotation, as shown in Listing 5-9.

Listing 5-9. Register Exception Mapper

```
@RegisterRestClient(baseUri="http://localhost:8080/wizard")
@RegisterProvider(WizardExceptionMapper.class)                    ①
interface WizardRestClient {
...
}
```

      ① Register WizardExceptionMapper for
        WizardRestClient.

Every exception that may occur during the service execution is handled gracefully.

Modifying Requests and Responses

You may probably notice that @RegisterProvider is used to register the exception mapper. It is also used to register different filters and modifiers.

You can use filters around requests and responses.

- **ClientResponseFilter** is invoked in order when a response is received from a remote service.

- **ClientRequestFilter** is invoked in order when a request is made to a remote service.

For example, if you want to log what request has been made, you should create a class implementing ClientRequestFilter. By overriding filter(ClientRequestContext requestContext) function, you can use any information about the current request, like headers, URLs, and so forth. You can get it from the ClientRequestContext object, which is passed as a parameter.

Listing 5-10. Request Filter

```
public class WizardRequestFilter implements
ClientRequestFilter {                        ①

    private static final Logger log =
            Logger.getLogger(String.valueOf(WizardRequest
            Filter.class));

    @Override
    public void filter(ClientRequestContext
    requestContext) {                        ②
        log.info("Request intercepted: " + requestContext.
        getHeaders());
    }
}
```

① Implement ClientRequestFilter.

② Override filter(...) and get information from ClientRequestContext.

The same can be done for Response Filters. You should create a class implementing ClientResponceFilter. In this case, log the response status.

Listing 5-11. Response Filter

```
public class WizardResponseFilter implements
ClientResponseFilter {          ①

    private static final Logger log =
            Logger.getLogger(String.valueOf(WizardResponse
            Filter.class));
```

```
    @Override
    public void filter(ClientRequestContext requestContext,
                                   ClientResponseContext
                                   responseContext) { ②
        log.info("Intercepted response status"
                         + responseContext.getHeaders());
    }
}
```

① Implement `ClientResponseFilter`.

② Override `filter(…)` and get information from `ClientResponseContext`.

Finally, you must register these filters with the `WizardRestClient`, as easy as the exception mapper, using the `@RegisterProvider` annotation, as shown in Listing 5-12.

Listing 5-12. Register Filters

```
@RegisterRestClient(baseUri="http://localhost:8080/wizard")
@RegisterProvider(WizardExceptionMapper.class)
@RegisterProvider(WizardRequestFilter.class)            ①
@RegisterProvider(WizardResponseFilter.class)           ②
interface WizardRestClient {

    ...
}
```

① Register `WizardRequestFilter`.

② Register `WizardResponseFilter`.

Now if you run the sorcery ministry app and call the /wizardClient endpoint in the log output, you see Listing 5-13.

Listing 5-13. Sample Output

```
{Accept=[application/json], Magic-Header=[Custom header
magic value]}
{content-length=[13], connection=[keep-alive], Date=[Wed, 28
Jan 2023 16:14:24 +0300], Content-Type=[application/json]}
```

The filters are working and returning header information as intended. Other interceptions and modifiers can be applied in the same way.

- **MessageBodyReader** is used when the entity should be read from the API response after invocation.

- **MessageBodyWriter** is used for a request body to be written in the request for @POST and @PUT operations and other HTTP methods that support bodies.

- **ParamConverter** is used for a parameter in a resource method to be converted to a format for a request or a response.

- **ReaderInterceptor** is a listener triggered when a read occurs against the response received from a remote service call.

- **WriterInterceptor** is a listener triggered when a write occurs to the stream to be sent on the remote service invocation.

Provider invocation priority can be controlled. @Priority is used when you want to set an explicit priority value, like @Priority(1000). This means that the annotated provider is used as one of the last. Both programmatically and via annotations, the builder pattern can be used to register providers. The providers that include the @RegisterProvider annotation are subordinate to those registered using a builder. The class's @Priority annotation is subordinate to the @RegisterProvider annotation.

Provider priorities can be overridden by various `Configurable` methods, which can take a `Provider` class, a `Provider` instance, and a priority and mappings of those priorities.

Handling Headers

HTTP headers are designed to enable the transfer of supplementary details between the client and server when sending an HTTP request or Response. A header comprises a name that is not case-sensitive, followed by a colon (:)and its corresponding value. Headers are crucial for implementing various security, authentication, tracing, and other mechanisms.

To specify headers for service calls, annotate a method parameter with the `@HeaderParam` annotation.

Listing 5-14. Header Parameters

```
@Path("/wizard")
public interface WizardRestClient {

    //.. other methods omitted

    @POST
    Response createWizard(@HeaderParam("Custom-Header")
                              String customHeader,       ①
                              Wizard wizard);

    @PUT
    @Path("/{name}")
    Response updateWizard(@BeanParam PutWizard putWizard,
                                        Wizard wizard);②

    @DELETE
    @Path("/{name}")
    Response deleteWizard(@CookieParam("AuthToken")
```

```
                                      String token, ③
                    @PathParam("name") String name);
}

public class PutWizard {                                    ④
    @HeaderParam("Custom-Header")
    private String custom;
    @PathParam("name")
    private String name;
    // ...
}
```

① Injects *Custom-Header* header.

② Injects an aggregate bean with fields annotated
   using the *...Param* annotation.

③ Injects AuthToken from a cookie.

④ This is a class with @HeaderParam and @PathParam
   annotated fields used in <2>.

But if you need to specify an HTTP Header without altering the
client interface method signature, you should use @ClientHeaderParam
annotation. It has three parameters.

- **name** is the header name.

- **value** is the header value, which must be String or
  string[], or a reference to a method that computes
  the value.

- **required** is a boolean value that determines whether
  a request should fail if the compute method throws an
  exception.

Listing 5-15. Client Header Parameters

```
@Path("/wizard")
public interface WizardRestClient {

    //.. other methods omitted

    @POST
    @ClientHeaderParam(name="Magic-Header",
        value="Custom header magic value",
        required=false)      ①
    Response postWizardCustomHeader(Wizard wizard) {...}
}
```

① Set a Custom header to the client method.

To add or distribute headers in bulk, ClientHeadersFactory is utilized. This factory contains only one method that accepts two read-only MultivaluedMap parameters. If the client is operating in a JAX-RS environment, the first map represents headers from the incoming JAX-RS request, whereas the second map includes headers specified using @ClientHeaderParam, @HeaderParam, @BeanParam, and so on that are sent. The returned result is MultivaluedMap, representing the "final" set of headers to be transmitted in the outbound processing flow.

Note   The final map of headers could still be changed by providers, such as filters, interceptors, and message body writers before the HTTP request is sent.

To add custom headers, you should implement ClientHeadersFactory and override the update method. There you have all the incoming and outgoing headers. As a result, you should return a map with the headers you want.

Listing 5-16. Client Headers Factory

```
public class WizardHeaderHandler implements
ClientHeadersFactory {                                       ①

    @Override
    public MultivaluedMap<String, String>
            update(MultivaluedMap<String, String>
            incomingHeaders,
                MultivaluedMap<String, String>
                clientOutgoingHeaders) {
        return new MultivaluedHashMap<>() {{
            put("Magic-Header",
                List.of("Custom header magic value"));   ②
        }};
    }
}
```

① Implements `ClientHeadersFactory`.

② Overrides `update` method returning a
   `MultivaluedHashMap` with the header desired.

Following the same paradigm as `Provider`, `WizardHeaderHandler`
must be registered with the REST client interface. It is achieved with the
`@RegisterClientHeaders` annotation.

Listing 5-17. Register Header Handler

```
...
@RegisterClientHeaders(WizardHeaderHandler.class)  ①
interface WizardRestClient {

    ...
}
```

① Registers the `WizardHeaderHandler`

Now there is a "magic header" in the headers.

Asynchronous Operations

MicroProfile Rest Client is a very powerful tool. If you must consume heavy or long-running requests, you can make them asynchronous so that these calls won't block your service. It is achieved very easily: a method should return `CompletionStage<>`. In our particular wizard client, replace the return type, as shown in Listing 5-18.

Listing 5-18. Asynchronous Operations

```
interface WizardAsyncRestClient {

    @GET
    CompletionStage<Response> getMostMightyWizard();        ①

    @Path("/{name}")
    @GET
    CompletionStage<Response>
        getWizardByName(@PathParam("name") String name); ②
}
```

① Asynchronous version of the
   `getMostMightyWizard` method

② Asynchronous version of the
   `getWizardByName` method

Now you can asynchronously process client requests using standard Java language features.

If you need to intercept and manipulate asynchronous calls, please consult the MicroProfile Rest Client documentation.

Programmatic APIs

MicroProfile Rest Client can also be created using a programmatic API via a builder obtained from `RestClientBuilder.newBuilder()`. This is the way to use MicroProfile RestClients outside the managed CDI environment. `RestClientBuilder` provides methods to configure client details and define the desired REST client interface.

Listing 5-19. Programmatic Operations

```
WizardRestClient client =
    RestClientBuilder.newBuilder()                              ①
        .baseUri(URI.create("http://localhost:8080/
        wizard"))    ②
        .followRedirects(true)                                  ③
        .proxyAddress("http://someobscureproxy.com:9000")  ④
        .build(WizardRestClient.class);

Wizard wizard = client.getMostMightyWizard();
```

① Uses a builder pattern to create the client.

② Sets `baseUrl`.

③ Sets `followRedirects` to `true`.

④ Configures the proxy.

You can set all the properties programmatically. For SSL setup, there are corresponding `trustStore` and `keyStore` objects.

Note   MicroProfile Rest Client instances created using builder are not injectable, as this usage is designed for operating outside the CDI container. So, if you create a client instance this way, it is not visible to the CDI container.

MicroProfile Rest Client Conclusion

As mentioned, MicroProfile Rest Client is a very powerful tool. This chapter covers the main usage cases of it. But it can do much more, like server-side events handling, its integrations with MicroProfile Config and fault tolerance, and other cool features.

Please refer to the official documentation for all details.

JAX-RS Client API

Another way to call other RESTful services in Helidon is to use the JAX-RS Client API. JAX-RS is an old but commonly used name for Jakarta EE specification called Jakarta RESTful Web Services Specification. It also has excellent inbuilt client capabilities.

The JAX-RS Client API is intended to facilitate a fluent programming model, and in Helidon, it is implemented using Jersey. This programming model differs from the one employed in the MicroProfile Rest Client. The JAX-RS Client API heavily employs the builder pattern to simplify configuration and execution. Additionally, unlike the MicroProfile Rest Client, the JAX-RS client lacks an annotations API.

If you use the full `helidon-microprofile` bundle, all the dependencies are available out of the box. If you chose to use the `helidon-microprofile-core`, to ensure correct JSON to Object mapping, you should include JSON-B support in our project `pom.xml` file, as shown in Listing 5-20.

Listing 5-20. MicroProfile Dependencies

```
<dependency>
    <groupId>io.helidon.microprofile.bundles</groupId>
    <artifactId>helidon-microprofile-core</artifactId> ①
</dependency>
```

```
<dependency>
    <groupId>jakarta.json.bind</groupId>
    <artifactId>jakarta.json.bind-api</artifactId>       ②
</dependency>
<dependency>
    <groupId>org.glassfish.jersey.media</groupId>
    <artifactId>jersey-media-json-binding</artifactId> ③
</dependency>
```

① MicroProfile Core dependency

② JSON-B support in Jersey

③ Jersey binding support dependency

Note   The JAX-RS Client API is a very powerful and versatile tool. It can be used with many services delivering XML, plain text, and binary streams. This book focuses only on RESTful services delivering JSON data, which is automatically marshaled/unmarshaled to Java objects.

To create and use the JAX-RS Client API, the following steps should be done: call `ClientBuilder.newClient()` static method to create a new `Client`. Then use `target()` method on the obtained client instance. A `WebTarget` is returned. Next, get `Invocation.Builder` using `target.request()` method on `WebTarget` instance obtained in the second step. Finally, execute `invocationBuilder.get()`, `put()`, `post()` or `delete()` methods to invoke corresponding REST calls.

Let's create and use the client by following the earlier four steps. First, create a `WebTarget` pointing to `http://localhost:8080`. Let's use `ClientBuilder.newClient()` for that as described. Next, use the created `client` to set the path to the `/wizard` endpoint, set `MediaType` to `APPLICATION_JSON` since we are working with JSON data, and call the

get method with the Wizard.class parameter. This way, the JAX-RS
Client API performs a GET call to the specified base URI and endpoint and
automatically maps the result to the Wizard class.

Listing 5-21. Resource with Endpoints

```
@ApplicationScoped
@Path("/wizardClient")
public class SorceryMinistryResource {

    private final WebTarget target =
                            ClientBuilder.newClient()
                                .target("http://
                                localhost:8080"); ①

    @GET
    @Path("/jaxrs")
    @Produces(MediaType.APPLICATION_JSON)
    public Wizard getWizardFromJaxrsClient() {
        return target
                .path("/wizard")                        ②
                .request(MediaType.APPLICATION_JSON)    ③
                .get(Wizard.class);                     ④
    }
}
```

① Creates a WebTarget by using a ClientBuilder
for creating a Client and setting a target. This is
a resource-heavy operation. (This is why we do it
once and cache it in a class field.)

② Sets the path to /wizard.

③ Builds an invocation with MediaType.APPLICATION_JSON.

④ Maps the JSON result to the Wizard class.

As simple as that. Just create a client using a static builder. After this, you can call the service using get(), put(), post(), or delete() methods on Invocation.Builder. This code achieves the same result as using the MicroProfile Rest Client. Bear in mind that the requests above are blocking. This means during the client call, the thread is blocked, and nothing useful can be done. Asynchronous and reactive execution is discussed later in this chapter.

Also, remember that WebTarget instances are immutable in terms of their URI. However, they are mutable in terms of configuration. Thus, configuring a WebTarget instance does not create new instances. Creating a WebTarget instance is considered a heavy operation.

An Invocation is a request that has been prepared and is ready for execution. You do not need to know how the invocation was prepared, but only how it should be executed—*synchronously* or *asynchronously*.

Client, ClientBuilder, and WebTarget are configurable, as they all implement a Configurable interface that supports the configuration of the following.

- **Properties** are name-value pairs for additional configuration.

- **Features** are special types of providers that implement the Feature interface and can be used to configure a JAX-RS implementation. Features are not covered in this book.

- **Providers** are classes or instances of classes that implement one or more interfaces of *entity providers*, *context providers*, and *exception mapping providers*. A provider can be a message filter, a context resolver, an exception mapper, and so forth. The usage of a *provider* is demonstrated later in this chapter.

Let's make a more complex demonstration by posting a new wizard instance to the endpoint. To demonstrate this, let's use the wizard service that was created in MicroProfile Rest Client. It has a /wizard/add POST endpoint, accepting JSON data.

To send our new wizard to the POST endpoint, let's use the post() request execution method. This method expects to receive Entity class instances to work properly. The Entity object holds metadata for sending the wizard entity over the network. The payload can be of any kind: XML data, text data, or a custom binary stream. In this case, create an Entity instance, which marks the wizard instance to be processed as a JSON document. It can be done using the Entity.json(wizard) method.

Listing 5-22. JAX-RS Client Usage

```
// other methods omitted

@GET
@Path("/jaxrs/add")
@Produces(MediaType.APPLICATION_JSON)
public Wizard addWizardAndCheck() {
    Wizard wizard = new Wizard();
    wizard.setName("NewWizard");                        ①

    client.path("/wizard/add")
            .request(MediaType.APPLICATION_JSON)
            .post(Entity.json(wizard);

    return client                                       ③
            .path("/wizard/NewWizard")
            .request(MediaType.APPLICATION_JSON)
            .get(Wizard.class);
}
```

① Creates a sample wizard.

② Marshals the new wizard to JSON using `Entity.json()` method and send data in a *post* request.

③ Synchronously queries the service for a new wizard and returns it.

When you call this method, it returns the new `wizard` object, which is saved in the wizard service.

Listing 5-23. Call the Client

```
curl -X GET http://localhost:8081/wizardClient/jaxrs/add
{"name":"NewWizard"}                                        ①
```

① Create a new `Wizard` object and query it back.

Providers

Providers in JAX-RS and its Client are responsible for various cross-cutting concerns such as filtering requests, converting representations into Java objects, and mapping exceptions to responses. A provider can be pre-packaged in the JAX-RS runtime or supplied by an application.

Let's implement the same logging filter used in the "MicroProfile Rest Client" section. For that, the JAX-RS Client API provides a conceptually close approach.

- Creates a class implementing `ClientRequestFilter` and/or `ClientResponseFilter`

- Registers this/these class(s) within `Client` or `WebTarget`, using `.register(...)` method

If you register a filter in `Client`, it is inherited by all `WebTarget` instances. Registering it within the current instance means no other `WebTarget` instance is affected.

To simplify the logging filter creation, let's create a single class implementing both interfaces. Override `filter(ClientRequestContext requestContext)` for `ClientRequestFilter`, and `filter(ClientRequestContext requestContext, ClientResponseContext responseContext)` for `ClientResponseFilter`. The class should look like Listing 5-24.

Listing 5-24. Request and Response Filters

```
public class LoggerFilter implements
              ClientRequestFilter, ClientResponseFilter {      ①

    private final Logger logger =
            Logger.getLogger(LoggerFilter.class.getName());

    @Override
    public void filter(ClientRequestContext requestContext) { ②
        logger.info(requestContext.getHeaders().toString());
    }

    @Override
    public void filter(ClientRequestContext requestContext,
                       ClientResponseContext
                       responseContext) { ③
        logger.info(responseContext.getHeaders().toString());
    }
}
```

① Class implementing `ClientRequestFilter` and
`ClientResponseFilter`.

② Override `filter(ClientRequestContext
requestContext)` to log request headers.

③ Override `filter(ClientRequestContext
requestContext, ClientResponseContext
responseContext)` to log response headers.

Only register this class in `Client`, since we want all `WebTargets` created
by this `Client` to have a logging filter registered.

Listing 5-25. Register Filter

```
WebTarget target = ClientBuilder.newClient()
          .register(new LoggerFilter())        ①
          .target("http://localhost:8080");
```

① Register `LoggerFilter` in the `WebTarget`.

Now all the headers from the requests and responses will be logged.

Let's run the sorcery ministry app and call the `/wizardClient/jaxrs`
endpoint in the log output, as shown in Listing 5-26.

Listing 5-26. Sample Output

```
{Accept=[application/json]}
{content-length=[13], connection=[keep-alive], Date=[Wed, 28
Sep 2022 16:26:55 +0300],
Content-Type=[application/json]}
```

Excellent, as expected!

There are many other providers of entity manipulation for media
type, working with contexts and exceptions. Please refer to the official
documentation for more details.

Asynchronous Operations

JAX-RS provides an *asynchronous* way of calling other services. It is achieved just by calling .async() method. Thus, the function immediately returns a Future instance, which contains a response once it is received.

Listing 5-27. Asynchronous Operations

```
public Future<Wizard> getAsyncWizardFromJaxrsClient() {
    return target
            .path("/wizard")
            .request(MediaType.APPLICATION_JSON)
            .async()                                    ①
            .get(Wizard.class);
}
```

① Invokes an asynchronous client call.

And even more than this. The requests can be processed *reactively*. And this is also achieved quite easily by calling the client's .rx() method. The function returns CompletableStage as a result.

Listing 5-28. Reactive Operations

```
public CompletableStage<Wizard>
                  getAsyncWizardFromJaxrsClient() {
    return client
            .path("/wizard")
            .request(MediaType.APPLICATION_JSON)
            .rx()                                       ①
            .get(Wizard.class);
}
```

① Invokes a *reactive* client call

The request execution immediately returns `CompletionStage`, which contains a `Wizard` instance once it processes the response. It can later be processed in a *reactive* means using standard Java language features.

These methods are suitable for heavy or long-running calls to avoid blocking the service thread.

JAX-RS Client API Conclusion

This chapter only scratched the surface of all the possibilities the JAX-RS Client API provides. The usage itself is worthy of its own thick book since it is a very powerful tool.

Please refer to the official documentation for more information.

CORS

Due to security reasons, browsers allow loading resources only from the same origin as the page was loaded. Previously, browsers allowed loading resources from any location, and this was a reason for much data to be stolen.

Still, sometimes, you need to allow requests from specific locations other than the origin. And CORS is made for this.

The *cross-origin resource sharing* (CORS) protocol allows the server to identify origins other than its own from which a browser should permit loading resources. It works based on HTTP headers.

Helidon can programmatically define the CORS behavior of your services using the Helidon CORS API. You can also configure it externally. Three built-in endpoints—health, metrics (see Chapter 4), and OpenAPI (see Chapter 9)—are integrated with CORS. Several annotations and configuration options allow you to easily control how our resources are exposed across origins. Please explore the Helidon official documentation for more information on all its features.

Add the Listing 5-29 dependency to the Helidon MP project's `pom.xml` file to enable CORS.

Listing 5-29. CORS Dependency

```
<dependency>
    <groupId>io.helidon.microprofile</groupId>
    <artifactId>helidon-microprofile-cors</artifactId>
</dependency>
```

In this example, let's refer to our wizard service.

The "sorcery ministry" at *sorceryministry.com* hosts an app that regulates wizards. A wizard service—a repo of all wizards—runs at *helidonserver.com/wizard*.

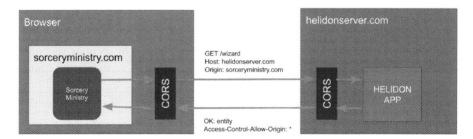

Figure 5-2. *Call hierarchy of the wizard service and the sorcery ministry application*

1. The browser loads the sorcery ministry app from *sorceryministry.com*, which is the origin of CORS.

2. The app requests GET `http://helidonserver.com/wizard`. *helidonserver.com* is the host. The browser's CORS implementation adds Host and Origin headers to the request.

3.   Helidon CORS checks that the Helidon application
     permits sharing of */wizard* via GET with
     sorceryministry.com. If so, it permits the request to
     reach the destination; if not, it rejects the request
     with "403 – Forbidden" status.

4.   Helidon CORS updates the response with *Access-
     Control-Allow-Origin: * (depending on how you
     have configured CORS for the Helidon application).

Now, let's add CORS to our wizard application. The goal is to permit
unrestricted sharing of the resource that returns wizards and restrict
sharing of the resource that gets the wizard so that only the origins `http://`
`sorceryministry.com` can get the information.

Listing 5-30. CORS Annotations Usage

```
@GET
@Produces(MediaType.APPLICATION_JSON)
@CrossOrigin(allowMethods = {"GET"},
        allowOrigins = {"http://sorceryministry.com"})    ①
public JsonObject getWizard() { }
```

① Declare CORS properties.

Use the `@CrossOrigin` annotation with the `allowMethods` and
`allowOrigins` parameters specified.

You can do the same using an external configuration. Add Listing 5-31
to the `microprofile-config.properties` file.

Listing 5-31. CORS Configuration

```
cors.paths.0.path-pattern=/wizard
cors.paths.0.allow-methods=GET
cors.paths.0.allow-origins=http://sorceryministry.com
```

This configuration enables the required CORS settings for the /wizard resource.

Helidon also lets us easily include health, metrics (see Chapter 4), and OpenAPI (see Chapter 9) services in our Helidon application. These services add endpoints to our application so clients can retrieve various telemetry and documentation information. As with the application endpoints you create, these endpoints represent resources that can be shared across origins.

By default, the integrated CORS support in all three services permits any origin to share their resources using GET, HEAD, and OPTIONS HTTP requests. You can override the default CORS behavior to those endpoints using the configuration. They are independent of the services created. For example, restrict the /health endpoint and the /metrics endpoint, provided by built-in components, to only the origin *http:// sorceryministry.com.*

Listing 5-32. Health and Metrics Configuration

```
...
health:
  cors:
    allow-origins: [http://sorceryministry.com]   ①
metrics:
  cors:
    allow-origins: [http://sorceryministry.com]     ②
...
```

> ① Allows /health to be accessible to the only origin
>   http://sorceryministry.com
>
> ② Allows /metrics to be accessible to the only
>   origin, http://sorceryministry.com

Now, if you try to access the /health endpoint, it rejects requests from origins that are not approved, as shown in Listing 5-33.

Listing 5-33. Sample Output

```
curl -i -H "Origin: http://sorceryministry.com"
http://helidonserver.com/health

HTTP/1.1 403 Forbidden
Date: Mon, 11 Jan 2023 12:06:55 +3:00
transfer-encoding: chunked
connection: keep-alive
```

And responds successfully only to cross-origin requests from *http://sorceryministry.com.*

Listing 5-34. Sample Output

```
curl -i -H "Origin: http://sorceryministry.com"
http://helidonserver.com/health


HTTP/1.1 200 OK
Access-Control-Allow-Origin: http://sorceryministry.com
Content-Type: application/json
Date: Mon, 11 Jan 2023 12:09:05 +3:00
Vary: Origin
connection: keep-alive
content-length: 461

{"outcome":"UP",...}
```

Summary

- Services call other services. Some services provide data, while others consume it.

- Helidon has multiple ways to communicate with other Microservices with REST.

- MicroProfile Rest Client and the JAX-RS Client API provide different programming models. Declarative for MicroProfile Rest Client and the builder pattern based on the JAX-RS Client API.

- Advanced header manipulations, filtering, and asynchronous operations can be done in MicroProfile Rest Client and the JAX-RS Client API.

- To ensure correct Cross-origin work, consider setting up CORS for your microservices. This is easily done using a few annotations in Helidon MP or external configuration.

- You can control the accessibility of built-in endpoints like /health, /metrics, and /openapi using external configuration.

CHAPTER 6

Accessing Data

This chapter covers the following topics.

- Microservices interacting with databases are nicely supported in Helidon in various ways

- Working with SQL and NoSQL using JDBC, JTA, and JPA in Helidon

- Accessing data using Micronaut Data in Helidon

We have heard at many conferences and read in many articles that the best microservices are stateless, and we should keep them stateless. Nevertheless, real-world practices have shown that most microservices must keep state and thus must talk to databases. That's why Helidon provides a convenient way to work with databases. Helidon offers multiple ways to work with a database, from low-level data access using JDBC to the complex Jakarta Persistence API and its implementations: Hibernate and EclipseLink. If you have ever worked with Enterprise Java, it takes no effort to learn it. Just work with it as you used to before. Just bear in mind that Helidon is not a full Jakarta EE container.

© Dmitry Kornilov, Daniel Kec, Dmitry Aleksandrov 2023
D. Kornilov et al., *Beginning Helidon*, https://doi.org/10.1007/978-1-4842-9473-4_6

From low-level to complex, these are the main options for working with a database in Helidon.

- At the lowest level of database interaction is JDBC, where physical connections are handled.

- **DataSource** provides an abstraction layer over JDBC, facilitating connection management and pooling.

- The **Jakarta Persistence API** is an object-relational mapping specification implemented with Hibernate and EclipseLink.

This chapter walks through all of them, explaining their pros and cons.

Low-Level Data Access with JDBC

Relational database management systems (RDBMS) and NoSQL databases are external software programs accessed through a database *driver* via some form of connection, usually TCP connections. Typically, the *database engine* functions as a *server*, with our code serving as the client. It is also acceptable to refer to it as a *database server*.

Java Database Connectivity (JDBC) is an API for the Java programming language that specifies how a client can access a database. It has been used since 1997, making it one of the oldest Java technologies.

The API is employed to load the appropriate drivers dynamically and register them in the JDBC DriverManager. The `DriverManager` functions as a connection factory for creating JDBC connections.

JDBC connections are used to create and execute *statements*, of which there are several kinds.

- **Statement** is a regular statement to read or alter data sent to a database.

- **PreparedStatement** is a cached statement; subsequently, the execution path is predetermined on the database server, enabling it to be executed repeatedly in a highly efficient manner.

- **CallableStatement** is for executing stored procedures on the database.

Query statements (e.g., SELECT) return a JDBC row result set. They represent the tabular data. The row result set has metadata describing the columns' names and their types.

Update statements (e.g., INSERT, UPDATE, and DELETE) alter data in the database and return the count of updates to indicate the number of affected rows.

Helidon MP does not include any database drivers; hence it is up to us to select the appropriate driver for our database and vendor and manually add its dependency to the pom.xml file of our application.

Let's dive into some code. To keep it simple, let's use H2—a small, in-memory database primarily used for unit testing. Listing 6-1 is its dependency.

Listing 6-1. H2 Driver Dependency

```
<dependency>
    <groupId>com.h2database</groupId>
    <artifactId>h2</artifactId>
    <scope>runtime</scope>                    ①
</dependency>
```

> ① The scope is runtime because JDBC drivers are runtime components not needed at compile time.

187

Now that you have the database driver, let's use it in the code.

Listing 6-2. JDBC Example

```
try {
        String url = "jdbc:h2:mem:sample";                        ①
        Connection connetion = DriverManager.getConnection
        (url,"sa","");                              ②
        Statement stmt = conn.createStatement();                  ③
        ResultSet rs = stmt.executeQuery("SELECT * FROM
        Wizards);      ④
        while ( rs.next() ) {
            String name = rs.getString("Name");
            System.out.println(name);
        }
        connections.close();                                      ⑤
    } catch (Exception e) {
        e.printStacktrace();                                      ⑥
    }
```

① Sets a database connection URL

② Creates a connection using `DriverManager`

③ Creates a statement

④ Executes a `SELECT` query, gets the `ResultSet`, and processes it

⑤ Closes the connection

⑥ Handles exceptions

This is a very straightforward and low-level way of accessing the data from a database. It is very inefficient. Creating a connection is a resource-heavy operation, and manually parsing data is not the best choice.

That is why the DataSource interface was created for managing connections.

Working with DataSource

DataSource is an interface with only two methods: getConnection() and getConnection(String username, String password), which is in the javax.sql package. Database vendors offer various implementations of this interface to provide distinct database functionality. Generally, these implementation classes contain methods that enable us to supply the database server particulars and user credentials.

The following are other common features provided by DataSource implementations.

- Connection pooling

- Caching PreparedStatement

- Connection timeouts

- Logging features

Helidon provides integration mechanisms to set up and inject DataSource into our code. The flow is easy: describe connection details in the microprofile-config.properties file and inject the DataSource using @Inject and @Named annotations. Helidon MP's named data source integration requires a connection pool implementation.

Two primary ones are currently supported: HikariCP and Oracle Universal Connection Pool (OCP). You can choose to use either, but not both. Just add the corresponding dependency for the selected option.

Listing 6-3 is for HikariCP.

Listing 6-3. HikariCP Dependency

```
<dependency>
    <groupId>io.helidon.integrations.cdi</groupId>
    <artifactId>helidon-integrations-cdi-datasource-hikaricp
    </artifactId>
    <scope>runtime</scope>
</dependency>
```

Listing 6-4 is for OCP.

Listing 6-4. OCP Dependency

```
<dependency>
  <groupId>io.helidon.integrations.cdi</groupId>
  <artifactId>helidon-integrations-cdi-datasource-ucp
  </artifactId>
  <scope>runtime</scope>
</dependency>
```

Note   Do not forget to add the database driver dependency to the
pom.xml file. Connection pools can work with different database
vendors, and drivers for them are not included in the dependencies.

Now that you have the required dependencies, let's configure
DataSource in microprofile-config.properties.

Listing 6-5. Typical Configuration

```
javax.sql.DataSource.wizardSource.dataSourceClassName=org.
h2.jdbcx.JdbcDataSource
javax.sql.DataSource.wizardSource.dataSource.
url=jdbc:h2:mem:test;DB_CLOSE_DELAY=-1
javax.sql.DataSource.wizardSource.dataSource.user=db_user
javax.sql.DataSource.wizardSource.dataSource.password=user_
password
```

Property names have a common pattern.

```
<objecttype>.<datasourcename>.<propertyname>
```

- `<objecttype>` is the fully qualified Java class name of
  the configured object. In our case, it is is.`javax.sql.`
  `DataSource`. It is followed by a period (`.`) as a separator.

- `<datasourcename>` is the name of the data source.
  It cannot contain a period "." In this case, it is
  `wizardSource`. A period (`.`) is a separator for the
  next part.

- `<propertyname>` supplies the connection pool or
  vendor-supplied `DataSource`-specific configuration
  property name. It may contain periods (`.`), such as `.url`
  (`.user` in our case).

Helidon reads this configuration and creates and configures the
desired `DataSource`. To use it in our Java code, inject it with the `@Named`
annotation.

Listing 6-6. Inject DataSource

```
@Inject
@Named("wizardSource")                                   ①
private DataSource wizardSource;
```

   ① Inject named DataSource "wizardSource"

Listing 6-7 uses a constructor.

Listing 6-7. Inject DataSource via Constructor

```
private final DataSource wizardSource;               ①

@Inject
public SomeObject(@Named("wizardSource")
                         DataSource wizardSource) {   ②
    this.dswizardSource = wizardSource;
}
```

   ① Defines the DataSource variable

   ② Injects the named DataSource to a constructor
      parameter

Now you can get a connection from the managed DataSource and use it in our code. This is a much more resource-friendly way to get a JDBC connection.

Data Access with JPA

The preceding sections discussed how the laborious task of managing database connections could be alleviated using DataSource. However, the challenge of dealing with low-level result sets remains. The data in a database exists in a completely different realm and is stored in tables with interrelations for relational databases. It does not consist of objects. As a result, manually converting this tabular data to Java objects and back is a time-consuming process. Various object-relational mapping (ORM) frameworks were developed to simplify this process. Essentially, they serve as an intermediary layer between the DataSource and user code, transforming the relational data stored in a database into Java objects and vice versa, thus reducing the required time.

But each of these frameworks provided its own API and usage model. A common specification was created since this is a typical problem in most enterprise applications. It is called the Jakarta Persistence API. This is not a ready-to-use solution; it is a document and a set of APIs that different vendors should implement. These implementations are usually called *JPA providers*.

JPA describes, among other things, how its implemented.

- Map Java objects to relational database tables.

- Manage such persistent Java objects.

- Interact with transactions (in this case, Jakarta Transactions).

- Interact with named data sources.

You must put a few annotations to our POJOs, and the JPA provider does all the magic for you. Those annotated objects are managed using special EntityManager and EntityManagerFactory classes, which are automatically configured and instantiated by Helidon. The code written with JPA is portable. This means it works the same way when you switch the provider, discussed later in the chapter.

JPA has two operation modes.

- In a **container-managed** entity manager, JPA management is handled entirely by the container; Helidon, in our case.

- In an **application-managed** entity manager, JPA management is handled by the application (better say, the developer).

This book talks only about the container-managed JPA, which means you learn how to tell Helidon to properly configure and run a JPA provider for you. Helidon takes of error handling, thread safety, and transaction management on behalf of the user, making the developer experience much better.

JPA providers are supported in Hibernate ORM and EclipseLink. You should choose one of them, but not both.

Note   This chapter only acquaints you with JPA in the context of Helidon. JPA is a vast topic. Please check other books about JPA for more details about this specification and its usage.

All of this may sound a little scary, but let's jump into the code, and you will see that it is quite easy.

Microservices working with a database is a common use case; there is a special Helidon QuickStart. It can be used as a template for our next Helidon service. Let's now generate a Quickstart database example at `https://helidon.io/starter`.

1. Select the **Helidon MP** flavor.

2. Select **Database**.

3. Choose **Jackson** or **JSON-B** for Media Support.

4. Select the following.

    - **Hibernate** as the JPA Implementation

    - **HipariCP** for Connection Pool

- **H2** for the Database Server

- **Auto DDL** for Automatic schema initialization

5.   Click the **Download** button.

Alternatively, you can go to https://helidon.io/starter/3.2.0?fl avor=mp&step=5&app-type=database, unzip the myproject.zip download, and open the folder in your favorite IDE.

Note   When this book was written, Helidon's latest version was 3.2.0. You may replace the version number with the latest version available to you.

Let's explore the generated project. It is a Pokemon repository service.

First, let's look at the dependencies in the pom.xml file. The most significant are those for *persistence*.

Listing 6-8. Persistence Dependencies

```
<dependency>
    <groupId>jakarta.persistence</groupId>
    <artifactId>jakarta.persistence-api</artifactId>      ①
</dependency>
<dependency>
    <groupId>io.helidon.integrations.cdi</groupId>
    <artifactId>helidon-integrations-cdi-jpa</artifactId>②
    <scope>runtime</scope>
</dependency>
<dependency>
    <groupId>io.helidon.integrations.cdi</groupId>
    <artifactId>helidon-integrations-cdi-hibernate</artifactId> ③
    <scope>runtime</scope>
</dependency>
```

```
<dependency>
    <groupId>io.helidon.integrations.cdi</groupId>
    <artifactId>helidon-integrations-cdi-datasource-hikaricp
    </artifactId>                                              ④
    <scope>runtime</scope>
</dependency>
```

① Jakarta Persistence API main dependency

② JPA CDI extensions

③ Since Hibernate was chosen as the JPA provider, Helidon integrates with it

④ Uses HikariCP for database connections management

In Helidon, you can set up and combine different technologies like Lego blocks. In this case, let's combine the HikariCP connection pool with JPA (Helidon uses CDI as an extension mechanism) and Hibernate as a JPA provider.

Let's look at the code, especially the Pokemon and PokemonType entities. These two entities depend on each other: Pokemon has a PokemonType as a property.

Listing 6-9. Pokemon Entity

```
@Entity(name = "Pokemon")                                    ①
@Table(name = "POKEMON")                                     ②
@Access(AccessType.PROPERTY)
@NamedQueries({                                              ③
        @NamedQuery(name = "getPokemons",
                    query = "SELECT p FROM Pokemon p"),
        @NamedQuery(name = "getPokemonByName",
```

```
                query = "SELECT p FROM Pokemon p WHERE
                p.name = :name")
})
public class Pokemon {

    private int id;
    private String name;
    private PokemonType pokemonType;

    @Id
    @Column(name = "ID", nullable = false, updatable =
    false)                    ④
    public int getId() {
        return id;
    }

    @Basic(optional = false)
    @Column(name = "NAME", nullable = false)                    ⑤
    public String getName() {
        return name;
    }

    @JsonIgnore
    @ManyToOne
    public PokemonType getPokemonType() {                    ⑥
        return pokemonType;
    }

    //.. constructor, other getters and setters omitted
}
```

① Declares an entity named "Pokemon"

② Entity is stored in a table called "POKEMON"

③ Several named queries for querying all Pokemons or to find a Pokemon by name

④ Id column, which should not be nullable and updatable

⑤ Name column described on a getter method should be titled "NAME" and not be empty

⑥ PokemonType field, described as a many-to-one dependency

Listing 6-10. PokemonType Entity

```java
@Entity(name = "PokemonType")                              ①
@Table(name = "POKEMONTYPE")                               ②
@NamedQueries({                                            ③
        @NamedQuery(name = "getPokemonTypes",
                    query = "SELECT t FROM PokemonType t"),
        @NamedQuery(name = "getPokemonTypeById",
                    query = "SELECT t FROM PokemonType t
                    WHERE t.id = :id")
})
public class PokemonType {

    @Id
    @Column(name = "ID", nullable = false, updatable = false)
                                                           ④

    private int id;

    @Basic(optional = false)                               ⑤
    @Column(name = "NAME")
    private String name;

    //.. constructor, getters, and setters omitted
}
```

① Entity named "PokemonType"

② Entity should be stored in a table called
   "POKEMONTYPE"

③ Several named queries used for querying all
   PokemonTypes or to find a PokemonType by ID

④ Id column, which should not be nullable and
   updatable

⑤ Name column described on a getter method
   should be titled "NAME" and not be empty

The following tables are generated in the database.

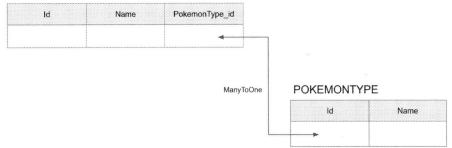

Figure 6-1. *Pokemon and PokemonTables represented in a database*

Figure 6-1 shows that the POKEMON table has a PokemonType_id
column. It is there to represent the relation between Pokemon and
PokemonType entities. JPA takes care of object mapping to those tables.

Now let's jump into configuration. In the microprofile-properties.
config file, you should describe the database connection properties
following the pattern described in the "Working with a DataSource"
section.

Listing 6-11. DataSource Configuration

```
javax.sql.DataSource.ds1.dataSourceClassName=org.h2.jdbcx.
JdbcDataSource          ①
javax.sql.DataSource.ds1.dataSource.url=jdbc:h2:mem:test;DB_
CLOSE_DELAY=-1          ②
javax.sql.DataSource.ds1.dataSource.user=db_user               ③
javax.sql.DataSource.ds1.dataSource.password=user_password       ④
```

① Driver class used

② Database connection URL

③ User name

④ Password

Helidon reads this config, prepares the DataSource object, sets up JPA, and provides EntityManager so you can inject it. Let's use it in or PokemonResource endpoint, where Pokemon CRUD operations are performed.

Listing 6-12. Pokemon Resource

```
@Path("pokemon")                                               ①
public class PokemonResource {

    @PersistenceContext(unitName = "pu1")
    private EntityManager entityManager;

    @GET
    @Produces(MediaType.APPLICATION_JSON)
    public List<Pokemon> getPokemons() {
        return entityManager
            .createNamedQuery("getPokemons", Pokemon.class).
            getResultList();                                   ②
    }
```

```
@GET
@Path("{id}")
@Produces(MediaType.APPLICATION_JSON)
public Pokemon getPokemonById(@PathParam("id") String id) {
    Pokemon pokemon = entityManager
            .find(Pokemon.class, Integer.valueOf(id));
    if (pokemon == null) {
        throw new NotFoundException("Unable to find
        pokemon with ID " + id);                            ③
    }
    return pokemon;
}

@GET
@Path("name/{name}")
@Produces(MediaType.APPLICATION_JSON)
public Pokemon getPokemonByName(@PathParam("name")
String name) {
    TypedQuery<Pokemon> query =
            entityManager.createNamedQuery("getPokemon
            ByName", Pokemon.class);                         ④
    List<Pokemon> list = query.setParameter("name", name).
    getResultList();
    if (list.isEmpty()) {
        throw new NotFoundException("Unable to find pokemon
        with name " + name);
    }
    return list.get(0);
}

// .. more methods to be described later.
}
```

① Sets `Path` endpoint to `/pokemon`

② Injects `EntityManager` using standard `@PersistenceContext` annotation with the `unitName` parameter set as "pu1" as set in the generator

③ Uses `entityManager` to execute the `getPokemons` query, maps each item to `Pokemon`, and returns a list of them

④ Uses `entityManager` to execute the `getPokemons` named query to find one by name, maps the result to the `Pokemon` class, and returns it

As you can see from the code, JPA takes care of all the calls to the database, querying the data, and automatically mapping the *relational data* to Java objects, which you can regularly use in our code.

Transactions

On occasion, a single significant action necessitates numerous interactions with a database. These interactions are grouped as a *transaction*. This implies that either all of the interactions are executed or none of them are. The database must not be left in a corrupted state, with some of the data modified and others left untouched. This is one of the key characteristics of database engines—to ensure ACID (atomicity, consistency, isolation, durability). These transaction properties are essential to guarantee data accuracy in the event of errors or failures.

For this, JPA requires a transactional engine to be used, and Jakarta Transactions API (or JTA) is used. It allows us to start, commit, and roll back transactions in a resource-agnostic way. Like JPA, JTA is not a tool or framework but an open standard specification that other vendors should implement. Helidon MP uses the Narayana transaction engine

as an implementation for JTA. It lets us use @jakarta.transaction.
Transactional to declare JTA transactions in our Java code. You just
annotate a method with the preceding annotation, and all the calls to the
database in this method are executed in a transaction. If something goes
wrong, the data will not be corrupted or saved in an intermediate state.
JTA is not bound to work with the database only. It can manage multiple
resources of different types (like messaging, for example) in a consistent
and coordinated manner.

Let's add some transactional methods to our Pokemon management
service. First, you need some Maven dependencies, as shown in
Listing 6-13.

Listing 6-13. Transaction Dependencies

```
<dependency>
    <groupId>jakarta.transaction</groupId>
    <artifactId>jakarta.transaction-api</artifactId>      ①
</dependency>
<dependency>
    <groupId>io.helidon.integrations.cdi</groupId>
    <artifactId>helidon-integrations-cdi-jta-weld
    </artifactId>                                          ②
    <scope>runtime</scope>
</dependency>
```

① Jakarta Transactions API core dependency

② Helidon Narayana CDI extension

The best candidates for transactional methods are the DELETE and
CREATE methods.

To use the DELETE method, the initial step involves verifying the
existence of the Pokemon. This entails retrieving it from the database. The
subsequent action involves deleting the Pokemon and saving the state, with

the entire process being an atomic action. If, for instance, Pokemon was retrieved the in the first step, there is a possibility that it may have already been altered or deleted before remove(pokemon) is executed in the same method but in another thread.

For the CREATE method, you first must retrieve the PokemonType from the database, then assign it to the newly created Pokemon instance. As in the previous situation, you must ensure this PokemonType exists. Thus, this sequence has to be performed as a single activity. You don't want a PokemonType to be deleted or altered before it is assigned to the new Pokemon.

Listing 6-14. Pokemon Resource

```
@Path("pokemon")
public class PokemonResource {

    //.. previous methods omitted

    @DELETE
    @Path("{id}")
    @Produces(MediaType.APPLICATION_JSON)
    @Transactional(Transactional.TxType.REQUIRED)          ①
    public void deletePokemon(@PathParam("id") String id) {
        Pokemon pokemon = getPokemonById(id);
        entityManager.remove(pokemon);                      ②
    }

    @POST
    @Consumes(MediaType.APPLICATION_JSON)
    @Transactional(Transactional.TxType.REQUIRED)          ③
    public void createPokemon(Pokemon pokemon) {
        try {
            PokemonType pokemonType = entityManager
```

```
            .createNamedQuery("getPokemonTypeById",
            PokemonType.class)                              ④
            .setParameter("id", pokemon.getType()).
            getSingleResult();
        pokemon.setPokemonType(pokemonType);
        entityManager.persist(pokemon);
    } catch (Exception e) {
        throw new BadRequestException("Unable to " +
                            "create pokemon with ID " +
                            pokemon.getId());
    }
  }
}
```

① Method should be part of a new transaction

② Uses entityManager remove method to delete a Pokemon from the database

③ All interaction with the database should be in a transaction

④ Assigns PokemonType to a given Pokemon, calls entityManager to execute the getPokemonTypeById named query to find a type, sets the type to a given pokemon, and uses entityManager to persist the data into a database

The topic of transactions is quite complex. It has a big part in computer science. This book does not go deep into how and where to use transactions, as this is nicely described in books about transactions. The same is about JPA and its providers—Hibernate and EclipseLink.

This chapter only scratched the surface of what JPA can do and much time it can save you by handling all the ORM jobs. But if you need complex object structures to be mapped to complex relational models, please consult specific books on the topic.

The main message of this part is to get us acquainted with JPA and JTA and that Helidon provides full support for JPA and JTA in container-managed mode.

Summary

- Microservices work with the database to persist data, and Helidon provides multiple ways of accessing and persisting the data.

- Helidon supports JDBC and DataSource for low-level work with JDBC-supported databases.

- Helidon supports standard ways of accessing data using JPA, with Hibernate or EclipseLink as providers. It can be used with almost no limitations as in regular Jakarta/Java EE applications.

CHAPTER 7

Resiliency

This chapter covers the following topics.

- Using the retry mechanism

- Defining the fallback method

- Invoking a method asynchronously

- Limiting the method execution time

- Controlling the number of parallel executions

- Combining Fault Tolerance features

Failure in your service is inevitable! Sounds grim, but it should be no surprise for any developer that something won't work as expected at some point in the program's life cycle. The more complex the system becomes, the bigger the chance is for failure. In the same way a car manufacturer needs to install airbags, you must prepare your code for failures with appropriate countermeasures. Network issue? Retry the call. Too many concurrent calls? Limit contention. The business method takes too long? Use timeout. Sending message fails? Store it in the error queue. It sounds easy, right? Use a try/catch block for a few cycles, start a monitor thread, and manage an extra thread pool.

Okay, it's not that easy, and you just don't need to reinvent the wheel each time. There can be a lot of *mission-critical code* that needs to be done right.

All this magic becomes a boilerplate when you realize the use cases are repeating and functionality can be done for you behind the scenes. There is a Helidon implementation of MicroProfile Fault Tolerance, with which you just annotate your bean method by appropriate annotation, to help you exactly in such situations when you expect your code could fail.

Fault Tolerance provides the following annotations to help you with various use cases.

- **Retry** retries an annotated bean method with a configured number of times when an exception is thrown.

- **Fallback** calls a configured handler or method if the annotated method throws an exception.

- **Asynchronous** executes an annotated method on a new thread.

- **Timeout** monitors annotated method execution time and interrupts it if it runs too long.

- **Circuit Breaker** keeps track of the ratio of annotated method execution failures and rejects new calls in case it reaches the limit.

- **Bulkhead** monitors contention on annotated method and blocks or rejects other threads when it gets too high.

Retry

Some operations can be unreliable by nature, and you must accommodate for it. A typical use case would be using the JAX-RS client. You never know what can happen on the network. Using old-school try/catch blocks in the cycle, as shown in Listing 7-1.

Listing 7-1. try/catch Block in the Cycle

```java
public String callWizardService() {
  RuntimeException retryError = null;
  for (int i = 0; i <= 2; i++) {
    try {
      System.out.println("Calling wizard service ...");
      return ClientBuilder.newClient()
              .target("http://wizard-service")
              .request()
              .get()
              .readEntity(String.class);
    } catch (RuntimeException e) {
      retryError = e;
    }
  }
  throw retryError;
}
```

Let's do one original invocation plus two retries if an exception is thrown.

```
Calling wizard service ...
Calling wizard service ...
Calling wizard service ...
2022.03.25 10:29:10 WARNING ...
java.net.ConnectException: Connection refused
```

Too much boilerplate just makes our business code needlessly complicated. Annotating the bean method with @Retry automatically does the same functionality done in Listing 7-1.

Listing 7-2. Retry

```
@Retry(maxRetries = 2)
public String callWizardService() {
    System.out.println("Calling wizard service ...");
    return ClientBuilder.newClient()
            .target("http://wizard-service")
            .request()
            .get()
            .readEntity(String.class);
}

Calling wizard service ...
Calling wizard service ...
Calling wizard service ...
2022.03.25 10:35:55 WARNING ...
java.net.ConnectException: Connection refused
```

Fallback

You have already learned how to do a retry. In case retrying doesn't
help, a default response might be needed. @Fallback simply provides a
value for returning in case our bean method fails. It's simple enough, so
let's combine it. You can return the default value if the wizard service is
unreachable.

Listing 7-3. Fallback Method

```
@Retry(maxRetries = 2)
@Fallback(fallbackMethod = "defaultWizardServiceResponse")
public String callWizardService() {
    System.out.println("Calling wizard service ...");
```

```
    return ClientBuilder.newClient()
        ...
}
String defaultWizardServiceResponse(){
    return "Wizard service is offline :-(";
}
```

This time method is invoked three times (remember: one original invocation plus two retries). When the last retry fails, the fallback method is invoked, and its result is returned by the `callWizardService()` method instead of the original wizard response.

Asynchronous

Spinning up a new thread in a DI application can be tricky. You never know what magic is happening in the thread context under the hood of your container. But the use case is quite common when you need to do something lengthy but can't afford to wait for the result.

@Asynchronous can be used on the business method, but annotation is not enough this time. Since the asynchronous method would return the value sometime in the future, you must change the return type to a callback. Java has a convenient API for callbacks right in the `java.util.concurrent` package. With `CompletableFuture,` you can create a callback and complete it either successfully `future.complete(value)` or exceptionally `.completeExceptionally(ex)`. `CompletionStage,` on the other side, is a superclass of `CompletableFuture`. It has fewer methods for a reason. Whereas `CompletionStage` is meant for the consumer of the future action, `CompletableFuture` is for the side controlling the completion.

By making the annotated method return CompletionStage<String>, you get a callback that you can listen to for the completion of the asynchronous method without blocking the calling thread. Without @Asynchronous, we would have to spin up our own thread or drive a special thread pool; either way, it is completely unmanaged by the container with a thread context unknown to the server.

Listing 7-4. Manual Asynchronous Execution

```
public CompletionStage<String> timeConsumingTask() {
  CompletableFuture<String> futureCallback =
                              new CompletableFuture<>();
  new Thread(() -> {
    try {
      Thread.sleep(2000);
    } catch (InterruptedException e) {
      futureCallback.complete("Long work interrupted!");
    }
    futureCallback.complete("Long work is done!");
  }).start();
  return futureCallback;
}
```

When the method is invoked, you get the CompletionStage instead of the actual result. You can use the thenAccept method and register a consumer lambda, which is invoked when the asynchronous work is done.

Listing 7-5. Long Task Call

```
System.out.println("Calling long task!");
CompletionStage<String> callback = bean.timeConsumingTask();
callback.thenAccept(s ->
    System.out.println("Task finished with result: " + s)
);
```

```
System.out.println("We didn't have to wait " +
"for task to finish to get here!");
```

The output of Listing 7-5 demonstrates that the parent thread will continue without waiting for asynchronous work to finish.

Listing 7-6. Long Task Call Output

```
Calling long task!
We didn't have to wait for task to finish to get here!
Task finished with result: Long work is done!
```

Fault Tolerance's @Asynchronous helps you with thread management behind the scenes. Although it looks as if you are returning a completed Future, the returned CompletionStage is actually completed when the asynchronous work is done.

Listing 7-7. The Same Functionality as Listing 7-4

```
@Asynchronous
public CompletionStage<String> timeConsumingTask() {
  try {
    Thread.sleep(2000);
  } catch (InterruptedException e) {
    return CompletableFuture
                .completedStage("Long work interrupted!");
  }
  return CompletableFuture
                .completedStage("Long work is done!");
}
```

The result is going to be the same.

```
Calling long task!
We didn't have to wait for task to finish to get here!
Task finished with result: Long work is done!
```

This time, the asynchronous thread has the correct server context and will work with other Fault Tolerance features, like timeout and retry.

Note   @Asynchronous can be conveniently combined with reactive messaging methods.

Timeout

Some tasks can take longer than expected or even get stuck forever. To effectively defend our application against such a situation, Fault Tolerance provides the @Timeout annotation. The run-time of the method with the annotation is being monitored, and if timeout is reached, the thread is interrupted, and the method throws TimeoutException.

There is a catch, however. When timeout is monitored on the same originating thread, the only way to stop it after the timeout is by interrupting it. An interruption doesn't have to be enough to stop the thread. The thread may be looping somewhere without checking for an interruption. In such cases, an exception is thrown long after the timeout is reached. No guarantees are given on the same thread. Combining @Timeout with @Asynchronous, on the other hand, offers much more control. While the new thread is monitored for timeout, our original thread doesn't have to wait for the asynchronous method to finish.

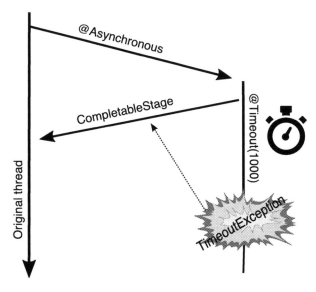

Figure 7-1. *Asynchronous timeout with exception propagated over CompletionStage*

TimeoutException wrapped in the ExecutionException is immediately provided through the returned Future or CompletionStage when the timeout occurs, whether the interruption succeeded or not.

Listing 7-8. Asynchronous Timeout with Fallback

```
@Asynchronous                                        ①
@Timeout(500)                                        ②
@Fallback(
        fallbackMethod = "longTaskFallback",        ③
        applyOn = TimeoutException.class)            ④
public CompletionStage<String> timeConsumingTask(Long mls)
throws InterruptedException {
    Thread.sleep(mls);                               ⑤
    return CompletableFuture
                .completedFuture(mls + " in time!");
}
```

```
private CompletionStage<String> longTaskFallback(Long p) {
    return CompletableFuture
                        .completedFuture(p + " timeout!");
}
```

① Run the method on a different thread to get the timeout immediately.

② Set the timeout for 500 milliseconds.

③ Define a fallback method to compensate in case of a timeout.

④ Use a fallback only in case of a timeout.

⑤ Delay for a certain number of milliseconds to check if the timeout kicked in.

Listing 7-9. Call Timeout

```
timeConsumingTask(490).get();      ① ②
timeConsumingTask(520).get();      ③

> 490 in time!
> 520 timeout!
```

① Uses `CompletionStage.get()` to block the current thread until the result is ready

② Sets lower delay to avoid timeout

③ Sets a higher delay to reach timeout

Circuit Breaker

You already learned how to do a retry and fallback in case of a failure and how to monitor a timeout. You do have basic tools now for coping with a certain degree of intermittent failure. Another tool for guarding the actual ratio of intermittent failures is Circuit Breaker.

Unlike the circuit breaker in your house that has only two states—on/off, this one is way smarter. Fault Tolerance's Circuit Breaker feature has three states.

- **Closed** means the failure ratio is low, and all executions are allowed.

- **Open** means the failure ratio is too high, and Circuit Breaker denies executions with `CircuitBreakerOpenException`.

- **Half-open** means the configured number of test executions is allowed to test if Circuit Breaker can switch back to a `Closed` state.

While the one in your basement opens the electric circuit with the first evidence of trouble and keeps it that way until you come with the flashlight to switch it back on again, Circuit Breaker analyzes the failure ratio in a rolling window to keep the quality of service at a configured level. A *rolling window* sounds fancy, but it's only the number of past execution attempts from which the success ratio is calculated. A "rolling window of 20" is the last 20 execution results the Circuit Breaker logic remembers for comparing the number of them that failed. If too many failures are registered, Circuit Breaker switches from `Closed` state to `Open,` and further executions are denied by throwing `CircuitBreakerOpenException`. You don't have to go there with the flashlight and turn it on again after a configured delay. Circuit Breaker switches to the third state: `Half-open`. In the `Half-open` state, configurable number executions are allowed to test if the situation improved and it's safe to switch back to the Closed state. If any of the executions in the Half-open state fail, Circuit Breaker returns to the Open state.

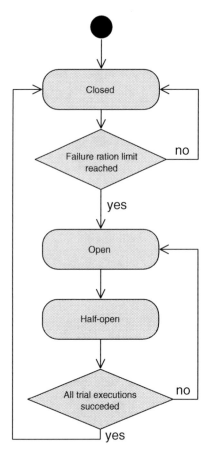

Figure 7-2. *Circuit breaker states*

Circuit Breaker can be combined with other Fault Tolerance annotations. For example, @Retry retries are counted as execution attempts, and @Fallback can compensate for denied execution with CircuitBreakerOpenException.

Bulkhead

Bulkhead functionality is best explained in a famous movie about the sinking of the *RMS Titanic* cruise ship. The *Titanic* had a known flood protection system: bulkheads. Waterproof bulkheads partitioned the ship's interior under the sea level so that possible hull breach would flood only the damaged compartments. The bulkheads would protect all the other compartments, as in Figure 7-3.

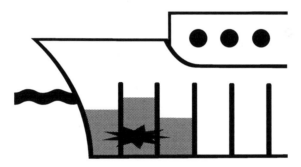

Figure 7-3. *Bulkheads isolating the flooded compartments*

Fault tolerance bulkheads work similarly, with a small difference that instead of stopping the flood of water, it stops the flood of concurrent requests.

Too many concurrent requests can be a problem, not only for our application but also for other services being invoked subsequently. Resources or services can be shared only by a limited number of contesting concurrent consumers. It's great when our service can survive a huge request peak, but what if it needs to call subsequent service multiple times per request? Such a situation could lead to cascading failure, and that's what bulkhead is for. It can effectively limit concurrent invocations of the annotated method.

In the same way that a ship's bulkhead needs to let sailors pass between the compartments, a fault tolerance bulkhead lets a configured number of threads through. It's like a valve in Figure 7-4, letting through

219

only configured number of threads at a time. When the bulkhead limit of threads currently executing our method is reached, any new thread trying to execute the method ends up with BulkheadException.

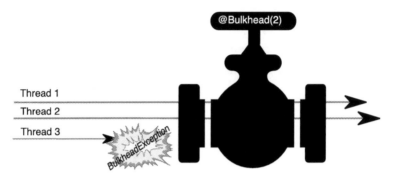

Figure 7-4. *Bulkheads regulating concurrent requests*

Bulkhead can be combined with @Asynchronous, which enables the waitingTaskQueue parameter. Since the bulkhead no longer works with simple semaphores but operates a thread pool, it is possible to keep threads in the queue until previous executions finish. When the queue is full, BulkheadException is thrown for any additional thread.

Listing 7-10. Bulkhead with Asynchronous

```
@Asynchronous
@Bulkhead(value = 2, waitingTaskQueue = 3)      ① ②
@Fallback(fallbackMethod = "bulkheadTaskFallback",
          applyOn = BulkheadException.class)      ③
public CompletionStage<Void> bulkheadTask(int task) {
    System.out.println("Executing - " + task);
    Thread.sleep(200);                            ④
    System.out.println("Finishing - " + task);
    return CompletableFuture.completedFuture(null);
}
```

```
private CompletionStage<Void> bulkheadTaskFallback(int t) {
    System.out.println("BulkheadException fallback - " + t);
    return CompletableFuture.completedFuture(null);
}
```

① Only two concurrent executions at a time are
allowed.

② Three threads can wait in a queue until previous
executions finish.

③ Invoke the fallback method instead in case
execution is rejected by @Bulkhead.

④ Spend some time on the method. Bulkhead
ensures there are always at most two threads
sleeping here at once.

Listing 7-11. Call Method with Bulkhead

```
for(int i = 1; i <= 7; i++){
    self.bulkheadTask(i);
}
```

```
>Executing - 1
>Executing - 2                        ①
>BulkheadException fallback - 6    ② ③
>BulkheadException fallback - 7
>Finishing - 1
>Executing - 3                        ④
>Finishing - 2
>Executing - 4
...
```

① Only two tasks are allowed concurrently.

② Notice how tasks 3 to 5 are waiting in the queue.

③ Tasks 6 and 7 are rejected because the queue is full already.

④ Let in task 3 as one of the previous tasks finished.

Note   All Fault Tolerance annotation parameter values can be overridden with configuration for each method, class, or whole service.

- `my.package.WizardBean/callWizardService/Retry/maxRetries=10`

- `my.package.WizardBean/Retry/maxRetries=10`

- `Retry/maxRetries=10`

- `Retry/enabled=false`

Fault Tolerance and CDI

MicroProfile Fault Tolerance uses CDI interceptors to intercept CDI bean method calls. CDI injects a proxy class instance instead of the actual instance of your bean class. This makes it possible to intercept method calls and enables other cool CDI features.

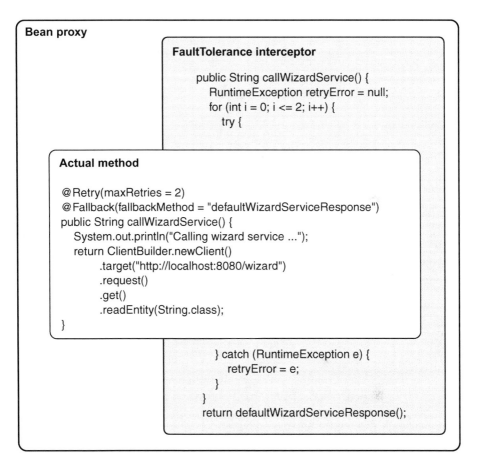

Figure 7-5. *Intercepting Fault Tolerance methods*

You need to remember to call the Fault Tolerance enabled method on the bean proxy, not the class itself. Calling a method from the same bean with this won't work. The method is executed, but Fault Tolerance has no chance to kick in.

Listing 7-12. Direct Method Call

```
public String otherBeanMethod() {
    return this.callWizardService();
}
```

You can, however, inject the bean inside itself, like in Listing 7-13, and use the reference for calling the method. This time the Fault Tolerance interceptor works.

Listing 7-13. Self Bean Method Call

```
@Inject
private WizardBean self;                    ①

public String otherBeanMethod() {
    return self.callWizardService();   ②
}
```

CDI injects proxy to the self field instead of the actual bean instance, making it possible to intercept method executions. The bean method called over the proxy instance has all the Fault Tolerance goodies.

Note   Don't call bean methods from the same class over this reference. It breaks CDI features as it misses the CDI proxy.

Summary

- Always invoke Fault Tolerance enabled methods over CDI proxy.

- The fallback method must have the same parameters and return type.

- Asynchronous methods must return `CompletionStage` or `Future`.

- All Fault Tolerance annotation arguments can be overridden with configuration.

CHAPTER 8

Security

This chapter covers the following topics.

- Using HTTPS encrypted with TLS 1.3

- Jakarta Security

- Using MicroProfile JWT tokens

- Authentication and authorization with OpenID Connect

- Encrypting secrets in configuration

Securing your application is a step that is often perceived as a very complicated task that requires security specialists with deep knowledge of all sorts of encryption mechanisms and black magic. Modern frameworks like Helidon provide tooling to simplify this task, even for developers with a basic understanding of this very important field. Since Helidon is a web server, let's start with setting up HTTPS so that you learn how to set up and use a server certificate. Then let's look at authentication and authorization by managing role-based access (RBAC) with the help of security annotations. Use OpenID Connect as a security provider. And finally, let's discuss how to use JSON Web Token (JWT) as a bearer token for easier communication between the applications and how to leverage the MicroProfile JWT extension to distribute roles within the JWT bearer token.

© Dmitry Kornilov, Daniel Kec, Dmitry Aleksandrov 2023
D. Kornilov et al., *Beginning Helidon*, https://doi.org/10.1007/978-1-4842-9473-4_8

Serving HTTPS

When you serve a plain HTTP protocol, capturing the packets on their way through the network and reading all the data is possible. You can try that yourself. Let's prepare a simple JAX-RS endpoint returning very sensitive information about whether our castle's gate is opened.

Listing 8-1. JAX-RS Method for Retrieving Gate State

```
@Path("/castle")
@ApplicationScoped
public class CastleResource {
    @GET
    @Produces(MediaType.APPLICATION_JSON)
    public JsonObject getCastle() {
        return JSON.createObjectBuilder()
                .add("gate", gateOpened.get())
                .build();
    }
}
```

Wireshark allows you to capture the packets when an endpoint is called.

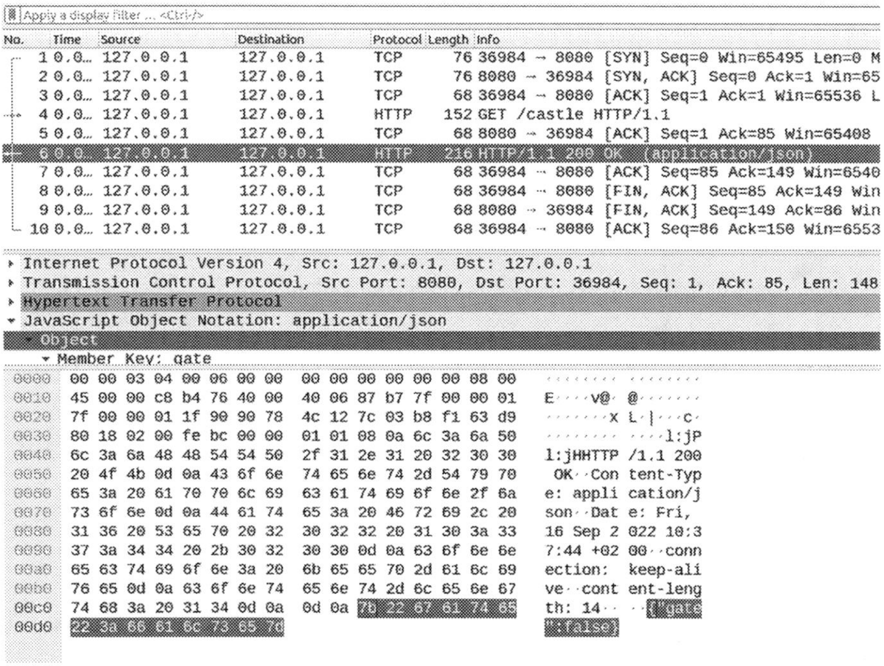

Figure 8-1. *Eavesdropping on HTTP communication with Wireshark*

As you can see, the payload {"gate":"false"} from our endpoint can be extracted easily.

And that's not even the worst attack you can suffer with HTTP. What if someone changes the DNS records, and you connect to a different server that mimics our castle service? You would call your service and get a falsified response without any way of knowing, leading your knights to the trap instead of the castle with an open gate.

Would you risk the security of your castle by using plain HTTP?

HTTPS comes to save the day. Not only can you sign server responses with our server certificate so nobody else can imitate our server, but you can also encrypt both requests and responses.

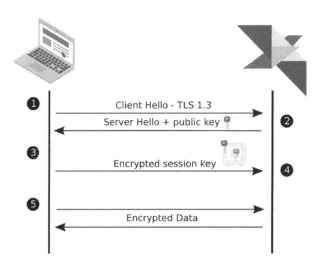

Figure 8-2. *HTTPS exchange*

1. After the initial TCP handshake, the client sends an initial "Hello" with the ALPN extension for selecting the proper protocol and the latest TLS version the client supports.

2. The server responds with its own "Hello" containing the selected protocol, TLS version, and server certificate with a public key within.

3. The client verifies the server certificate with the list of trusted certification authorities, ensuring the server is who it claims to be. Then the client generates a one-time session key, encrypts it with the server public key he just got, and verifies it is genuine.

4. The client sends the encrypted session key to the server, and only the server can decrypt the session key with its original private key(the server key). The server now has the session key, generated by the client, transferred to the server securely, so it can be used for symmetric data encryption from both sides.

5. The client can use its session key for data encryption. The server knows how to decrypt it and vice versa.

Enabling HTTPS with TLS 1.3 is not complicated with Helidon. All you need is a trusted server certificate. To obtain one, you need a private key that nobody else has. You can generate one with OpenSSL.

Listing 8-2. Create Private Key for Server Certificate

```
openssl genrsa -des3 -passout pass:'password' -out server-
private.key 4096
```

Next, you need to create a *certificate signing request* (CSR), which is the file you can send to the certification authority (CA) containing the public key from the previously generated server private key and subject data identifying our organization and domain name for signing our server certificate. Certification authorities are usually commercial companies providing the services of physically validating CSR data before actual signing by their root CA certificates. For example, around 150 root certificates are trusted by the Mozilla Firefox web browser.

Note   You can easily become a CA and sign your certificates yourself (self-signed certificate). The only problem is that no one trusts your CA. With cURL, for example, you need to use the -k option or add your CA to the cert store.

Listing 8-3. Create CSR

```
openssl req -key server-private.key -passin pass:'password' \
-subj "/C=CZ/ST=Prague/L=Prague/O=Apress/OU=BeginningHelidon/
CN=castle.beginning-helidon.apress.com" \
-new -out server.csr
```

CA creates a new server certificate for the `castle.beginning-helidon.apress.com` domain based on our CSR. To use a newly issued server certificate in a Java environment, a conversion to PKCS12 may be needed.

Listing 8-4. Convert CA Issued Server Certificate to PKCS12 Format

```
openssl pkcs12 -inkey server-private.key \
-in server.crt -export \
-passin pass:'password' \
-passout pass:'password' \
-out server.p12
```

Finally, the `server.p12` certificate file is used in Helidon with just a simple configuration.

Listing 8-5. Configure Helidon to Use TLS 1.3

```
server.tls.private-key.keystore.resource.resource-
path=server.p12
server.tls.private-key.keystore.passphrase=password
```

This time it is practically impossible to decode the data exchange between the Helidon server and the client without a securely exchanged session key.

```
Apply a display filter ... <Ctrl-/>

No.   Time    Source        Destination    Protocol Length Info
  1 0.0...  127.0.0.1     127.0.0.1      TCP      76 44618 → 8080 [SYN] Seq=0 Win=65495 Len=0 MSS=65495 SACK_PE
  2 0.0...  127.0.0.1     127.0.0.1      TCP      76 8080 → 44618 [SYN, ACK] Seq=0 Ack=1 Win=65483 Len=0 MSS=65
  3 0.0...  127.0.0.1     127.0.0.1      TCP      68 44618 → 8080 [ACK] Seq=1 Ack=1 Win=65536 Len=0 TSval=18159
  4 0.0...  127.0.0.1     127.0.0.1      TCP     585 44618 → 8080 [PSH, ACK] Seq=1 Ack=1 Win=65536 Len=517 TSva
  5 0.0...  127.0.0.1     127.0.0.1      TCP      68 8080 → 44618 [ACK] Seq=1 Ack=518 Win=65024 Len=0 TSval=181
  6 0.2...  127.0.0.1     127.0.0.1      TCP    2337 8080 → 44618 [PSH, ACK] Seq=1 Ack=518 Win=63872 Len=2269 T
  7 0.2...  127.0.0.1     127.0.0.1      TCP      68 44618 → 8080 [ACK] Seq=518 Ack=2270 Win=63872 Len=0 TSval=
  8 0.2...  127.0.0.1     127.0.0.1      TCP     132 44618 → 8080 [PSH, ACK] Seq=518 Ack=2270 Win=65536 Len=64
  9 0.2...  127.0.0.1     127.0.0.1      TCP      68 8080 → 44618 [ACK] Seq=2270 Ack=582 Win=65536 Len=0 TSval=
 10 0.2...  127.0.0.1     127.0.0.1      TCP     174 44618 → 8080 [PSH, ACK] Seq=582 Ack=2270 Win=65536 Len=106
 11 0.2...  127.0.0.1     127.0.0.1      TCP      68 8080 → 44618 [ACK] Seq=2270 Ack=688 Win=65536 Len=0 TSval=
 12 0.2...  127.0.0.1     127.0.0.1      TCP    1850 8080 → 44618 [PSH, ACK] Seq=2270 Ack=688 Win=65536 Len=178
 13 0.2...  127.0.0.1     127.0.0.1      TCP      68 44618 → 8080 [ACK] Seq=688 Ack=4052 Win=64128 Len=0 TSval=
 14 0.3...  127.0.0.1     127.0.0.1      TCP     254 44618 → 8080 [PSH, ACK] Seq=4052 Ack=688 Win=65536 Len=186
 15 0.3...  127.0.0.1     127.0.0.1      TCP      68 44618 → 8080 [ACK] Seq=688 Ack=4238 Win=64896 Len=0 TSval=
 16 0.3...  127.0.0.1     127.0.0.1      TCP      92 44618 → 8080 [PSH, ACK] Seq=688 Ack=4238 Win=65536 Len=24
 17 0.3...  127.0.0.1     127.0.0.1      TCP      68 8080 → 44618 [ACK] Seq=4238 Ack=712 Win=65536 Len=0 TSval=
 18 0.3...  127.0.0.1     127.0.0.1      TCP      68 44618 → 8080 [FIN, ACK] Seq=712 Ack=4238 Win=65536 Len=0 T
 19 0.3...  127.0.0.1     127.0.0.1      TCP      68 8080 → 44618 [FIN, ACK] Seq=4238 Ack=713 Win=65536 Len=0 T
 20 0.3...  127.0.0.1     127.0.0.1      TCP      68 44618 → 8080 [ACK] Seq=713 Ack=4239 Win=65536 Len=0 TSval=

▶ Frame 12: 1850 bytes on wire (14800 bits), 1850 bytes captured (14800 bits) on interface 0
  Linux cooked capture
▶ Internet Protocol Version 4, Src: 127.0.0.1, Dst: 127.0.0.1
▶ Transmission Control Protocol, Src Port: 8080, Dst Port: 44618, Seq: 2270, Ack: 688, Len: 1782

0000  00 00 03 04 00 06 00 00  00 00 00 00 00 08 00       ............. ..
0010  45 00 07 2a 9e 11 40 00  40 06 97 ba 7f 00 00 01    E··*··@· @·······
0020  7f 00 00 01 1f 90 ae 4a  23 4a 57 14 3c 01 2a fd     ·······J #JW·<·*·
0030  80 18 02 00 05 1f 00 00  01 01 08 0a 6c 3c 86 bb    ··········· ·l<··
0040  6c 3c 86 7d 17 03 03 06  f1 c1 bb 0b 63 b2 1a 65    l<·}······· ·c··e
0050  c3 eb f2 4e 88 e1 7a 93  9d 75 18 dd 36 3b cb 20    ···N··z· ·u··6;·
0060  10 1d 33 49 97 29 c3 01  c7 0d e9 5a 41 c0 7c 57    ··3I·)·· ···ZA·|W
0070  5b 29 10 3c fd dc b1 b2  dc f2 bf fd c7 db 5a 72    [)·<···· ······Zr
0080  52 c7 0d 19 00 e4 bb dd  66 1d 89 cc f1 34 69 d9    R······· f····4i·
```

Figure 8-3. *Eavesdropping on HTTPS communication with Wireshark*

Helidon Security

Every HTTP server needs a way to limit access to its resources to specific users with specific rights. We developers build our own fortresses and castles with walls and gates to keep uninvited users away from the precious data and functionalities that are hidden inside. Let's imagine this castle of ours. Not everyone in a medieval castle can open the main gate; otherwise, anyone can access it. And what point would those high walls have if the gate is unrestricted? It's necessary to know who is who (authentication) and who has what rights (authorization). In our medieval castle, guards surely can recognize (authenticate) its residents. For example, if they recognize Gyles, the gatekeeper, they already know he can operate the gate because of his role as the gatekeeper. The warden, also well known to the guards, who can do almost anything, can control the gate. Among many others, he has the gatekeeper role too.

Helidon, instead of guards with swords and armor, provides a system of security providers for authentication, authorization, and role-mapping. Each can be added as a stand-alone dependency and configured to work together.

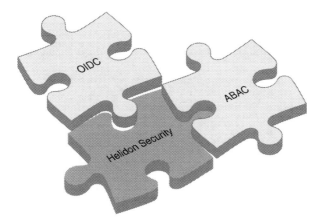

Figure 8-4. *Helidon security providers*

Security providers are designed to work together, configured by a common configuration structure.

Listing 8-6. Security Configuration Structure

```
security:
  providers:
    - <provider-name>: ①
      <provider-settings> ②
    - <another-provider-name>:
      <provider-settings>
  web-server:
    defaults: ③
```

```
    <default-settings>
paths:
  - path: "/greeting[/{*}]" ④
    <path-specific-sec-settings>
  - path: "/helloworld[/{*}]"
    <path-specific-sec-settings>
```

① Enabled providers (e.g., abac, http-basic-auth,
   or oidc)

② Provider-specific configuration

③ Default configuration for all web resources

④ Custom security configuration per resource path

For securing JAX-RS resources in Helidon, a combination of security-related Jakarta Annotations (JSR-250) and Helidon security annotations can be used.

- io.helidon.security.annotations.Authenticated
  enables or disables authentication on JAX-RS classes or
  methods.

- io.helidon.security.annotations.Authorized
  enables or disables authorization on JAX-RS classes or
  methods.

- jakarta.annotation.security.RolesAllowed defines
  the list of roles to be authorized for this resource.

- jakarta.annotation.security.PermitAll signifies
  that all roles are authorized for this resource.

- jakarta.annotation.security.DenyAll signifies that
  no roles are authorized for this resource.

- io.helidon.security.abac.policy.
  PolicyValidator.PolicyStatement validates security
  attributes with the ABAC provider's Java EE policy
  expression language (EL).

- io.helidon.security.abac.role.RoleValidator.
  Roles validates roles with the ABAC provider.

- io.helidon.security.abac.scope.ScopeValidator.
  Scope validates scopes with the ABAC provider.

Most typical use cases can be solved with only @RolesAllowed and
@Authenticated. Let's look at how to secure the gate of our castle so only
users with gatekeeper and warden roles can open it.

Listing 8-7. JAX-RS Method with Authentication and Authorization

```
@PUT
@Path("/gate/open")
@Authenticated      ①
@RolesAllowed({"gate-keeper", "warden"})      ②
public Response openGate() {
    if (gateOpened.compareAndSet(false, true)) {
        return Response.ok().build();
    } else {
        return Response.notModified().build();
    }
}
```

① Enables authentication for this endpoint; can also
   be enabled at class level

② Defines roles with access to this method

Listing 8-7 defines needed roles and authentication for specific JAX-RS methods. JAX-RS endpoint security can be disabled with `security.jersey.enabled` security key.

Security annotations don't set your security in stone. Security settings can be overridden by Helidon configuration mapped to the actual path in the following manner.

Listing 8-8. JAX-RS Methods Secured by Configuration

```
security:
  web-server:
    defaults:      ①
      authenticate: false
    paths:
      - path: "/castle/gate[/{*}]" ②
        authenticate: true
        roles-allowed: [ "gate-keeper", "warden" ]
      - path: "/castle[/{*}]"
        methods: [ "get" ]
        authenticate: true
        roles-allowed: "warden"
```

① Properties applied to all paths

② Path with wildcards to apply security
   configuration to

One more thing that is needed is an actual security provider to make it work.

Basic Authentication

Basic authentication is the simplest but not very practical or secure approach to enable authentication and authorization in production. A weak part of the basic access authentication is providing an unencrypted password over the authorization HTTP header in the form of a base64 encoded username and password delimited by a colon. For example, a `Basic am9lbDpqb2Vs` authorization header can be easily decoded as `joel:joel`.

When used without TLS, anyone can easily intercept our password. When accessed without this header, the endpoint returns `401 Unauthorized` with `WWW-Authenticate` header populated by `Basic realm="beginning-helidon"`. The client knows then that basic authentication is required. The browser typically shows a simple login dialog and retries the request with an authorization header populated by provided username and password.

Figure 8-5. *Basic authentication dialog in the browser*

Listing 8-9. Basic Authentication Configuration

```
security:
  providers:
    - abac: ①
    - http-basic-auth: ②
        realm: "beginning-helidon"
        users: ③
          - login: "gyles"
            password: "gyles"
            roles: ["gate-keeper"]
          - login: "alad"
            password: "alad"
            roles: ["flag-keeper"]
          - login: "joel"
            password: "joel"
            roles: ["warden"]
```

① Enable ABAC provider

② Enable basic auth provider

③ User store from configuration

Users with roles and passwords are provided by user stores. The configuration shown in Listing 8-9 provides the simplest user store. Another way to supply a custom user store is to implement io.helidon. security.providers.httpauth.spi.UserStoreService over service locator.

> **Note**   A user store is registered as a service provider. If you are
> working on a classpath-based project, create a provider-configuration
> file with `my.package.MyCustomUserStoreService` as its
> content.
>
> `META-INF/services/io.helidon.security.providers.`
> `httpauth.spi.UserStoreService`
>
> Config runtime finds your converter over the service loader facility.
>
> Don't forget to use `module-info.java` when registering
> a service provider in a JPMS module-based project. Just
> add the `provides io.helidon.security.providers.`
> `httpauth.spi.UserStoreService` with `my.package.`
> `MyCustomUserStoreService;` clause to `module-info.java`.

Only one simple dependency is needed for basic auth support in
Helidon MP with no other third-party transitive dependency.

Listing 8-10. Dependency Needed for Basic Authentication
Provider

```
<dependency>
    <groupId>io.helidon.security.providers</groupId>
    <artifactId>helidon-security-providers-http-auth</
    artifactId>
</dependency>
```

JSON Web Token

One of the easiest yet very secure approaches to authentication is token-based authentication. Authentication tokens, often called bearer tokens, are unique short-lived text strings, verifiable to be issued by a genuine identity manager. Services can pass along such a token without needing to authenticate repeatedly. Just imagine a knight in our example kingdom with a decree from the castle warden allowing him passage through any part of the kingdom during his travels. The decree has a seal, so anyone can verify the warden has issued it. It is valid only for a short time necessary for the particular quest and only for the knight it has been issued for. All those knightly qualities mentioned and more provides JWT.

There are several enigmatic acronyms. Let's break it down so you don't get lost.

- JWT is the acronym for JSON Web Token.

- JWS is the acronym for JSON Web Signature. It is a JWT base64 format signed for verification; the content is not encrypted.

- JWE is the acronym for JSON Web Encryption, another JWT format in which payload is safely encrypted.

- JWK is the acronym for JSON Web Key, a cryptographic key representation.

- JWKS is the acronym for JSON Web Key Set. It is a simple JSON format for handling multiple JWK keys. Keycloak provides those at `/realms/my-realm/protocol/openid-connect/certs`.

- OIDC is the acronym for OpenID Connect.

- OpenID Connect Discovery is a mechanism for
  fetching metadata about OIDC identity providers like
  REST resources for obtaining JWT tokens or JWKS
  public key sets. Keycloak provides those at `/realms/`
  `my-realm/.well-known/openid-configuration`

JWT is a simple, standardized JSON structure encoded as a base64
token carrying an identity claims map, usually signed by a private
certificate of the issuer (JWS) or fully encrypted (JWE). In the JWS format,
you need only the issuer's public key (JWK) to check the validity of the JWT
token. Keys can be provided to Helidon services locally or downloaded at
Helidon service startup as JWKS from an identity provider with OpenID
Connect Discovery protocol unless the custom public key is configured,
depending on the used security provider. When the JWT token is signed,
Helidon security can easily check if the correct identity authority created
it. No additional communication with the identity manager is needed once
Helidon has access to the issuer's public key. Checking JWT token validity
can be fast and localized.

JWT token issuer can be a specialized identity provider like the
Keycloak server in this chapter's examples or the Helidon service. The
data carried inside the token payload are structured in JSON format in the
claims. While there are many IANA authority registered claims with a given
structure, JWT tokens can also carry custom claims, making JWT tokens
highly customizable.

Listing 8-11. JWT Token Payload Claims Issued by Keycloak

```
{
  "exp": 1671647530, ①
  "iat": 1671647230, ②
  "jti": "2bfdb114-2dfd-4696-a8ac-0ffcf9dc4257", ③
  "iss": "http://localhost:8979/realms/beginning-helidon", ④
  "aud": ["kingdom-audience", ...], ⑤
```

```
"sub": "14515518-1856-4564-855f-3d44814c5ba4", ⑥
"typ": "Bearer",
"azp": "beginning-helidon-client",
"nonce": "9a358080-a589-4b47-a870-7e8e5e8ae145",
"session_state": "4b7307f6-5e69-47e3-9af1-00921adb6181",
"acr": "1",
"allowed-origins": ["http://localhost:8080"],
"realm_access": {"roles": ["warden", ...]},
"scope": "openid microprofile-jwt profile email kingdom-
jwt-scope",
"sid": "4b7307f6-5e69-47e3-9af1-00921adb6181",
"upn": "joel", ⑦
"name": "Joel Driffin",
"groups": ["warden", ...],⑧
"preferred_username": "joel",
"given_name": "Joel",
"family_name": "Driffin"
}
```

① Token expiration time

② Token issue time

③ Unique identifier of the token

④ Issuer identification

⑤ Audience to validate if a token was issued for this particular resource group

⑥ Unique identifier of the subject

⑦ Preferred username

⑧ Groups claim to carry roles added in Keycloak by the microprofile-jwt scope mapper

JWT is especially practical for service-to-service communication as each service doesn't have to be able to reach JWT token issuer and can validate (JWS) or decrypt (JWE) a JWT token locally.

Warning   Although the JWT payload is verifiably genuine in JWS format, it is not encrypted like in the JWE format!

JWT tokens are usually carried along over the SESSIONID cookie, parameters, or the Authorization header. Helidon JWT-aware security providers take care not only of incoming tokens but Helidon also provides outbound security features for calling other services with JWT tokens.

MicroProfile JWT RBAC

MicroProfile JWT specification brings CDI-friendly official API for your JAX-RS resources. Let's manually call the JAX-RS watchtower service with cURL.

Listing 8-12. Calling MicroProfile JWT Enabled JAX-RS Resource with cURL

```
curl -d "http://localhost:8080" \
-H "Authorization: Bearer $JWT_TOKEN" \
localhost:8082/watchtower/signal
```

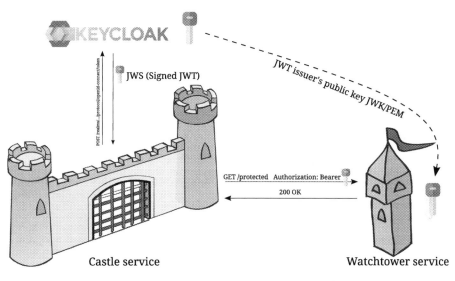

Figure 8-6. *Service-to-service communication with JWT*

Watchtower service doesn't have to contact any other service to
validate the JWS token. All it needs is a public key of the JWT token
issuer. Public key content can be provided directly with `mp.jwt.verify.`
`publickey` or via link to its location with `mp.jwt.verify.publickey.`
`location`. Location can be a file path, classpath, or URL. MicroProfile JWT
supports the following formats.

- JWK

- JWKS

- PKCS#8 base64 encoded PEM format

Keycloak exposes JWKS keys at `/realms/my-realm/protocol/`
`openid-connect/certs`, for example. When configured, Hélidon MP JWT
implementation lazily and automatically downloads the key set when
needed; no other calls are needed since.

Listing 8-13. Configuration of MP JWT

```
mp.jwt.verify:
  issuer: "http://${keycloak.host}:${keycloak.port}/realms/
  beginning-helidon" ①
  audiences: "kingdom-audience" ②
  publickey:
    location: ${mp.jwt.verify.issuer}/protocol/openid-connect/
    certs ③
```

① Value to verify issuer claim

② Value to verify audiences claim

③ Load public key for verifying JWS directly from
   Keycloak as JWKS

MicroProfile JWT decodes the bearer JWT token and injects its claims into your JAX-RS resource. When you inspect JWT more carefully, you find it implements `java.security.Principal`. That is because JsonWebToken is principal accessible with JAX-RS `SecurityContext. getUserPrincipal()`. Among others, MP JWT supports `groups` claims, as defined in RFC-7643, to propagate authorization data with the JWT token's principal identity. Yes, you can access roles. That is why the specification has RBAC in its name! `SecurityContext.isUserInRole` is checked against actual groups from the JWT token, and `@RolesAllowed` works too.

Most identity providers must be configured to add MP JWT claims to the JWT token. Keycloak, for example, provides prepared `microprofile-jwt` built-in scope, which, when enabled, adds MicroProfile JWT–required `upn` and `groups` scopes.

Note   You can stick to the same annotations in the business code and easily switch between security providers.

Listing 8-14. JAX-RS Resource with MP JWT RBAC Support

```
@Inject
@Claim(standard = Claims.iss)
private ClaimValue<String> issuer;①

@Inject
private JsonWebToken jwt; ②

@POST @Path("/signal")
@RolesAllowed({"warden"}) ③
public void signal(@Context SecurityContext securityContext,
String msg) {
    String user = securityContext.getUserPrincipal().getName();
    jwt.getGroups().forEach(s -> {
        if (securityContext.isUserInRole(s))
            System.out.println(user + " is in role " + s); ④
    });
```

① Injecting JWT token claim

② Injecting whole JWT token used for actual request

③ RolesAllowed is mapped to the groups claim
  by default

④ JWT claims are mapped to Jakarta WS security
  context; the user is in all the JWT groups

Warning   Keep in mind that each request has its own bearer JWT token. Always inject Instance or ClaimValue when working with the @ApplicationScoped JAX-RS bean.

To enable MicroProfile JWT support in a JAX-RS application, @LoginConfig annotation is needed with the authMethod value, MP-JWT.

Listing 8-15. JAX-RS Enabled to Use MicroProfile JWT RBAC

```
@LoginConfig(authMethod = "MP-JWT")
@ApplicationScoped
public class ProtectedApplication extends Application {
```

Once again, only one simple dependency is needed for MP JWT support in Helidon MP with no other third-party transitive dependency except the actual MicroProfile API.

Listing 8-16. Dependency Needed for MicroProfile JWT Authentication Provider

```
<dependency>
    <groupId>io.helidon.microprofile.jwt</groupId>
    <artifactId>helidon-microprofile-jwt-auth</artifactId>
</dependency>
```

OpenID Connect

Let's look at a more serious approach to solve authentication and authorization to make our castle security more professional and production ready. Our example uses the Keycloak identity manager with single sign-on (SSO). Identity managers are stand-alone services for managing users and their attributes, like roles. Identity managers usually provide authentication and authorization services over protocols like old-timer XML-based SAML (Security Assertion Markup Language) or modern and popular OIDC.

JSON-based OIDC is an extension of OAuth 2.0, adding the means of authentication. OIDC is a protocol over which authentication and authorization are realized with JSON-based REST API. When a client doesn't have a proper identity JWT token, the Helidon application with OIDC support redirects the call to the Keycloak SSO page. Users can sign in with their credentials to obtain the authorization code needed by the Helidon application and the client ID and client secret to obtain a JWT identity token.

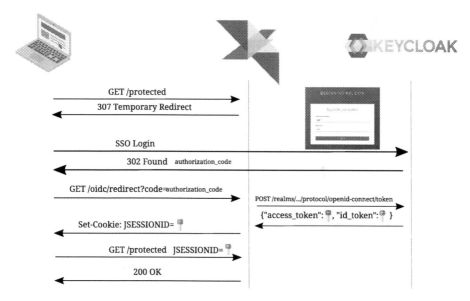

Figure 8-7. *Helidon with Keycloak as identity manager*

① Accesses protected resources without JWT ID

② Helidon redirects the unauthenticated request to the Keycloak SSO login page with 307

③ After a successful SSO login, the client obtains an authorization code

④ Client is redirected back to Helidon special
resource /oidc/redirect with authorization code

⑤ Helidon uses the authorization code, client ID,
and client secret to obtain JWT identity token

⑥ Client uses JWT identity token as JSESSIONID for
subsequent calls

While the authorization code is obtained by SSO login, the client ID
and secret are configured with the application's OIDC configuration and
used for basic authorization during token requests.

Let's use Keycloak as an identity manager for our castle example. All
you need to do is configure the OIDC security provider with the client
secret, the Keycloak URL, and the client ID. Notice that we have added
RBAC capability by adding a microprofile-jwt scope mapper for the
groups claim in the Keycloak. You don't need any special support for
MicroProfile JWT RBAC on the Helidon side because the groups claim is
used for fetching subject groups by default if available (can be disabled
with oidc.use-jwt-groups: false).

Listing 8-17. Keycloak OIDC Configuration

```
keycloak:
  host: localhost
  port: 8979
security:
  providers:
    - abac: ①
    - oidc:
        audience: "kingdom-audience" ②
        client-id: "beginning-helidon-client" ③
        redirect: true
```

```
# Client secret is updated by startKeycloak.sh
client-secret: pYSJjHAymzLqw61x7bsePp4AR6GVdC1s ④
identity-uri: "${keycloak.url}/realms/
beginning-helidon"
frontend-uri: "http://localhost:${server.port}" ⑤
logout-enabled: true
post-logout-uri: /
```

① Adds abac provider

② Audience to compare with the one inside the JWT
token so the issuer's certificate can be reused

③ Identifies the client for identity manager

④ Uses as password for basic authorization
when requesting JWT token from OIDC
identity manager

⑤ Where should the identity manager redirect back
from the SSO page

You can switch security providers by changing configuration and
dependency, while the annotated example resource stays the same.
Business code doesn't need to change between the test and production
environment.

Listing 8-18. Dependency Needed for OIDC Support

```xml
<dependency>
    <groupId>io.helidon.microprofile</groupId>
    <artifactId>helidon-microprofile-oidc</artifactId>
</dependency>
```

251

Token Propagation

After learning about the JWT bearer token and how to authenticate and even authorize against it with our web server, the next logical step is sending it with a client call. Most of the security providers in Helidon support outbound security. Unlike inbound, which secures web resources, outbound helps with client calls to other services. When discussing clients in Helidon MP, JAX-RS client or MicroProfile Rest client should be the first and best choice. But how do you propagate the JWT token you have received in our JAX-RS resource? You can most certainly access the bearer token. It can come within the `Authorize` header or `JSSESSIONID` cookie.

Listing 8-19. Raw JWT Token from Cookies Propagated Manually to Jersey JAX-RS Client

```
@POST
@Path("/send-signal")
public Response signalToWatchTower(@CookieParam("JSESSIONID")
Cookie cookie) {
    Response res = ClientBuilder.newBuilder()
        .register(OAuth2ClientSupport.feature(cookie.
        getValue()))
        ...
```

Another more elegant approach is to use the MicroProfile JWT support in Helidon and access raw JWT tokens over injected API. Remember that the JWT token is request-specific, but CDI injected `JsonWebToken` proxy is updated according to your request context on the fly.

Listing 8-20. Injected JWT Token Propagated Manually to Jersey
JAX-RS Client

```
@Inject
JsonWebToken jwt;

@POST
@Path("/send-signal")
public Response signalToWatchTower() {
    Response res = ClientBuilder.newBuilder()
        .register(OAuth2ClientSupport.feature
        (jwt.getRawToken()))
        ...
```

Such approaches are very explicit, but must you repeat this every time
you use a JAX-RS client? You don't because Helidon provides an implicit
configurable solution in the shape of outbound security of relevant
security providers.

Listing 8-21. Enabled JWT Token Propagation with OIDC Security
Provider

```
security:
  providers:
    - abac:
    - oidc:
        audience: "kingdom-audience"
        client-id: "beginning-helidon-client"
        redirect: true
        client-secret: 9rnQEI3gV6FuBMk41UeYqYfNlCutgaN1
        identity-uri: "${keycloak.url}/realms/
        beginning-helidon"
        frontend-uri: "${app.castle-url}"
        logout-enabled: true
```

```
post-logout-uri: /
propagate: true ①
outbound:
  - name: "propagate-token" ②
    hosts: ["watchtower.local"] ③
```

① Enables JWT token propagation to the clients

② Arbitrary name for the outbound configuration;
   choose any application-wide unique name

③ Filters target hosts to propagate to; supports
   wildcards

The bearer token is used automatically for specified hosts whenever you use a JAX-RS client from a secured context with propagation. Outbound propagates a token to all hosts when the hosts config is missing. Host filtering supports wildcards to match subdomains easily hosts: ["*.local"] allow JWT token propagation to both watchtower.local and castle.local hosts.

Listing 8-22. Automatic JWT Propagation with JAX-RS Client and OIDC Provider Outbound

```
@POST
@Path("/send-signal")
public Response signalToWatchTower() {
    Response res = ClientBuilder.newBuilder() ①
        .target("http://watchtower.local:8082/watchtower") ②
        .path("/signal")
        ...
```

① No need to provide JWT token manually with
   OIDC provider outbound propagation

② Hosts `watchtower.local` matches to allow hosts
   for propagation

OIDC token flow gets easy with Helidon because you can control service-to-service token propagation simply by configuration. There is much more than a security provider's outbound feature can do. It is not only good for JWT token propagation. You can define your headers or create and sign a brand-new JWT token!

Configuration of Secrets

Did you ever wonder how secure it is to leave your database passwords, usernames, and other sensitive data in the configuration file? It is secure as long as you can protect your configuration files. Configuration tends to be shared, copied, transformed, and distributed a lot, and not all passwords can be or need to be externalized to specialized vaults or as K8s secrets. Helidon provides encryption capability for configuration values to keep your secret values safely encrypted. It doesn't matter if you store your passwords in the config file, vault, or database. Only a Helidon application with the right master password or decryption key can use your configured secrets.

Two encryption options are available.

- **AES-GCM encryption** is symmetric; both the encrypting and decrypting sides need the same master password.

- **RSA encryption** is asymmetric; the value is encrypted with a public key and decrypted with a private key.

AES-GCM Encryption

AES encryption uses a single master password for encryption and decryption; no keys are required. Encryption can be done with the `helidon-config-encryption` artifact, which is conveniently copied to the `target/lib` directory when you build your Helidon application. Encrypt any text value from CLI by providing an AES cipher, the password needed for eventual decryption, and the actual value to be encrypted as arguments.

```
java -jar ./target/libs/helidon-config-encryption-3.0.2.jar aes
masterPassword superSecretPassword
```

Output in the format ${GCM=⋯} can be used as a value in Helidon Config. Helidon Config encryption knows it should use AES-GCM for decryption when the actual value is needed.

Listing 8-23. AES Encrypted Config Value in YAML Configuration File

```
app.pass: ${GCM=ALOsq65u5NkJ3VlQTPeBrD4piMMD+zTaYxtOtAHFGnvnnFS
tcIuOnILUjOfNVANr+tH7+VPIZfSRrGn1QprX}
```

To allow Helidon to decrypt encrypted configuration values, the master password used for encryption needs to be provided via the environment variable `SECURE_CONFIG_AES_MASTER_PWD`.

Listing 8-24. Master Password Env Variable Provided via K8s Config Map

```
apiVersion: v1
kind: ConfigMap
metadata:
  name: castle-config
data:
  SECURE_CONFIG_AES_MASTER_PWD: masterPassword
```

In your Helidon application, you get the decrypted value since it would be a plain text config value.

RSA Encryption

RSA encryption makes it possible to encrypt value by a public key and later let Helidon decrypt it via a private key from the same pair. Helidon configuration encryption tool can load keys directly from a key store.

```
java -jar ./libs/helidon-config-encryption-3.0.2.jar rsa
./server.p12 password 1 superSecretPassword
```

The generated encrypted form of our secret value can be placed directly in the Helidon configuration.

Listing 8-25. RSA Encrypted Config Value in YAML Configuration File

```
app.pass: ${RSA-P=cU2cL/j......YmwwLudo=}
```

Once again Helidon config encryption feature knows it should use RSA for decryption when the actual value is needed, thanks to the RSA-P prefix. Helidon application needs to know where to find the private key for decryption. You can provide the location, alias, and password for the keystore containing the private key.

Listing 8-26. Keystore Location env Variable Provided via K8s Config Map

```
apiVersion: v1
kind: ConfigMap
metadata:
  name: castle-config
data:
```

```
SECURE_CONFIG_RSA_PRIVATE_KEY: /helidon/server.p12
SECURE_CONFIG_PRIVATE_KEY_ALIAS: 1
SECURE_CONFIG_PRIVATE_KEYSTORE_PASSPHRASE: password
```

Plain Text Password Detection

Encryption of secret configuration values is practical for production use but may be too demanding and unnecessary in a test environment. Simply replacing the encrypted value with plain text value in a test environment is an obvious solution, but it brings the danger of accidentally leaking such value to actual production.

To avoid this danger, you can define a special unencrypted value detectable by the Helidon Config encryption feature.

Listing 8-27. Detectable Unencrypted Config Value in YAML Configuration File

```
app.pass: ${CLEAR=superSecretPassword}
```

By default, when the Helidon application requests such a config value, an exception is thrown.

```
ConfigEncryptionException: Key "app.pass" is a clear text password, yet encryption is required
```

In a test environment, the check can be disabled.

Listing 8-28. Encryption Check Turned Off in Testing Environment

```
security.config.require-encryption: false
```

This ensures that no sensitive test configuration is used in production by accident.

Configuration encryption adds another security layer. You can provide secret values to your application over various, less secure channels. You can even send configuration examples to a friend without the need for tedious checks if you are not sharing any secrets by doing so.

Listing 8-29. Dependency Needed for Config Encryption

```
<dependency>
    <groupId>io.helidon.config</groupId>
    <artifactId>helidon-config-encryption</artifactId>
</dependency>
```

In this chapter, you learned how to secure the Helidon web server with TLS 1.3 and what annotations, regardless of the security provider, can be used for authentication and authorization. You also learned to set up basic authorization for test cases and OpenID Connect for production. This chapter covered a very popular part of OIDC, JWT tokens, and took a tour of MicroProfile JWT tooling to use JWT tokens in modern DI applications built on top of Helidon MP.

Don't forget to check out the security examples accompanying this book, where you can start Keycloak identity provider with an already configured realm and experiment with our OIDC and MicroProfile JWT–secured castle application.

Summary

- Use TLS to avoid man-in-the-middle attacks.

- Use different security providers without changing the business code.

- JWT is easy to use with MicroProfile API.

- Service doesn't have to call the JWT issuer to verify JWS or decode JWE.

- OIDC security provider supports JWT token propagation.

- Configuration secrets can be encrypted right in the configuration source.

CHAPTER 9

Using OpenAPI

This chapter covers the following topics.

- Documenting your code using OpenAPI

- Reading generated API information using out-of-the-box endpoints

- Generating clients using OpenAPI Generator

About OpenAPI

In today's technological landscape, it is of utmost importance for modern applications to have APIs, and RESTful APIs are at the forefront of the API economy. With the ability to transform any application into a language-independent service that can be accessed from any location and with any language, RESTful APIs have become an integral part of software development.

MicroProfile provides the OpenAPI 3.x specification to facilitate the development of RESTful APIs. This specification offers Java developers diverse programming models and interfaces that enable them to natively generate OpenAPI documents from their REST services. By simplifying the process of creating OpenAPI documents, MicroProfile empowers developers to streamline their API development workflows and rapidly create high-quality, interoperable APIs that clients can easily consume.

© Dmitry Kornilov, Daniel Kec, Dmitry Aleksandrov 2023
D. Kornilov et al., *Beginning Helidon*, https://doi.org/10.1007/978-1-4842-9473-4_9

Helidon implements OpenAPI 3.0 out of the box. It is already included in the full `helidon-microprofile` bundle. To use OpenAPI with all other MicroProfile options, our `pom.xml` file should include the code in Listing 9-1.

Listing 9-1. MicroProfile Bundle Dependency

```
<dependency>
    <groupId>io.helidon.microprofile</groupId>
    <artifactId>helidon-microprofile</artifactId>
</dependency>
```

If more fine-grained control is preferred and `helidon-microprofile-core` is used, add the dependency shown in Listing 9-2 to the project's `pom.xml` file.

Listing 9-2. OpenAPI Dependencies

```
<dependency> ①
    <groupId>org.eclipse.microprofile.openapi</groupId>
    <artifactId>microprofile-openapi-api</artifactId>
</dependency>

<dependency> ②
    <groupId>io.helidon.microprofile.openapi</groupId>
    <artifactId>helidon-microprofile-openapi</artifactId>
    <scope>runtime</scope>
</dependency>
```

① MicroProfile OpenAPI annotations dependency

② Helidon MP OpenAPI runtime support
   dependency

Basic Usage

To generate a precise OpenAPI document that effectively describes an application's API, the primary approach is to use OpenAPI standard annotations to annotate the relevant functions. These annotations provide crucial metadata that helps create an accurate and complete OpenAPI document.

Once the application is started, the Helidon MP runtime automatically identifies the annotated endpoints and utilizes the provided metadata to create the OpenAPI document. This streamlined process eliminates the need for manual documentation and ensures that the API documentation remains up-to-date and in sync with the application's implementation. Additionally, by adhering to the OpenAPI standard, the resulting API documentation is easily shareable. It can be consumed by many tools and platforms, enabling easy integration with other systems.

Listing 9-3 is an example.

Listing 9-3. OpenAPI Annotations in Use

```
@GET
@Operation(summary = "Returns a Wizard", ①
        description = "General Wizard Name and Licence
        information ")
@APIResponse(description = "Simple JSON containing Wizard name
and license information", ②
        content = @Content(mediaType = "application/json",
                           schema = @Schema(implementation =
                           Wizard.class)))
@Produces(MediaType.APPLICATION_JSON)
public JsonObject getWizard() {...}
```

① @Operation gives information about this
endpoint.

② @APIResponse describes the HTTP response and
declares its media type and contents.

The Helidon application creates an additional /openapi endpoint,
and it returns the OpenAPI document describing the endpoints in our
application. According to the MicroProfile OpenAPI spec, the OpenAPI
document's default format is YAML. application/vnd.oai.openapi is a
suggested media type for OpenAPI documents that has some support but
has not yet been adopted by the IANA YAML standard.

Listing 9-4 calls an /openapi endpoint.

Listing 9-4. Retrieve OpenAPI Information with cURL

```
curl -X GET http://localhost:8080/openapi
```

Listing 9-5 shows the output.

Listing 9-5. Result Output with OpenAPI Data

```
components:
  schemas:
    Wizard:
      properties:
        message:
          type: object
      type: object
info:
  title: Generated API
  version: '1.0'
openapi: 3.0.3
paths:
  /wizard:
```

```
get:
  description: 'General Wizard Name and Licence information'
  responses:
    default:
      content:
        application/json:
          schema:
            $ref: '#/components/schemas/Wizard'
      description: Simple JSON containing Wizard name and
      license information
  summary: Returns Wizard Information
```

Note   A client can specify *Accept* as either application/vnd.
oai.openapi+json or application/json to request JSON.

Here are some of the main annotations used to describe your code.

- **@Schema** allows you to define inputs and outputs.

- **@Operation** describes an operation or usually an
  HTTP method for a particular path.

- **@Content** provides schema and examples for a specific
  media type.

- **@Link** represents a possible design-time link for
  the answer.

- **@Parameter** represents a single parameter in an
  OpenAPI operation.

- **@Callback** describes a set of requests.

- **@RequestBody** represents the request body in an operation.

- **@APIResponse** represents the response in an activity.

- **@Tag** represents tags for an operation or an OpenAPI definition.

- **@Server** represents the servers for an operation or an OpenAPI definition.

Please consult the official specification for more information.

Static OpenAPI Files

In addition to using OpenAPI annotations to generate an API's documentation, Helidon MP also offers the option of utilizing a static file to provide the API's description. This static file—named `openapi.yml`, `openapi.yaml`, or `openapi.json`—can be added to the application's `/META-INF` folder. Helidon's OpenAPI implementation automatically picks up this file and incorporates its contents into the resulting document.

To make creating this static file easier, tools such as Swagger can generate the OpenAPI document. Once the document is created, it can be added to the application's `/META-INF` folder, and Helidon's OpenAPI implementation handles the rest.

It's worth noting that Helidon MP OpenAPI can incorporate data from all the sources mentioned, including annotations, static files, and programmatic configuration. This allows for flexibility in documenting the API and enables developers to choose the best approach for their needs. Ultimately, the goal is to generate an accurate and comprehensive OpenAPI document that effectively describes the API's functionality and can be easily consumed by other systems.

Automatic Client Generation

OpenAPI can also be used for automatic client generation. Once an OpenAPI document is available for an API, a client can be generated for that API in a variety of programming languages. It can significantly reduce the time and effort required to create a client for the API and ensure that the client is generated accurately and consistently.

Additionally, using an OpenAPI-generated client can provide a standardized way of interacting with the API, making it easier for developers to consume the API from other applications. It can help to improve interoperability and reduce the likelihood of errors caused by inconsistencies in how different clients interact with the API.

Full information about the tool can be found on the official website at `https://openapi-generator.tech/`.

Using OpenAPI Generator, clients in many languages and frameworks can be generated, like Helidon, Jersey, MicroProfile, and many more.

OpenAPI Generator is distributed as a single JAR file. But there are also many "native" distributions for different operating systems, which can be installed using appropriate packet managers or simply by downloading the executables.

The most generic version is just the executable JAR. You download it and then run the following command with the wizard application running.

```
> java - jar openapi-generator.jar generate -g java --library
microprofile -i http://localhost:8080/openapi ①
```

> ① Checks that *http://localhost:8080/openapi* has
>   started and is running

Since the `microprofile` option is specified as a parameter, the generated code is based on the MicroProfile Rest Client spec and looks close to one written by hand in Listing 9-6.

Listing 9-6. Generated Code Based on OpenAPI Document

```
@RegisterRestClient
@RegisterProvider(ApiExceptionMapper.class)
@Path("/wizard")
public interface DefaultApi{
    @GET
    @Produces({ "application/json" })
    public Object wizardGet() throws ApiException,
    ProcessingException; ①
}
```

① Generated code based on working microservice

The generated code can provide a ready-to-use API client communicating with the target API. This can significantly reduce the amount of manual coding required to consume the API. Additionally, since the client code is generated directly from the OpenAPI document, it ensures that the client code is always in sync with the API documentation.

Using this plugin, developers can automate the code generation process during the build phase of their projects. This can save significant time and effort in the development process and help ensure the client code is consistent with the API.

Note Some generated code is fully ready for execution, like this one generated with target `jaxrs`. Some others are not, like the one in Listing 9-6.

A Maven plugin named openapi-maven-plugin can generate client code based on the OpenAPI document. The plugin generates a client interface and a set of data models that represent the data structures used in the API. The generated code can be easily customized using templates provided by the plugin or by creating custom templates.

Summary

- With only a few annotations, you can easily document our API.

- Another way is to create a separate YAML/JSON file and keep it separate from the code.

- You can generate clients out of the openapi information provided automatically by Helidon.

- Generated clients may have different flavors, libraries, and even programming languages.

## CHAPTER 10

Testing Your Helidon Application

This chapter covers the following topics.

- Testing your application with Helidon infrastructure based on JUnit and TestNG

- Creating highly customizable test fixtures using a rich set of annotations

- Testcontainers for integration testing

Testing in Helidon

Software testing is undeniably crucial, yet motivating ourselves to create those tests can be challenging. However, as soon as you begin incorporating tests, you'll quickly discover that the quality of your application improves as well. By running automated tests, you can identify potential issues and bugs before they cause major problems, which saves time and resources in the long run.

Thankfully, Helidon offers excellent support for testing with both JUnit 5 and TestNG. These testing frameworks provide many features that make it easy to test different code aspects and identify potential issues.

© Dmitry Kornilov, Daniel Kec, Dmitry Aleksandrov 2023
D. Kornilov et al., *Beginning Helidon*, https://doi.org/10.1007/978-1-4842-9473-4_10

With Helidon's support, you can create and run tests with minimal effort, ensuring that your application is of the highest quality and is free of bugs or errors. Testing with Helidon can help you build more robust, reliable, and maintainable applications.

Testing with JUnit 5

Helidon provides extended functionality to test your applications with JUnit 5. Just add Listing 10-1.

Listing 10-1. Helidon JUint5 Dependency

```
<dependency>
    <groupId>io.helidon.microprofile.tests</groupId> ①
    <artifactId>helidon-microprofile-tests-junit5</artifactId>
    <scope>test</scope>
</dependency>
```

① Helidon JUnit 5 integration dependency

And you get an extended set of annotations to easily test your applications. Let's dive directly into the code.

The first step is to include the @HelidonTest annotation in the test class. This custom annotation automates various tasks, such as launching the Helidon server on a random port and configuring the environment to mimic actual Helidon usage. Thanks to this annotation, the Helidon testing framework initializes the container before creating the test class and shuts it down after the final test.

Usually, the primary goal of testing is to call the server and verify the output. Helidon offers additional convenience by injecting a WebTarget configured to the currently running server. You can leverage this preconfigured target to call the endpoint and confirm the result.

Listing 10-2 tests the wizard app discussed in Chapter 5.

Listing 10-2. @HelidonTest Annotation Usage

```
@HelidonTest                                             ①
public class WizardResourceTest {

    @Inject
    private WebTarget webTarget;                         ②

    @Test
    void testWizard() {
        JsonObject jsonObject = webTarget.path("/wizard") ③
                .request()
                .get(JsonObject.class);

        validateWizard(jsonObject, "Oz");                ④
    }

    @Test
    void testWizardByName() {
        JsonObject jsonObject = webTarget.path("/wizard/
        Skylar")                          ⑤
                .request()
                .get(JsonObject.class);

        validateWizard(jsonObject, "Skylar");
    }

    private void validateWizard(JsonObject jsonObject,
                                    String nameExpected){
        String actual = jsonObject.getString("name");
        assertEquals(nameExpected, actual,
                        nameExpected + " is expected");
    }
}
```

① Annotate a Test class with @HelidonTest to start the container.

② Inject a WebTarget automatically configured by JUnit Extension.

③ Use WebTarget to call an endpoint.

④ Validate the result.

⑤ Reuse the same webTarget to call another endpoint.

In addition to the benefits mentioned, this approach of launching the Helidon container at the beginning and keeping it active until the completion of the final test also offers several other advantages.

First, it reduces the overall testing time as the container is not repeatedly started and stopped for each test case. This can save time, especially when testing large and complex applications.

Second, it enables the reuse of resources and dependencies across different test cases, improving the overall efficiency of the testing process. By keeping the container active, the resources and dependencies required by the application can be loaded and shared among multiple tests, eliminating the need for redundant loading and initialization.

This approach is commonly used among users and applies to most testing situations, covering more than 90% of all tests.

But what if you need to test some features, which are initialized at the startup time, and there is a different setup for these features? Should you write a separate test class for them? The answer is no. If you set resetPerTest = true parameter in @HelidonTest, the framework restarts the Helidon container on each test. And there are even more features. You can apply different annotations directly on the test method level and inject WebTarget directly into the method as a parameter. Let's create another test:

Listing 10-3. Wizard Test

```
@HelidonTest(resetPerTest = true)                        ①
class WizardTitleTest {

    @Test
    void testDefaultTitle(WebTarget webTarget) {         ②
        String result = webTarget.path("wizard/title")
                .request()
                .get(String.class);

        assertEquals("The Greatest!", result);
    }

    @Test
    @AddConfig(key = "app.title", value = "The Mighty!") ③
    void testModifiedTitle(WebTarget webTarget) {

        String result = webTarget.path("wizard/title")
                .request()
                .get(String.class);

        assertEquals("The Mighty!", result);
    }
}
```

① Enable resetPerTest.

② Inject WebTarget as a method parameter.

③ Use @AddConfig annotation to override the app.
   title property for the specific test.

Here the Helidon container reset on each test method execution. Since it runs on a random port, a new WebTarget is configured with the new container parameters and injected as a method parameter.

For the second test, override the `app.title` config value, which is present in the *microprofile-config.properties* file. This is easily achievable using `@AddConfig(key = "app.title", value = "The Mighty!")` annotation applied to the method. Thus, when the Helidon container starts for the new test, it reads the configuration from this annotation.

`@AddConfig` annotation can also be applied on the class level, thus affecting all test methods.

Advanced Usage

The Helidon testing framework supports a few additional annotations that allow more fine control of the test configuration and execution.

- **@DisableDiscovery** annotation: This is used when a required test class is isolated from the rest of the CDI environment.

- **@AddBean(SomeBean.class)** annotation: If the Bean Discovery is disabled or a specific bean is not available in the current CDI environment, it can be manually added to the current test with this annotation. It is added as an ApplicationScoped bean by default, but the scope can be specified as a parameter. For example, `scope = Dependent.class`. Usually used together with `@DisableDiscovery` annotation to create a very specific set of CDI beans to be tested.

- **@AddExtension(SomeCdiExtension.class)** annotation: If there is a need to extend the current test with a specific CDI Extension, it can easily be done using this annotation.

- **@Configuration(configSources = "some-test-config.properties")** annotation: If a whole specific configuration, either on a classpath or on an absolute path, is required for the current test, it can be set using this annotation.

Listing 10-4 creates a more sophisticated test using some of the features mentioned.

Listing 10-4. Advanced Test

```
@HelidonTest
@DisableDiscovery                                           ①
@AddExtension(ServerCdiExtension.class)                     ②
@AddExtension(JaxRsCdiExtension.class)
@AddExtension(CdiComponentProvider.class)
@AddBean(WizardNoDiscoveryTest.MiniWizard.class)            ③
class WizardNoDiscoveryTest {

    @Inject
    private WebTarget injected;                             ④

    @Test
    void testSpell() {
        String response = injected.path("/spell")          ⑤
                .request().get(String.class);
        Assertions.assertEquals(response,"I put a spell
        on you!");
    }
```

```
@Path("/spell")
public static class MiniWizard {                    ⑥
    @GET
    public String saySpell() {
        return "I put a spell on you!";
    }
}
}
```

① Disable Bean Discovery for this particular test.

② Add CDI Extensions.

③ Add an internal class as a managed bean.

④ WebTarget should point to the MiniWizard resource.

⑤ Check if the endpoint responds correctly.

Here CDI Bean discovery is disabled for the particular test. The internal class MiniWizard is a subresource with only one function: "Say a spell." Using @AddBean annotation, add this class as a bean to the current test. Also, use @AddExtension annotation to make the endpoint work correctly and be correctly injected to WebTarget, to be tested correctly.

The Helidon testing framework provides a wide range of features to test the most typical use cases and some very sophisticated scenarios. This allows developers to tailor their tests to suit their specific needs, ensuring their applications are thoroughly tested under all conditions.

Testing with TestNG

This part is concise. It has the same functionality described earlier but with TestNG. The annotation set is absolutely the same! Just add the Listing 10-5 Maven dependency.

Listing 10-5. Helidon TestNG Dependency

```
<dependency>
    <groupId>io.helidon.microprofile.tests</groupId>
    <artifactId>helidon-microprofile-tests-testng</
    artifactId>                        ①
    <scope>test</scope>
</dependency>
```

① Helidon TestNG support dependency.

Work with Testcontainers

Testcontainers is a Java library that supports JUnit tests, automating the management and life cycle of different applications, databases, and testing environments provided as containers.

The Testcontainers for Java website says it is perfect for the following tests.

- **Data access layer integration tests** running MySQL, PostgreSQL, or Oracle database in a container to test your data access layer code for complete compatibility. No complex local installation and configuration are required. Everything is in an isolated container.

- **Application integration tests** run your application in a container as a black box.

- **UI/Acceptance tests** use containerized web browsers compatible with Selenium for conducting automated UI tests.

And it's hard to argue with that. Testcontainers are widely used beyond the Java world.

Note   To use the Testcontainers library, you need Docker installed on your machine. For more information, go to `https://www.docker.com`.

Testcontainers bring integration testing to another level. You can test Helidon running inside a container running as a black box.

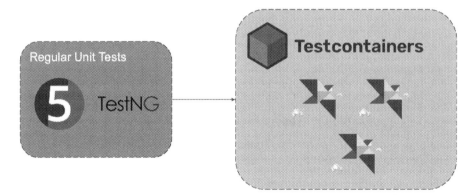

Figure 10-1. *Unit tests work with Helidon applications as a black box*

First, you need to build an image of the application. As you generate your project using CLI with `helidon init` or download the generated project from `https://helidon.io/starter`, a `Dockerfile` is generated (if the corresponding checkboxes are selected).

To prepare an image of the application, run the Listing 10-6 command in the project's root.

Listing 10-6. Build Docker Image

```
docker build -t wizard-app .
```

Then try to run the app locally.

Listing 10-7. Run the Created Container

```
docker run --rm -p 8080:8080 wizard-app:latest
```

Now, you can use our Helidon application with Testcontainers. In our tests, you can create a generic testcontainer that uses the image with the application.

Listing 10-8. Testcontainers Setup

```
static final GenericContainer<?> APPLICATION
                            = new GenericContainer<>("wizard-
    app:latest")                           ①
    .withExposedPorts(8080)
    .withNetwork(Network.newNetwork())
    .withNetworkAliases("HelidonWizardApplication")
    .waitingFor(Wait.forHealthcheck());                    ②
static {
    APPLICATION.start();                              ③
}
```

① Create a Generic Container with the Wizard Helidon application.

② Configure the container to expose port 8080.

③ Start the container and wait for it to be ready.

Using the @HelidonTest annotation on your test class is no longer necessary to perform tests on this container. Because the application is now operating inside a docker container, you can regard it as a "black box" and test it. To accomplish this, you must establish a WebTarget that directs to "localhost" utilizing the indicated open port.

Listing 10-9. Wizard Test

```
public class WizardTest {                                    ①

    WebTarget webTarget = ClientBuilder
                          .newClient()
                          .baseURL("http://localhost:8080") ②

    @Test
    void testWizard() {
        JsonObject jsonObject = webTarget.path("/wizard")    ③
                .request()
                .get(JsonObject.class);

        String actual = jsonObject.getString("name");
        assertEquals("Oz", actual, "Should be Oz");          ④
    }
}
```

① No need to run the Helidon container; it is already in a container

② Creates WebTarget with BaseURL configured as with Docker container

③ Calls the desired endpoint.

④ Verifies the result

This way, you can do a "black box" interrogation testing the application. For the test, it is just a service running on localhost on some port. Testcontainers automates bringing this service up and shutting it down after test execution. Every time the service starts brand new with no trailing artifacts, which can pollute the environment.

The Other Way Around

Helidon can be configured to use resources from external services running inside Testcontainers to perform integration testing.

For instance, you would want to check if Kafka is being properly used for communications and if MySQL is working correctly as the database for your application. For testing purposes, they run within Testcontainers. To make your application use the database and messaging in Testcontainers, you merely need to change the configuration. Use standard @HelidonTest annotation to set up and run the application on your local machine. But since the database and message broker are now running in containers, the configuration has to be overridden. This is easily done using the annotation @Configuration(useExisting = true).

Prepare containers and run Listing 10-10.

Listing 10-10. Setup Testcontainers and Run

```
private static MySQLContainer db = new MySQLContainer()   ①
    .withDatabaseName("mydb")
    .withUsername("test")
    .withPassword("test");
static KafkaContainer kafka = new KafkaContainer();        ②

@BeforeAll
public static void setup() {                               ③
    kafka.start();
    Map<String, String> configValues = new HashMap<>();
```

```
configValues.put("mp.initializer.allow", "true");
configValues.put("mp.messaging.incoming.from-kafka.
connector", "helidon-kafka");
...
configValues.put("javax.sql.DataSource.test.
dataSourceClassName", "com.mysql.cj.jdbc.MysqlDataSource");
configValues.put("javax.sql.DataSource.test.dataSource.
url", db.getJdbcUrl());
...

org.eclipse.microprofile.config.Config mpConfig =
ConfigProviderResolver.instance()
        .getBuilder()
        .withSources(MpConfigSources.create(configValues))
        .build();

ConfigProviderResolver.instance().registerConfig(mpConfig,
Thread.currentThread().getContextClassLoader());
}
```

① Defines and sets up MySQL testcontainer

② Defines Kafka container

③ Starts Kafka container and provides configuration
   as properties to Helidon

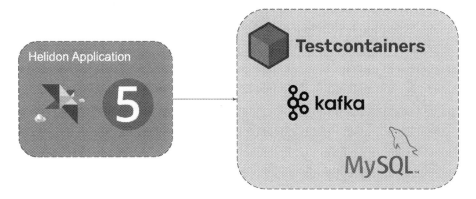

Figure 10-2. *Helidon testing external services as a disposable black box*

Upon executing this test, Testcontainers launch the images, establish the properties, and eventually run the Helidon application. Following preparation, all testing is conducted on those containers. Consequently, all database inquiries are routed through MySQL, while all messaging passes through Kafka. Once testing is complete, Testcontainers is terminated, and the associated resources are freed.

Summary

- Testing your application is essential, and Helidon provides a well-developed infrastructure.

- Helidon provides integration with JUnit 5 and TestNG.

- You can test your Helidon as a black box inside a test container.

- You can run a Helidon application against Testcontainers images.

CHAPTER 11

Scheduling Tasks

This chapter covers the following topics.

- Scheduling is essential for enterprise microservices, and it is easily done in Helidon

- Scheduling using annotations in code and external configuration

- Scheduling with Kubernetes

In the enterprise environment, scheduling plays a critical role in ensuring that various tasks and processes are executed promptly and efficiently. With Helidon, scheduling is easy thanks to its built-in implementation of scheduling functionality, based on the open source cron-utils library.

cron-utils is a powerful Java library that allows us to define, parse, validate, and migrate cron expressions. It provides a simple and intuitive way to work with crons, commonly used in scheduling tasks. Additionally, cron-utils can generate human-readable descriptions of cron expressions, making it easier for developers to understand and modify them as needed.

With Helidon's scheduling functionality, you can leverage the power of cron-utils to create scheduled tasks and processes in our enterprise applications. This allows us to automate various tasks and ensure that they are executed on time, leading to increased efficiency and productivity.

Scheduling can also be configured in the Kubernetes environment because it has full CronJob support. This is discussed later in the chapter.

© Dmitry Kornilov, Daniel Kec, Dmitry Aleksandrov 2023
D. Kornilov et al., *Beginning Helidon*, https://doi.org/10.1007/978-1-4842-9473-4_11

Scheduling in Helidon

Add the Maven dependency shown in Listing 11-1 to enable scheduling.

Listing 11-1. Helidon Scheduling Dependency

```
<dependency>
    <groupId>io.helidon.microprofile.scheduling</groupId>
    <artifactId>helidon-microprofile-scheduling</artifactId>   ①
</dependency>
```

① Helidon scheduling support dependency

In Helidon, a function can be configured to run with a certain schedule using @Scheduled annotation. This annotation receives a value of a string with a *cron expression*. The word *cron* originates from the Greek word *chronos*, meaning "time." cron is a preeminent command-line tool for scheduling jobs on Unix-like operating systems.

In Unix-based systems, it is customary to write a CronJob in files such as *crontab*. Each line in these files comprises a schedule definition and the corresponding command to be executed. The first five characters, each separated by a space, is the schedule definition.

Figure 11-1. *Cron expression definition*

In Helidon, you don't have a command after the expression; you just use the scheduling expression in the annotation @Scheduled, which is put on a method that should run with a certain schedule.

Listing 11-2. Scheduled Task Example

```
@Scheduled("0 5 1 * *", concurrentExecution = false)
public void magicJob() { ... }
```

This method is executed "At 05:00 on day-of-month 1." No concurrent execution is allowed. The string follows the cron model to describe the scheduled calls.

Note   Ensure that the annotated with @Scheduled method is in an ApplicationScoped bean.

Cron expressions are really powerful. Just with a few symbols, you can describe quite a complex schedule. In Helidon, you can do even more complex scheduling scenarios, as the cron-utils library enables them. For example, instead of, writing 0 0 1 * * ? *, 0 0 10 * * ? *, 0 15 3 * * ? * and 0 0 7 * * ? * you can wrap it into 0 0|0|15|0 1|10|3|7 * * ? *

If you need more metadata about each cron invocation, it is available through the CronInvocation object, injected as a method parameter.

Listing 11-3. Scheduled Task Invocation Details Injection

```
@Scheduled("0 11 4 * *")
public void magicJob(CronInvocation inv) {                    ①
    String description = invocation.description();            ②
 }
```

① Injects CronInvocation as a parameter

② Uses invocation data

This data can be used for logging or debugging purposes.

@Scheduled annotation properties can be overridden using application.yaml properties.

Listing 11-4. Scheduled Task Configuration

```
fully.qualified.ClassName.methodName:    ①
  schedule:
    cron: "* * * * *"                    ②
    concurrent: false                    ③
```

① Fully qualified class name on which to define scheduled execution

② cron expression

③ Concurrent execution (set it to false)

The following configuration properties are available.

- **property** (description)

- **cron** (string containing cron setup)

- **concurrent** (boolean, equivalent concurrentExecution property of @Scheduled, default true)

Now you know how to create and configure *scheduled tasks* with Helidon!

Simple Scheduling in Helidon

While Cron expressions can be useful for handling more complex scheduling scenarios, there are situations when a simpler solution is needed. For instance, when a fixed rate invocation interval is sufficient, using the @FixedRate annotation is often the easiest way to schedule a recurring task invocation. Just annotate a method with what is shown in Listing 11-5.

Listing 11-5. Fixed Rate Task

```
@FixedRate(initialDelay = 2, value = 15, timeUnit = TimeUnit.
SECONDS)
```

A method annotated this way is executed every 15 seconds with an initial delay of 2 seconds.

Note   Ensure that the annotated with @FixedRate function is in an ApplicationScoped bean.

The same functionality can be achieved with external configuration. As with @Scheduled, all values defined with the annotation can be overridden from the config.

Listing 11-6. Configuration Example

```
fully.qualified.ClassName.methodName: ①
  schedule:
    initial-delay: 0                    ②
    delay: 30                           ③
    time-unit: MINUTES                  ④
```

① Fully qualified class name on which to define scheduled execution

② Initial delay

③ Delay between calls

④ Time unit

The FixedRateInvocation injected method parameter provides access to metadata such as interval descriptions that are easy for humans to read and configured values.

Listing 11-7. Invocation Details Injection

```
@FixedRate(initialDelay = 5, value = 10, timeUnit = TimeUnit.
MINUTES)
public void magicJob(FixedRateInvocation invocation) {      ①
    String description = invocation.description();          ②
}
```

① Injects FixedRateInvocation as a parameter

② Uses invocation data

This data can be used for debugging or logging purposes.

Scheduling in Kubernetes

Scheduling in Helidon is fine if you use a single microservice with a single instance running on a bare metal machine. This is a rare case nowadays. Most microservices are executed in a *Kubernetes* environment somewhere in the clouds, with multiple *replicas* and a *load balancer* set.

Whenever you schedule a CronJob in our code or configuration, this scheduled code runs, and *all* replicas of the application. This is often not the behavior you want. Usually, you want only application to make a scheduled job.

But this can be easily solved on a Kubernetes level itself. Kubernetes provides CronJob support. And as with everything in Kubernetes, you just need to create a yaml file.

Note   Here we assume that you are familiar with Kubernetes and the `kubectl` CLI utility; otherwise, please consult the official Kubernetes documentation.

Imagine you want to run a "magic cleanup" job every morning at 2 a.m. As with everything in Kubernetes, you should create the `yaml` spec shown in Listing 11-8.

Listing 11-8. CronJob Configuration

```
apiVersion: batch/v1
kind: CronJob                                    ①
metadata:
  name: CleanSomeMagic                           ②
spec:
  schedule: "* 10 5 * *"                         ③
  jobTemplate:
    spec:
      template:
        spec:
          containers:
          - name: CleanSomeMagic
            image: wizardCleaningApp:latest      ④
```

① Document `kind` is `CronJob`

② Name of the job

③ Job execution schedule: every day at 2 a.m.

④ An image with Helidon application

The Magic Cleanup Job is a hypothetical Helidon application packaged as a Docker image and published in a Docker image registry.

As the descriptor is applied, you can *watch* the status of the job executions.

Listing 11-9. Monitor the Job

```
> kubectl get jobs --watch

NAME                COMPLETIONS    DURATION    AGE
CleanSomeMagic      0/1                        0s
CleanSomeMagic      1/1            12s         12s
```

Alternatively, you can simply call describe to see all the information about the job. The output also includes the run history.

When you no longer need a CronJob, you simply delete it.

A full description of how to construct CronJob specifications is available in the official documentation.

Indeed, while the topic of scheduling may seem simple, it is critical to the success of many enterprise applications. Fortunately, Helidon makes it easy to manage complex tasks and process scheduling.

In addition, if you are deploying your Helidon application to Kubernetes, you can use Kubernetes' built-in scheduling capabilities. Kubernetes allows us to define and manage complex schedules for your applications, including support for cron expressions and other advanced scheduling features.

Whether you're using Helidon's built-in scheduling framework or leveraging Kubernetes' scheduling capabilities, you can be sure that your application can handle even the most complex scheduling scenarios with ease.

Summary

- With only two annotations—@Scheduled or
  @FixedRate—you can schedule a task with an easy or
  complex schedule.

- You can schedule tasks both with annotations or with
  configuration.

- To schedule a job on one Pod in Kubernetes, use its
  built-in cron capabilities.

## CHAPTER 12

Integration with Other Technologies

This chapter covers the following topics.

- Integrating Helidon with other famous technologies

- Creating graph database-backed microservices with Neo4j

- Integrating with Coherence CE whenever fast, scalable, and persistent caching is required

- Deploying microservices to the clouds with Verrazzano

Neo4j

Neo4j is a graph database management system developed by Neo4j, Inc. Neo4j's native graph storage and processing capabilities make it an ideal choice for applications that manage complex relationships between data points.

One of the key benefits of using Neo4j with Helidon is the ability to take advantage of both technologies' strengths. Helidon's lightweight and modular architecture makes building and deploying microservices easy, while Neo4j's graph database capabilities allow you to manage complex

© Dmitry Kornilov, Daniel Kec, Dmitry Aleksandrov 2023
D. Kornilov et al., *Beginning Helidon*, https://doi.org/10.1007/978-1-4842-9473-4_12

data relationships. This combination of strengths makes it easy to build powerful, scalable, and highly performant applications that can handle even the most complex data challenges.

The integration with Neo4j is ensured by configuring and initializing Neo4j driver from the standard Helidon configuration.

Add the following dependency to the project's `pom.xml` file to start using it.

Listing 12-1. Neo4j Helidon Integration Dependency

```
<dependency>
    <groupId>io.helidon.integrations.neo4j</groupId>        ①
    <artifactId>helidon-integrations-neo4j</artifactId>
</dependency>
```

① Neo4j Helidon dependency

After that, you should specify all the connection details in the `microprofile-config.properties` file.

Listing 12-2. Neo4j Configuration

```
neo4j.uri=bolt://localhost:7687              ①
neo4j.authentication.username=neo4j          ②
neo4j.authentication.password=secret         ③
```

① Neo4j server URI using *Bolt* protocol

② Server username

③ Server password

Now you can simply inject the driver into the code.

Listing 12-3. Inject Neo4j Driver

```
@Inject
public WizardsRepository(Driver driver) {                    ①
    this.driver = driver;
}
```

① Injects Neo4j driver

Here it is done using the constructor. So, when Helidon starts, the driver is automatically injected into our class.

As the driver is set up and injected, you can do Cypher queries to the Neo4j database, as shown in Listing 12-4.

Listing 12-4. Example of a Cypher Request

```
public List<Wizard> findAllWizards() {        ①
      var session = driver.session()                      ②
      var result = session.run("MATCH (Wizard) RETURN
      wizard").list()                                     ③

      return result;
  }
```

① Sample Neo4j Cypher query

② Initializes a session using driver

③ Executes a Cypher query and gets the result

This data can then be processed and returned using a typical Helidon endpoint.

To play more with Helidon and Neo4j, please check out a full-scaled Helidon Neo4j example based on a Movie database in Helidon Official GitHub Repository.

Enabling Metrics and Health Checks

The extent of Neo4j's support goes beyond the driver configuration and initialization. You can include two additional dependencies if you require greater insight into the database's performance.

Listing 12-5 is the code for health checks.

Listing 12-5. Neo4j Health Checks

```
<dependency>
    <groupId>io.helidon.integrations.neo4j</groupId>       ①
    <artifactId>helidon-integrations-neo4j-health</artifactId>
</dependency>
```

① Neo4j health checks dependency

Listing 12-6 is the code for metrics.

Listing 12-6. Neo4j Metrics Dependency

```
<dependency>
    <groupId>io.helidon.integrations.neo4j</groupId>       ①
    <artifactId>helidon-integrations-neo4j-metrics</artifactId>
</dependency>
```

① Neo4j metrics dependency

By adding them, the observability data from Neo4j is injected into Helidon standard /health and /metrics endpoints output.

Note   Metrics on the server side should be enabled by setting the neo4j.pool.metricsEnabled to true in the Helidon config.

Now, run the following in the command line.

```
> curl -X GET http://localhost:8080/metrics
```

Neo4j metrics information is printed.

And the following shows available Neo4j health check information.

```
> curl -X GET http://localhost:8080/health
```

Coherence

Oracle Coherence CE is an implementation of `java.util.Map` that offers a concurrent, fault-tolerant key/value store. It can scale and distribute across multiple JVMs, servers, and data centers while providing automatic data sharding, highly redundant data storage, and integrated messaging. Moreover, it offers events that notify of any changes to the data or the cluster and user-friendly APIs.

This system is stateful and capable of vertical and horizontal scaling. It can be reconfigured to utilize more or fewer CPUs, RAM, and storage, allowing for vertical scaling. In typical scenarios, data access operations in Coherence CE only require a few milliseconds and, in some cases, even less than a millisecond for simple key-based operations.

Integrating with Helidon

To start using Coherence with Helidon MP, include the following Maven dependencies.

Listing 12-7. Coherence Dependencies

```
<dependency>
    <groupId>com.oracle.coherence.ce</groupId>          ①
    <artifactId>coherence-cdi-server</artifactId>
</dependency>
```

```xml
<dependency>
  <groupId>com.oracle.coherence.ce</groupId>          ②
  <artifactId>coherence-mp-config</artifactId>
</dependency>
<dependency>
  <groupId>com.oracle.coherence.ce</groupId>          ③
  <artifactId>coherence-mp-metrics</artifactId>
</dependency>
```

① Coherence CDI integration dependency

② Coherence Helidon MP config integration

③ Coherence Helidon MP metrics integration

The main magic is concentrated in the NamedMap object. Coherence CE's NamedMap extends the java.util.Map interface and functions as a distributed data structure with data partitioned across multiple JVMs, machines, or data centers. The mentioned dependencies provide full integration of Helidon with Coherence CE. They care for setting up and configuring all necessary for this NamedMap to be simply injected in our code.

Listing 12-8. Spell Resource

```java
public class SpellRepository extends AbstractRepository<String,
Spell> {                                                 ①

    @Inject
    private NamedMap<String, Spell> spells;              ②

    //omitted for simplicity
}
```

① `AbstractRepository` is provided by
     Coherence CE

② `NamedMap` injected in Helidon application by
     Coherence CDI Support.

For this example, `Spell` is a simple POJO containing two fields: the wizard's name (used as a key) and their spell.

Listing 12-9. Spell POJO

```
public class Spell implements Serializable { ①

    private String wizardName;

    private String spell;
    // getters and setters omitted
}
```

① Simple spell POJO must be serializable

The spell POJO can be serialized in two distinct formats: Java serialization, which Coherence CE utilizes for storage purposes, and JSON-B, which is used by the REST APIs. Alternatively, the application could have used JSON as a transport format and Coherence Portable Object Format (POF) for storage instead.

Since there is a repository and domain objects, they can be used in Helidon's typical REST endpoint, where you can do CRUD operations.

Listing 12-10. Spell Resource

```
@Path("/api/spell")
@ApplicationScoped
public class SpellsEndpoint {
    @Inject
    private SpellRepository spellRepository;               ①
```

```
@POST
@Consumes(APPLICATION_JSON)
public Spell createSpell(JsonObject spell) {
    Spell result = new Spell(spell.getString("wizardName"),
                                    spell.
                                    getString("spell"));
    return spellRepository.save(result);            ②
}

@GET
@Produces(APPLICATION_JSON)
@Path("{wizardName}")
public Spell findSpell(@PathParam("wizardName") String
wizardName){                                         ③
    return spellRepository.get(wizardName);
}

@GET
@Produces(APPLICATION_JSON)
public Collection<Spell> getSpells() {               ④
    return spellRepository.getAll();
}

@DELETE
@Path("{wizardName}")
public Spell deleteSpell(@PathParam("wizardName") String
wizardName) {                                        ⑤
    return spellRepository.removeById(wizardName, true);
}

@PUT
@Path("{wizardName}")
@Consumes(APPLICATION_JSON)
```

```
public Spell updateSpell(@PathParam("wizardName")
                                   String wizardName, Spell
                                   spell) {                    ⑥
    spellRepository.update(wizardName,
                       Spell::setSpell, spell.
                       getSpell());
    return findSpell(wizardName);
  }
}
```

① Inject the repository.

② Create a new spell using `spellRepository.
  save` method.

③ Find a spell by wizard name using the
  `spellRepository.get` method.

④ Get all spells using the `spellRepository.
  getAll` method.

⑤ Delete a spell using `spellRepository.
  removeById`.

⑥ Update a spell using `spellRepository.get`.

Coherence CE provides an abstraction `AbstractRepository` for
a repository, simplifying the work with `NamedMap` for typical CRUD
operations.

Now run the application. Helidon starts, configures, and runs a
Coherence CE cluster. Since Coherence CE is just a library, it runs inside
the application. No external server connections are required.

Using cURL to call the endpoint, it can get, create, update, and delete
the spells by simply using the following.

```
curl -X GET "http://localhost:8080/api/spell"
```

The preceding code fetches all the spells.

```
curl -X POST -H "Content-Type: application/json" -d
'{"wizardName" : "Oz", "spell":"Bless you!"}' http://
localhost:7001/api/spell
```

This creates a new Spell item.

Coherence CE is extremely scalable.

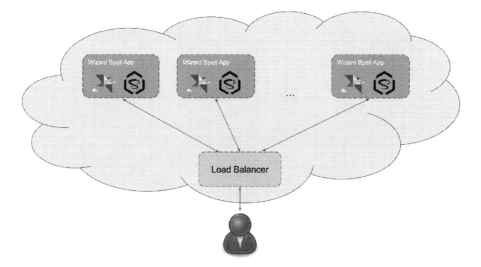

Figure 12-1. *Helidon with Coherence CE in a Cloud*

To demonstrate how easy it is to scale our application, imagine it is deployed in the Kubernetes-managed clouds. You can easily do the following.

```
kubectl scale --replicas=1000 -f spells.yaml
```

This scales the spells app to 1000 nodes and shards and replicates all data across these nodes—and all are *stateful*! Another good part is that Coherence CE can be configured directly in Helidon's microprofile-config.properties because there is full integration.

Verrazzano

Verrazzano is a comprehensive end-to-end corporate container platform that can deploy cloud-native and legacy applications in hybrid and multi-cloud environments. It comprises a thoughtfully curated selection of open-source components, some familiar and essential, while others are purpose-built to integrate all the parts seamlessly into a user-friendly platform.

Figure 12-2. *Verrazzano Enterprise cloud platform*

Verrazzano offers a lot of capabilities like facilitation of DevOps and GitOps practices, out-of-the-box application monitoring; management of hybrid and multi-cluster workloads; custom handling of WebLogic, Coherence, and Helidon applications; administration of multi-cluster infrastructure; and security handling.

Helidon is a "first-class citizen" in the Verrazzano world. There is special support for Helidon out of the box.

It is very easy to run a Helidon application in the cloud using Verrazzano. Let's deploy the wizard app in it!

Deploying the Helidon Wizard Application

Note   First, please install Verrazzano by following the installation instructions.

We assume that you are familiar with Kubernetes since the operations in Verrazzano are done within a terminal using the kubectl command. If not, please learn more about Kubernetes on its official website.

Note   The following instructions are applicable for the Kubernetes environment like OKE.

Let's do it!

It is usually a good idea to create a namespace for the application and add a label identifying the namespace as managed by Verrazzano.

```
$ kubectl create namespace wizard-helidon                  ①
$ kubectl label namespace wizard-helidon verrazzano-
managed=true istio-injection=enabled                       ②
```

① Creates Helidon namespace

② Labels Helidon namespace

You must create two descriptor files to make the Helidon Wizard app run properly in Verrazzano.

First, you create the component `wizard-helidon-comp.yaml` file, describing the Helidon workload, as shown in Listing 12-11.

Listing 12-11. Helidon Verrazzano Component

```
apiVersion: core.oam.dev/v1alpha2
kind: Component                                    ①
metadata:
  name: wizard-helidon-component                   ②
  namespace: wizard-helidon
spec:
  workload:
    apiVersion: oam.verrazzano.io/v1alpha1
    kind: VerrazzanoHelidonWorkload               ③
    metadata:
      name: wizard-helidon-workload
      labels:
        app: wizard-helidon
    spec:
      deploymentTemplate:
        metadata:
          name: wizard-helidon-deployment
        podSpec:
          containers:
            - name: wizard-helidon-container
              image: "ghcr.io/verrazzano/wizard-helidon-
              app"                                 ④
              ports:
                - containerPort: 8080
                  name: http
```

① Describes a component

② Name and namespace of the component

③ Uses special Helidon workload to autoconfigure
   all service endpoints

④ Docker image with the app

Helidon is a "first-class citizen" in Verrazzano and has its own workload: VerrazzanoHelidonWorkload. This means that Verrazzano not only configures, deploys, and runs your Helidon application but also configures and deploys other services, such as Prometheus and Grafana, to gather metrics and monitor the service activity, for example.

Note   The image property points to the location of the Docker image with the wizard app.

Then you need to create the app wizard-helidon-comp.yaml file, describing the deployment of the workload, as shown in Listing 12-12.

Listing 12-12. Helidon Application Verrazzano Descriptor

```
apiVersion: core.oam.dev/v1alpha2
kind: ApplicationConfiguration                          ①
metadata:
  name: wizard-helidon-appconf                          ②
  namespace: wizard-helidon
  annotations:
    version: v1.0.0
    description: "Wizard Helidon application"
spec:
  components:
    - componentName: wizard-helidon-component           ③
```

```
traits:
  - trait:
      apiVersion: oam.verrazzano.io/v1alpha1
      kind: MetricsTrait
      spec:
          scraper: verrazzano-system/vmi-system-
          prometheus-0
  - trait:
      apiVersion: oam.verrazzano.io/v1alpha1
      kind: IngressTrait
      metadata:
        name: wizard-helidon-ingress
      spec:
        rules:
          - paths:
              - path: "/wizard"
                pathType: Prefix
```

① Application configuration config

② Name and metadata of the config

③ Components description

Note   For more information about each config field, please refer to the official Verrazzano documentation.

And you just need to apply them with kubectl.

Listing 12-13. Apply Configuration with kubectl

```
$ kubectl apply -f wizard-helidon-comp.yaml   ①
$ kubectl apply -f wizard-helidon-app.yaml    ②
```

① Apply component configuration

② Apply application configuration

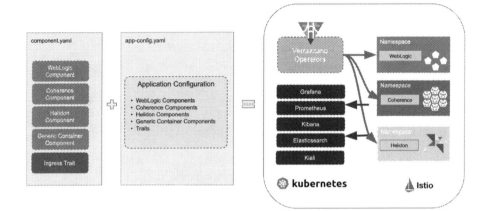

Figure 12-3. *Verrazzano deployment*

The wizard Helidon application implements a REST API endpoint */wizard*, which returns a message {"name":"Oz"} when invoked.

To access the application using the command line, type Listing 12-14 in the terminal.

Listing 12-14. Use cURL to Access the Application

```
$ curl -X GET https://wizard-helidon-appconf.wizard-
helidon.11.22.33.44.nip.io/wizard                    ①

{"name":"Oz"}
```

① Uses curl to get a response from the application
in the cloud

This means that our wizard application is successfully deployed in the cloud and managed by Verrazzano.

Note   Check the Verrazzano documentation on how to obtain the correct URL.

There is a variety of endpoints that get automatically created, deployed, and associated with our application. They are available to further explore the logs, metrics, and such. They include famous tools like Grafana, Kibana, Prometheus, and ElasticSearch. And they all were automatically deployed and set up by Verrazanno, thus saving a lot of DevOps work.

You can get the list of available services with the command shown in Listing 12-15.

Listing 12-15. Get Ingress Data

```
$ kubectl get ing -n verrazzano-system          ①
NAME                      CLASS     HOSTS
                          ADDRESS        PORTS      AGE
verrazzano-ingress          <none>    verrazzano.
default.11.22.33.44.nip.io  11.22.33.44   80, 443    7d2h
vmi-system-es-ingest        <none>    elasticsearch.vmi.system.
default.11.22.33.44.nip.io  11.22.33.44   80, 443    7d2h
vmi-system-grafana          <none>    grafana.vmi.system.
default.11.22.33.44.nip.io  11.22.33.44   80, 443    7d2h
vmi-system-kibana           <none>    kibana.vmi.system.
default.11.22.33.44.nip.io  11.22.33.44   80, 443    7d2h
vmi-system-prometheus       <none>    prometheus.vmi.system.
default.11.22.33.44.nip.io  11.22.33.44   80, 443    7d2h
```

① Gets various Verrazzano components' host and
   address information

Deployment of Helidon applications to Verrazzano is really easy.
When you create a new Helidon project using CLI or `http://helidon.`
`io/starter`, you can specify that you need a docker file and a Verrazzano
descriptor. Two files are generated: `component.yaml` and `application.`
`yaml`. Apply them with the `kubectl` command, and Verrazzano does all
the rest!

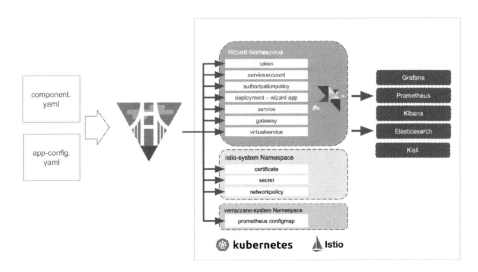

Figure 12-4. *What Verrazzano does*

To get all the details of the configuration and deployment of a Helidon
application, please follow the official Verrazzano guide.

This chapter only scratched the surface of all functionalities provided
by Verrazzano. Please consult the official website for a full description of
the functionalities.

Summary

- Helidon is not a closed ecosystem and provides easy integrations with the most famous technologies on the market.

- Neo4J integration is not just an injection of the driver but also integration with health and metrics.

- Coherence CE provides an easy way to have highly scalable cashing and persistence in Helidon.

- Helidon is a "first-class citizen" in Verrazzano. You can easily deploy the services in multi-cloud environments with only two YAML files.

CHAPTER 13

Going Reactive

This chapter covers the following topics.

- Using Reactive Streams instead of simple callbacks on asynchronous APIs

- Understanding the inner structure of Reactive Streams

- Connecting streams together

- Using Helidon's reactive stream operators, producing and consuming data

The last few years have seen emerging technological trends in the never-ending chase after better performance. APIs started to change from a *here is my thread—block it until things are ready* blocking manner to less intuitive asynchronous promises, futures, or callbacks, providing means for *my thread time is precious–call me back through this callback on your own thread when things are ready*.

It has had huge performance advantages as switching the thread contexts during all the blocking and yielding is expensive. But it is more difficult to orient yourself in all the callbacks and futures not mentioning loss of natural backpressure of the blocking APIs. The need for setting a standard was obvious.

© Dmitry Kornilov, Daniel Kec, Dmitry Aleksandrov 2023
D. Kornilov et al., *Beginning Helidon*, https://doi.org/10.1007/978-1-4842-9473-4_13

Reactive Streams

Reactive Streams is a standard for asynchronous communication with built-in flow control, known as *backpressure*. We can describe it as two parallel pipes through which messages flow under very strict conditions. Let's call the sending side of the pipes *upstream* and the receiving side *downstream*. While one pipe is used for requesting the exact amount of the data or canceling by the downstream, the other one is used for sending the actual data by the upstream.

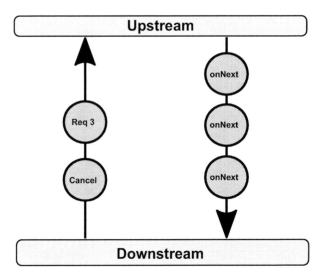

Figure 13-1. *Simplified reactive stream*

Upstream or the publishing side usually implements `Publisher` while downstream, the consuming side implements `Subscriber`. Every publisher has a method `void subscribe(Subscriber<? super T> subscriber)` which registers the subscriber, it's downstream. Publisher signals the subscriber with `onSubscribe` and gives him the subscription to request more data or cancel the stream. Publishers can never send more data than what was requested; that way, downstream regulates the volume and not get overwhelmed, this mechanism is known as a *backpressure*.

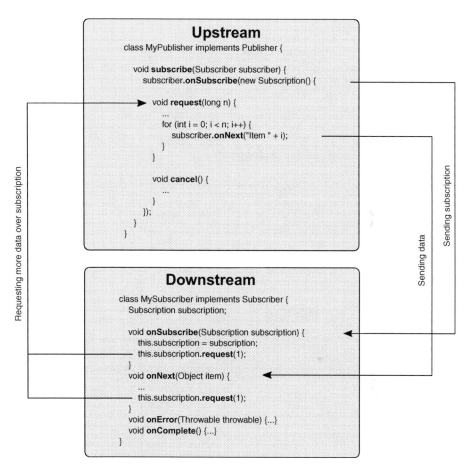

Figure 13-2. Reactive Streams API

Reactive Streams API is available in two packages for Java nowadays,
older but still widely used `org.reactivestreams` available as stand-alone
library and newer `java.util.concurrent.Flow` added to JDK in version 9.
Despite that both are semantically identical, package names differ. Until
all reactive libraries are migrated to JDK's Flow variant, simple conversion
between the two is possible with `org.reactivestreams.FlowAdapters`.

The API itself isn't very practical except for connecting reactive streams together. It gets much more practical with tooling built around those APIs, providing specialized publishers, subscribers and operators provided by specialized reactive libraries. Operators are intermediate operations you can define to augment the stream of the data coming through the pipe.

Caution   Implementation of the Reactive Streams interfaces can be tricky, while interfaces look simple, rules they need to comply with are complex and require advanced knowledge of Java concurrent programming.

Reactive Operators

Reactive streams can operate with an infinite amount of data. When you want to work with potentially huge amounts of items flowing down the stream without blocking, you need to create some kind of intermediate operation which is applied on every item coming down the stream. Helidon has its own implementation of the various operators you can chain together with a builder like API, that is part of Helidon's reactive engine with API built on top of the new `java.util.concurrent.Flow` interfaces.

Listing 13-1. Reactive Operators in Helidon

```
Multi.just("1", "2", "3", "4")                              ①
        .limit(3)                                           ②
        .map(Integer::parseInt)                             ③
        .forEach(i -> System.out.println("Received: " + i)); ④
```

① Defines finite reactive stream of four string values

② Limits operator canceling when three items
  are passed

③ Maps operator parsing every string item to integer

④ Terminal operator, subscriber of the stream

Helidon operators are used on all the Helidon SE APIs, even so Helidon MP leverages mainly imperative coding approach, there is reactive streams abstraction defined by the MicroProfile Reactive Streams Operators specification. That is clever abstraction over an actual implementation of the operators, so you can switch implementation without changing your business code.

Listing 13-2. MicroProfile Reactive Streams Operators

```
ReactiveStreams.of("1", "2", "3", "4")
        .limit(3)
        .map(Integer::parseInt)
        .forEach(i -> System.out.println("Received: " + i))
        .run();
```

MicroProfile Reactive Streams are used mainly with another MicroProfile Reactive Messaging specification, as discussed later. Let's look at the operators first. Describing which operator does what can be complicated, so there is a special kind of diagram used for such a description.

Marble Diagrams

As little marbles on an arrow are depicted items in the stream on a marble diagram.

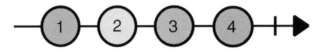

Figure 13-3. *Marble diagram: stream*

While marbles are representing subscriber onNext calls, error is represented by X mark and stream completion by |.

Figure 13-4. *Marble diagram legend*

The stream above the operator depicted in Figure 13-4 is upstream, the source of the data. The stream under the operator is downstream, the result of operation.

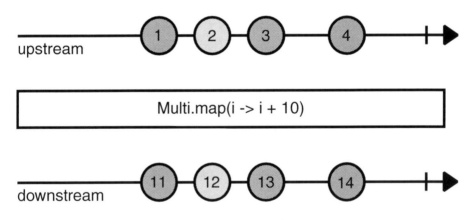

Figure 13-5. *Marble diagram: map*

On the map operator marble diagram, you can see immediately what happens to each item coming through the operator. You can see that the number of the items is not affected, only the value is. Also, the complete signal | is not affected by the operator and passes downstream as is.

MicroProfile Reactive Streams Operators

MicroProfile Reactive Streams Operators is an abstraction bound by specification in the way in which you can port your business code without any changes. Using reactive streams, you can switch from RxJava to Mutiny or Helidon operators without changing your code.

Portability is not the only feature by far, MP Reactive Streams API is structured around builders for units representing operators called *stages*.

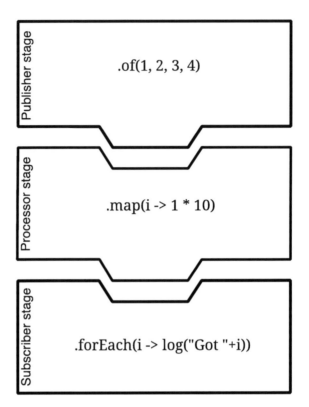

Figure 13-6. *Reactive stream stages in a closed graph*

Stage builder creates reactive streams publisher, processor, or subscriber. You can structure your streams with *stages* into larger reusable parts called *graphs*. Graphs can be composed together into larger graphs like a toy building kit.

Listing 13-3. RS Stages in a Closed Graph

```
ReactiveStreams
        .of(1, 2, 3, 4)                          ①
        .map(i -> i * 10)                        ②
        .filter(i -> i < 35)
        .forEach(i -> log("Got " + i))           ③
        .run();                                  ④
```

① Publisher stage of

② Processor stage map

③ Subscriber/terminal stage

④ Invoke subscription between the stages

Graph is a combination of stages, depending on stage types, graphs can be distinguished to four types.

- The publisher graph starts in the publisher stage and optionally ends in the processor stage.

- The processor graph is only in the processor stages.

- The subscriber graph optionally starts with processor stage and always ends in the subscriber stage.

- The closed graph starts in the publisher stage, ends in the subscriber stage, and optionally has processor stages in between.

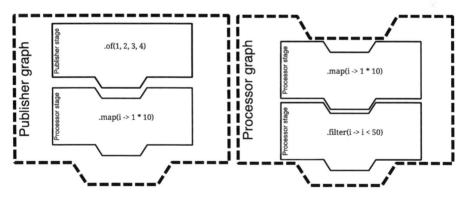

Figure 13-7. *Publisher and processor graphs*

Separate publisher and processor stages can be grouped into larger graphs with .via(processor).

Listing 13-4. Combining RS Stages in Graphs

```
var publisherStage =
        ReactiveStreams.of(1, 2, 3, 4);

var processorStage =
        ReactiveStreams.<Integer>builder()
                .map(i -> i * 10);

var publisherGraph =
        publisherStage.via(processorStage);
```

For creating subscriber or closed graphs, `.to(subscriber)` method is used. While the publisher graph connected with the subscriber graph over the `.to()` method creates a closed graph, the processor connected with the subscriber graph creates the subscriber graph. Only the closed graph is runnable, with the `run()` method actual subscription is done and the whole stream starts.

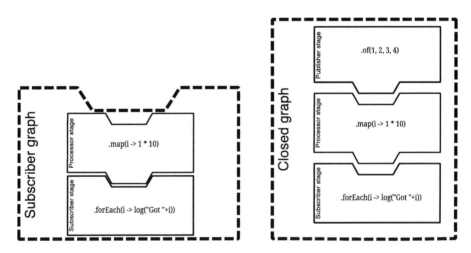

Figure 13-8. *Subscriber and closed graph*

This extensive granularity of MP Reactive Streams allows reusing whole chains of operators. Following stream example repeats the whole sequence of operators.

Listing 13-5. Closed Graph with Repeated Stages

```
ReactiveStreams
        .of(1, 2, 3, 4, 5)
        .filter(i -> i < 5)
        .filter(i -> i > 2)
        .map(i -> i * 10).map(i -> i - 5)
        .map(i -> i * 10).map(i -> i - 5)  ①
        .map(String::valueOf)
        .forEach(i -> log("Got " + i))
        .run();
```

① Repeated operators

You can decompose the same reactive stream into multiple graphs, combine them, and reuse the repeated graph.

Listing 13-6. Combining Graphs

```
var publisherGraph =
        ReactiveStreams.of(1, 2, 3, 4, 5)
                .filter(i -> i < 5)
                .filter(i -> i > 2);

var processor1Graph =
        ReactiveStreams.<Integer>builder()
                .map(i -> i * 10)
                .map(i -> i - 5);

var processor2Graph =
        ReactiveStreams.<Integer>builder()
                .map(String::valueOf);
```

```
var subscriberGraph =
        ReactiveStreams.<String>builder()
                .forEach(i -> log("Got " + i));

publisherGraph
        .via(processor1Graph)
        .via(processor1Graph)   ①
        .via(processor2Graph)
        .to(subscriberGraph)    ②
        .run();   ③
```

① Connecting the same graph with repeated
   operators twice

② Closing the graph with subscriber

③ Invoking actual subscription

Running the stream doesn't immediately yield the result nor blocks
the current thread as the completion of the stream may (or may not)
be asynchronous. Instead of the actual value Java's CompletionStage is
returned as a promise callback to be completed in the future successfully
with the result value from the terminal operator or exceptionally with the
Throwable in case the onError signal terminated the reactive stream.

CompletionStage has its own operators you can use to react on
asynchronous completion like whenComplete, thenApply and many
more. It is also possible to block the current thread until asynchronous
operation completes, but it is a very dangerous thing to do in any reactive
environment. When you are sure that the current thread can be blocked,
either because it is a virtual thread or a physical thread you have under
control; either .join() on converted CompletableFuture or .await() on
Helidon-proprietary Single can be used.

Listing 13-7. Blocking Current Thread Until Stream Completes

```
CompletionStage<List<String>> cf =
        ReactiveStreams.of("1", "2", "3", "4")
        .toList()
        .run();

List<String> resultJoin = cf.toCompletableFuture()
        .join();   ①
List<String> resultAwait = Single.create(cf, true)
        .await();   ②
```

      ① Way of blocking with `CompletableFuture.join()`

      ② Way of blocking with `Single.await()`

Warning   Keep in mind that blocking in reactive context is always harmful and quickly leads to deadlock or event pool exhaustion.

---

of

The of operator is a publisher emitting downstream given items supplied over the vararg parameter.

Listing 13-8. of Operator Publishing Given Items

```
ReactiveStreams.of(1, 2, 3, 4)
        .toList()     ①
        .run()
```

      ① Result list contains [1, 2, 3, 4]

empty

The empty operator sends an onComplete signal downstream after the
subscription happens.

Listing 13-9. empty Operator Immediately Completing the Stream

```
ReactiveStreams.empty()
        .peek(i -> log("This is never executed"))  ①
        .onComplete(() -> log("Completed immediately"))  ②
        .toList()
        .run()
```

① peek is never executed, as no onNext signals come.

② OnComplete is executed right away.

failed

The failed operator sends an onError signal downstream with the
supplied Throwable as the cause after subscription happens.

Listing 13-10. failed Operator Immediately Failing the Stream

```
ReactiveStreams.failed(new Exception("BOOM!"))
        .peek(i -> log("This is never executed"))  ①
        .onComplete(() -> log("This is never executed"))  ②
        .onError(t -> log("Stream failed because of " +
        t.getMessage()))  ③
        .toList()
        .run()
```

① No onNext signals are sent

② No onComplete happens

③ Stream finishes with onError signal

generate

The generate operator executes given supplier once for each requested item, returned item is emitted downstream as an onNext signal.

Listing 13-11. generate Operator Invoking Supplier for Each Requested Item

```
AtomicLong seq = new AtomicLong();
ReactiveStreams.generate(() -> {
        log("Generating " + seq.incrementAndGet());  ①
        return seq.get();
    })
    .limit(3)
    .toList()  ②
    .run();
```

① Logged exactly three times

② Result list contains [1, 2, 3] as requested items are
   limited to three

iterate

The iterate operator first emits provided seed item and executes a provided function to generate an item for each subsequent emit with the previously emitted item as a parameter.

Listing 13-12. iterate Operator Generates Subsequent Items from Previous One

```
ReactiveStreams.iterate(10, i -> i + 2)
        .limit(3)
        .toList()   ①
        .run()
```

     ① Result list contains [10, 12, 14]

fromCompletionStage

The fromCompletionStage operator creates a reactive stream from the CompletionStage promise. When the supplied completion stage is completed with a value, it is emitted downstream as an onNext item immediately followed by an onComplete signal.

Listing 13-13. fromCompletionStage Operator Creates Reactive Stream from Completion Stage

```
ReactiveStreams.fromCompletionStage(CompletableFuture.
completedStage(1))
        .onComplete(() -> log("Completed!"))   ①
        .peek(i -> log("Got " + i))   ②
        .onError(t -> log("Not executed!"))   ③
        .ignore()
        .run()
```

     ① An onComplete signal is sent right after the item

     ② Item is intercepted when CompletionStage is completed

     ③ No onError signal intercepted

When CompletionStage is completed exceptionally, an onError signal is emitted downstream with the original Throwable as a cause.

Listing 13-14. fromCompletionStage Operator Creates Reactive Stream from Failed Completion Stage

```
CompletionStage<Object> cs = CompletableFuture.failedStage(new
Exception("BOOM!"));
ReactiveStreams.fromCompletionStage(cs)
        .onComplete(() -> log("Not executed!"))  ①
        .peek(i -> log("Not executed!"))  ②
        .onError(t -> log("Failed with " + t.getMessage()))  ③
        .ignore()
        .run()
```

① Not executed as there is no onComplete signal

② Not executed as there is no onNext signal

③ Error from failed CompletionStage intercepted

fromCompletionStageNullable

While CompletionStage allows null values, reactive streams do not. Null cannot be carried as the onNext item within the reactive stream. When the fromCompletionStage operator is supplied with CompletionStage completed by null, the stream gets failed by the onError signal with NullPointerException as the cause.

The fromCompletionStageNullable operator drops null items and emits onComplete immediately.

fromPublisher

The fromPublisher operator can construct a stream from a raw reactive publisher. This is very practical when connecting reactive streams to other reactive APIs.

Listing 13-15. fromCompletionStage Operator Creates Reactive Stream from Publisher

```
SubmissionPublisher<Integer> sp = new
SubmissionPublisher<>();   ①
Publisher<Integer> rawPublisher = FlowAdapters.
toPublisher(sp);   ②
CompletionStage<List<Integer>> resultCs =
        ReactiveStreams.fromPublisher(rawPublisher)
                .toList()
                .run();
sp.submit(1);   ③
sp.submit(2);
sp.submit(3);
sp.close();   ④
List<Integer> list = resultCs.toCompletableFuture().join();   ⑤
```

① Java Flow.Publisher

② Adapted Reactive Stream Publisher

③ Emitting items with Flow.Publisher

④ Completing stream with Flow.Publisher

⑤ Result list contains all emitted items [1, 2, 3]

concat

The concat operator connects two publisher graphs together the way that when first stream completes, the second one continues to publish instead.

Listing 13-16. concat Connecting Two Streams to One

```
ReactiveStreams.concat(
                ReactiveStreams.of(1, 2),
                ReactiveStreams.of(3, 4)
        )
        .toList()  ①
        .run();
```

> ① Result list contains items from both streams in the
>   correct order [1, 2, 3, 4]

map

The map operator is a notoriously known wrench in your reactive toolbox. Its parameter is a function executed for each onNext signal coming through the stream. Incoming value is provided to the function, and the returned value is sent downstream to the next operator.

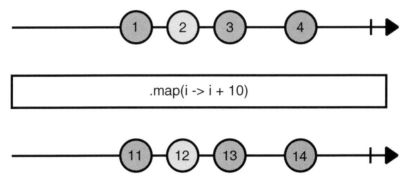

Figure 13-9. *Map operator*

The type of the returned value decides the inbound type of the next downstream operator.

Listing 13-17. map Operator Changing Type of Outbound Value

```
List<String> upstreamData = List.of("1", "2", "3", "4");
CompletionStage<List<Integer>> resultFuture =
        ReactiveStreams.fromIterable(upstreamData)  ①
                .map(Integer::parseInt)  ②
                .toList()  ③
                .run();
```

① Upstream sends string items

② Mapping function changes the type from string to integer

③ Terminal operator toList already collects strings

peek

The peek operator never augments the stream data. It executes the provided consumer for each onNext signal coming through the stream.

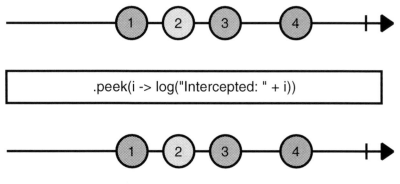

Figure 13-10. *Limit operator*

Each item is consumed by the consumer which is never executed in parallel. The onNext signal sends the item to the next operator only after the peek consumer function is executed. The only way peek can affect the stream is when an exception is thrown in its consumer function, then upstream is canceled, and the onError signal is sent downstream with exception cause as a Throwable parameter.

Unlike Java's Stream.peek which may get ignored because of downstream optimization, Reactive Streams peek is guaranteed to be executed for each onNext signal. It can be used for creating intentional side effects.

filter

The filter operator allows throwing away selected items coming down the stream. Its predicate function gets executed for each onNext signal with item as its parameter. The onNext signal is sent downstream only when the filter's predicate function returns true.

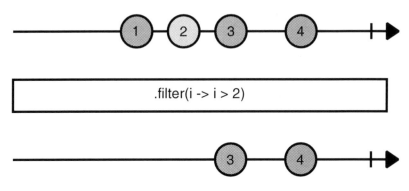

Figure 13-11. *The filter operator*

The filter function is always executed serially, as all the operator functions are.

Listing 13-18. filter Operator Letting Through Only Selected Items

```
ReactiveStreams.of(1, 2, 3, 4)
        .filter(i -> i > 2)  ①
        .toList()  ②
        .run()
```

① Only numbers greater than 2 can pass downstream

② Result list contains [3, 4] because 1 and 2 were filtered out

limit

The limit operator limits the number of items sent downstream; its only parameter is a long number of items that can pass the limit operator. Limit operator counts onNext signals passing through. When limit number is reached, limit completes the stream by canceling upstream and sending the onComplete signal downstream.

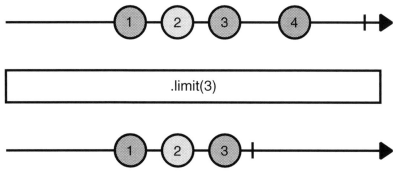

Figure 13-12. *The limit operator*

The limit parameter can be only a positive number or 0. When a negative number is supplied, IllegalArgumentException is raised.

takeWhile

The takeWhile operator lets through items until supplied predicate returns true, takeWhile functions similarly to the filter operator, but completes the stream when predicate returns false.

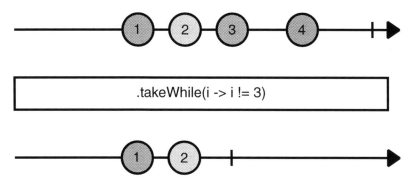

Figure 13-13. *takeWhile operator*

Listing 13-19. takeWhile Operator Letting Items Through While Predicate Is True

```
ReactiveStreams.of(1, 2, 3, 4)
        .takeWhile(i -> i != 3)  ①
        .toList() ②
        .run()
```

① Items can pass downstream only until the predicate returns false

② Result list contains [1, 2] because 3 caused stream completion

dropWhile

The dropWhile operator drops all items coming with onNext signal, not sending them to the next operator downstream until its predicate returns false.

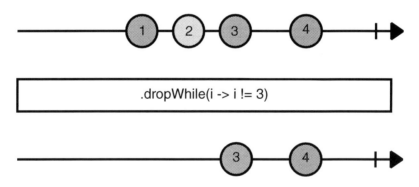

Figure 13-14. *DropWhile operator*

Predicate function is executed for each onNext signal with item as its parameter until first time predicate returns false, after first false result is not executed anymore.

Listing 13-20. dropWhile Operator Dropping Items While
Predicate Is True

```
ReactiveStreams.of(1, 2, 3, 4)
        .dropWhile(i -> i != 3)  ①
        .toList()  ②
        .run()
```

① Items can pass downstream only after the
predicate returns false for the first time

② Result list contains [3, 4] because 1 and 2
were dropped

skip

The skip operator drops given number of items, after that all subsequent
onNext signals are allowed to pass downstream.

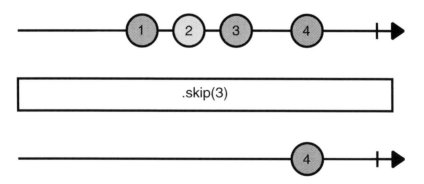

Figure 13-15. *Skip operator*

Skip parameter can be only a positive number or 0. When a negative
number is supplied IllegalArgumentException is raised.

flatMap

The flatMap operator executes a given function for each item, where another reactive stream is expected as a result. flatMap inlines all items from the resulting stream, sending each of its items separately downstream.

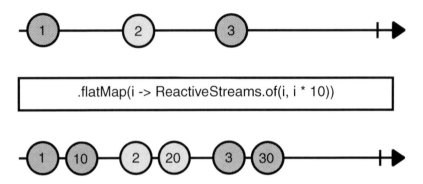

Figure 13-16. flatMap operator

This ability allows multiplying items based on the provided logic.

Listing 13-21. flatMap Operator Multiplying Items

```
ReactiveStreams.of(1, 2, 3)
        .flatMap(i -> ReactiveStreams.of(i, i * 10))  ①
        .toList()  ②
        .run()
```

① Items are converted to streams containing themselves and their multiple

② Result list contains [1, 10, 2, 20, 3, 30] because for each item, its multiple was added

Whereas a basic MP Reactive Streams flatMap expects a publisher builder, its alternative, flatMapRsPublisher, behaves the same but expects a Publisher type.

flatMapCompletionStage

The flatMapCompletionStage operator safely aligns CompletionStage callbacks in the reactive stream so that execution of the next operator happens when a given completion stage is completed.

While normally it is very dangerous to block or obstruct reactive operators, flatMapCompletionStage provides a way of offloading the blocking or obstructing operation to another thread. This approach is necessary in case upstream uses a limited number of threads, for example event loop model, otherwise other workers would be deprived of their thread time.

Listing 13-22. flatMapCompletionStage Operator Aligning Asynchronous Execution

```
ReactiveStreams.of(1, 2, 3)
    .flatMapCompletionStage(i ->
            CompletableFuture.consumeAsync(() -> {
                workForFewMinutes();  ①
                return i;
            }, executorService))
    .toList()  ②
    .run()  ③
```

      ① Asynchronous work is done serially; each execution starts only after the previous is done

      ② Result list contains [1, 2, 3]

      ③ Streams CompletionStage is completed when all async works are finished and results collected

flatMapIterable

The flatMapIterable serializes supplied iterable's items downstream as separate stream items.

Listing 13-23. flatMapIterable Operator Multiplying Items

```
ReactiveStreams.of(1, 2, 3)
        .flatMapIterable(i -> List.of(i, i * 10))  ①
        .toList()  ②
        .run()
```

① Items are converted to streams containing themselves and their multiple

② Result list contains [1, 10, 2, 20, 3, 30] because for each item, its multiple was added

onComplete

The onComplete operator never augments the stream. It executes provided runnable for onComplete signal coming through the stream.

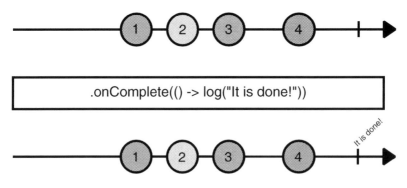

Figure 13-17. OnComplete operator

The onComplete runnable is executed before the onComplete signal continues downstream.

onError

The onError operator never augments the stream. It executes a provided consumer for the onError signal coming through the stream. The consumer gets a Throwable, with the cause of the error as a parameter.

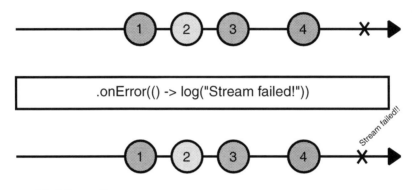

Figure 13-18. onError operator

The onError consumer is executed before the onError signal continues downstream.

onErrorResume

The onErrorResume operator can convert the onError signal to a single new item and send it downstream as the onNext signal.

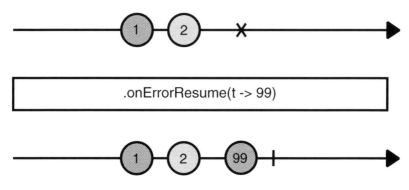

Figure 13-19. *OnErrorResume operator*

The operator function receives a Throwable cause if the onError signal is a parameter. A new item of the same type as the previous is expected to be returned.

Listing 13-24. onErrorResume Operators Reviving Failed Stream

```
ReactiveStreams.concat(
            ReactiveStreams.of(1, 2),
            ReactiveStreams.failed(new Exception("BOOM!"))
    )
    .onErrorResume(t -> 99)  ①
    .toList()  ②
    .run()
```

① Error is converted to a single item sent downstream as onNext instead of the onError signal

② Result list contains [1, 2, 99] because onError was converted to a single additional item

onErrorResumeWith

The onErrorResumeWith operator converts the onError signal to a new stream and flatmap it downstream.

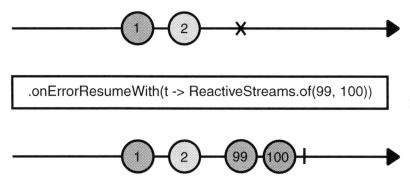

Figure 13-20. *onErrorResumeWith Operator*

The operator function receives a Throwable cause if the onError signal as a parameter, new stream is expected to be returned.

Listing 13-25. onErrorResumeWith Operators Reviving Failed Stream

```
ReactiveStreams.concat(
            ReactiveStreams.of(1, 2),
            ReactiveStreams.failed(new Exception("BOOM!"))
    )
    .onErrorResumeWith(t -> ReactiveStreams.of(99, 100))  ①
    .toList()  ②
    .run()
```

① Error is converted to flat-mapped stream
   downstream instead of the onError signal

② Result list contains [1, 2, 99, 100] because onError
   was converted to a stream of additional items

347

onTerminate

The onTerminate operator never augments the stream. It executes
provided runnable for the onComplete or onError signal coming through
the stream. The onTerminate runnable is executed before the onComplete
or onError signal continues downstream.

cancel

cancel is a terminal operator, meaning it subscribes upstream, and
no other operators follow. The cancel operator sends the cancel signal
upstream after the onSubscribe signal is received. It is not possible to do it
earlier because the onSubscribe signal carries the subscription needed to
send the cancel signal upstream.

Listing 13-26. cancel Operator Canceling the Whole Stream

```
ReactiveStreams.of(1, 2, 3)
        .peek(i -> log("This is never executed"))  ①
        .cancel()  ②
        .run()
```

① peek is not executed as the cancel signal is sent to
   the publisher and no request signal

② cancel sends cancel signal as soon as
   onSubscribe is signaled upstream

reduce

reduce is a terminal operator, and its parameter is an accumulator bi-
function that takes two parameters. The first parameter is the first item
if executed for the first time or a result of the previous execution of the
accumulator. The second parameter is always the next item.

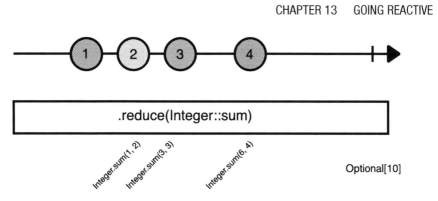

Figure 13-21. *Reduce operator*

Reduce operator aggregates the stream items with the provided accumulator function.

Listing 13-27. reduce Operator Applying Accumulator

```
Optional<Integer> result =  ②
        ReactiveStreams.of(1, 2, 3, 4)
                .reduce((sum, next) -> sum + next)  ①
                .run()
                .toCompletableFuture()
                .join();
```

① Accumulator is executed three times with
   parameters (1,2), (3,3), and (6,4)

② Result is Optional[10], the sum of all the
   stream items

distinct

The distinct operator removes duplicities from the stream by comparing the items with Object.equals.

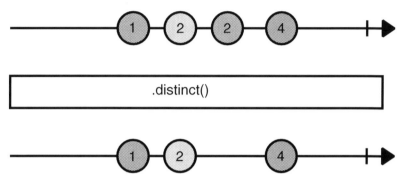

Figure 13-22. *Distinct operator*

Distinct is keeping the references to all the already passed unique values until onError, onComplete or *cancel* signal passes the operator. Need for keeping the references for future comparison should be considered when using the distinct operator on a larger stream.

Listing 13-28. distinct Operator Removing Duplicities

```
ReactiveStreams.of(1, 2, 2, 4)  ①
        .distinct()
        .toList()  ②
        .run()
```

① Notice the second and third items are the same

② Result contains only distinct values [1, 2, 4]

findFirst

The findFirst operator is a terminal operator, it returns the first item coming with onNext signal from upstream if any. When onComplete is received before any onNext signal, findFirst returns an empty optional.

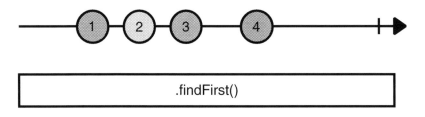

Optional[1]

Figure 13-23. *findFirst operator*

findFirst sends a cancel signal immediately after the first onNext signal is received, ignoring any subsequent onNext signals.

Listing 13-29. findFirst Operator Returning First Item or Empty Optional

```
ReactiveStreams.of(1, 2, 3, 4)  ①
        .findFirst()  ②
        .run()

ReactiveStreams.empty()  ③
        .findFirst()  ④
        .run()
```

① Stream with first item 1

② Result is Optional[1]

③ Empty stream has no first item

④ Result is Optional.empty

forEach

The forEach operator is a terminal operator, it executes provided supplier function for each onNext signal with the item as its parameter. forEach sends a request(Long.MAX_VALUE) signal upstream right after the onSubscribe signal is received, requesting the unbounded data, with no backpressure applied.

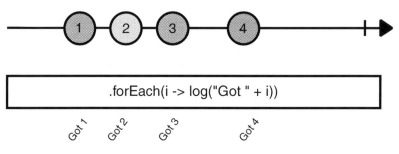

Figure 13-24. *ForEach operator*

When an exception is thrown in the supplier function, forEach sends a cancel signal upstream, and the resulting CompletionStage is completed exceptionally.

Listing 13-30. forEach Operator Executing Consumer for Each Item

```
ReactiveStreams.of(1, 2, 3, 4)
        .forEach(i -> log("Got " + i))  ①
        .run()

ReactiveStreams.of(1, 2, 3, 4)
        .forEach(i -> {
            throw new RuntimeException("BOOM!");
        })
        .run()  ②
```

① Each item is logged

② Resulting `CompletionStage` is
   `[Completed exceptionally: java.lang.`
   `RuntimeException: BOOM!]`

ignore

The `ignore` operator is a terminal operator; it works like the `forEach` operator with a loop function. The `ignore` operator ignores each `onNext` signal separately and completes the resulting `CompletionStage` when the `onComplete` signal is received.

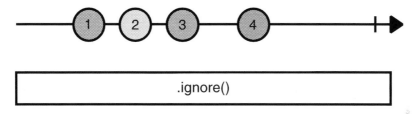

Figure 13-25. *The ignore operator*

toList

The `toList` operator is a terminal operator, it collects all the items from stream to `java.util.List` and returns `CompletionStage<List<T>>` completed when `onComplete` signal is received.

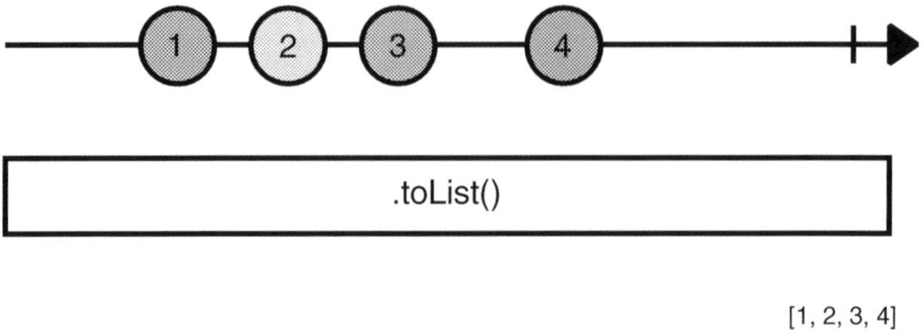

[1, 2, 3, 4]

Figure 13-26. *toList operator*

Listing 13-31. The toList Operator Collects All Items to List

```
List<Integer> result =
        ReactiveStreams.of(1, 2, 3, 4)
                .toList()
                .run()
                .toCompletableFuture()
                .join();
```

to

to is a composition and terminal operator that allows connection of prepared subscriber graphs to a publisher or processor graph builder.

Listing 13-32. to Operator Connect Subscriber Graph to a Builder

```
SubscriberBuilder<Integer, Void> subscriberGraph =  ①
    ReactiveStreams.<Integer>builder()
        .forEach(i -> log("Got " + i));

ReactiveStreams.of(1, 2, 3)
        .to(subscriberGraph)  ②
        .run()
```

① Prepared subscriber graph

② Connecting prepared subscriber to a builder

via

via is a composition operator that allows connecting processor graphs in a builder. Unlike the to operator, via is not terminal; other operators can follow it.

Listing 13-33. via Operator Connect Processor Graph to a Builder

```
ProcessorBuilder<Integer, Integer> processorGraph =  ①
        ReactiveStreams.<Integer>builder()
                .map(i -> i * 10)
                .map(i -> i - 5);

ReactiveStreams.of(1, 2, 3)
        .via(processorGraph)  ②
        .forEach(i -> log("Got " + i))
        .run()
```

① Prepared processor graph

② Connecting prepared processor graph to a builder

Helidon Reactive Operators

Helidon has its own set of reactive operators on top of which are all the reactive features in Helidon built. Each reactive API in Helidon SE is exposing Helidon operators. And because Helidon MP is built on top of Helidon SE, you almost always have Helidon reactive operators on the classpath.

Even under the MicroProfile Reactive Stream Operators implementation in Helidon are hidden Helidon operators.

Helidon operators are constructed by two main classes, `Multi` for streams with 0–n items and `Single` for streams with only 0–1 items.

Listing 13-34. Multi and Single Streams

```
Single<String> single =
        Multi.range(1, 10)  ①
                .limit(3)
                .map(String::valueOf)
                .first();  ②

Integer result = single
        .map(Integer::parseInt)
        .await();  ③
```

① Create a new multistream

② Get only the first item → Single

③ Block till single is completed, don't do this in a
   reactive context

Single is a promise with all the features of reactive stream publisher, but it implements publisher and `CompletionStage`.

Listing 13-35. Single Is CompletionStage

```
Single.just(1)
        .whenComplete((i, t) -> log("Complete!"))
        .toCompletableFuture()
        .join();
```

This makes `Single` versatile for usage with other asynchronous but not reactive streams compatible APIs.

Listing 13-36. Single As CompletionStage

```
ReactiveStreams.of(1, 2)
        .flatMapCompletionStage(Single::just)  ①
        .toList()
        .run();
```

> ① Single flat-mapped by unsuspecting MP
>   reactive stream

This dual personality of Single has a catch: reactive streams are forbidden to have null as an item, and CompletionStages are okay with nulls. Single overcomes this similarly to MP Reactive Streams fromCompletionStageNullable by converting null to an empty stream when instructed.

Listing 13-37. Single from Nullable CompletionStage

```
CompletionStage<Void> csWithNull =
        CompletableFuture.completedStage(null);
Single.create(csWithNull, true)  ①
        .peek(unused -> log("Not invoked"))
        .onComplete(() -> log("Completed!"))  ②
        .ignoreElement();
```

> ① Null means empty parameter set to true

> ② Only onComplete signal

Unlike the MicroProfile Reactive Stream Operators implementing the org.reactivestreams API, Helidon operators implement Java's java.util.concurrent.Flow reactive stream API. These are identical APIs, first in a stand-alone library for pre–Java 9 environments, later a part of Java API since version 9.

Same APIs but in different packages, but don't worry conversion is quite easy. Reactive Streams API library brings with it handy adapter utility `org.reactivestreams.FlowAdapters`.

Listing 13-38. Converting Helidon Publisher to RS

```
Flow.Publisher<String> flowPublisher =
        Multi.just(1, 2, 3, 4)
                .map(String::valueOf);   ①
Publisher<String> rsPublisher = FlowAdapters.
toPublisher(flowPublisher);   ②
ReactiveStreams.fromPublisher(rsPublisher)   ③
        .map(Integer::parseInt)
        .toList()
        .run();
```

① Helidon map operator

② Adapter between RS Publisher and Flow.Publisher

③ MP Reactive Streams connected to adapted
   Helidon operator

Reactive Messaging

Messaging is an important feature of any runtime, bringing the means for asynchronous communication, and a way to loosen strong coupling between the components. On the first look MicroProfile messaging strongly resembles well-known messaging beans.

Listing 13-39. Simple Incoming Message Handler Method

```
@Incoming("channel-1")
public void receive(String payload) {
    System.out.println("Received payload:" + payload);
}
```

The Reactive Messaging API is much richer, and it's no coincidence the "Reactive" has much to do with it.

Reactive systems are defined in the famous reactive manifesto as responsive, resilient, elastic and message-driven. Yes, message-driven messaging makes it easy for the system to be easily scalable and fail proof if, and that is important, if it can provide feedback to the producing side. Feedback for acknowledging message reception and regulating the flow. You already know the concept of acknowledgment from JMS or offset committing from Kafka without acknowledgment messages present. When one server crashes, another can take over its unacknowledged messages.

Great approach to regulation of incoming messages flow is known from reactive streams, it's called backpressure. Instead of re-creating reactive APIs, Reactive Messaging uses Reactive Streams for constructing *channels.*

Channel

A *channel* is a reactive stream with a publisher and single subscriber constructed from reactive streams stages. Channels are identified by names, either in annotations (see Listing 13-40) or in the configuration (see Listing 13-41).

Listing 13-40. Messaging Annotations Channel Names

```
@Incoming("channel-1")
...
@Channel("channel-1")
```

Listing 13-41. Messaging Channel Configuration

```
mp.messaging:
  incoming:
    channel-1:        ①
      connector: helidon-jms
      destination: ./TestJMSModule!TestQueue
```

> ① Named channel with channel-specific
>   configuration

Every channel, since it's in fact a reactive stream, needs to have both publisher and subscriber. When it doesn't, the container won't start successfully.

The simplest possible channel is a combination of @Incoming and @Outgoing annotated methods.

Listing 13-42. Simple Reactive Messaging Channel

```
@Outgoing("channel-1")
public PublisherBuilder<String> registerPublisher() {
    return ReactiveStreams.of("first", "second", "third");
}

@Incoming("channel-1")
public void consume(String payload) {
    System.out.println(">" + payload);
}

>first
>second
>third
```

Listing 13-42 shows the publisher is supplied with MicroProfile Reactive Streams operator's `PublisherBuilder`, which is a prepared chain of reactive operators called a *stage*.

The consuming method still looks like it was taken from a message-driven bean; but behind the scenes, it is a hidden terminal `forEach` operator. You can tweak the example to supply a `SubscriberStage` doing the same.

Listing 13-43. Incoming Method with Explicit forEach

```
@Outgoing("channel-1")
public PublisherBuilder<String> registerPublisher() {
    return ReactiveStreams.of("first", "second", "third");
}

@Incoming("channel-1")
public SubscriberBuilder<String, Void> consume() {
    return ReactiveStreams.<String>builder()
            .forEach(payload -> {
                System.out.println(">" + payload);
            });
}

>first
>second
>third
```

When the reactive stream is no longer hidden, you can construct more advanced reactive pipelines and employ more operators, such as `.map()` to transform payloads to uppercase.

Listing 13-44. Incoming Method with Reactive Operators

```
@Incoming("channel-1")
public SubscriberBuilder<String, Void> consume() {
    return ReactiveStreams.<String>builder()
            .map(payload -> payload.toUpperCase())
            .forEach(payload -> {
                System.out.println(">" + payload);
            });
}
```

```
>FIRST
>SECOND
>THIRD
```

For consuming, instead of providing a subscriber with the incoming method, you can also access the channel's publisher directly by letting messaging inject it into your bean's field or constructor parameter.

Note   Since MicroProfile Reactive Messaging 2.0

Listing 13-45. Injected Publisher

```
@Inject
@Channel("channel-1")
Publisher<String> channelOnePublisher;
```

Channels can be connected with processor methods; processor method can combine both @Incoming and @Outgoing annotations. It can work like a map operator when a method with one parameter is invoked for each stream item; or it can provide a reactive streams graph with operators to be aligned as a processor between the two channels.

Listing 13-46. Processor Method

```
@Incoming("channel-1")
@Outgoing("channel-2")
public ProcessorBuilder<String, String> processor() {
    return ReactiveStreams.<String>builder()
            .map(payload -> payload.toUpperCase());
}

@Incoming("channel-2")
public void consume(String payload) {
    System.out.println(">" + payload);
}

>FIRST
>SECOND
>THIRD
```

Emitter

Note   Since MicroProfile Reactive Messaging 2.0

Publishing messages from imperative code to reactive stream can be technically quite challenging. There is a convenient SubmissionPublisher shipped with JDK since version 9 and newer, you can just register it as a publisher with the @Outgoing messaging method, and you are good to go.

While it is a working solution, SubmissionPublisher is a big gun covering much more ground than you need by spinning up unnecessary threads, ready to serve multiple subscribers.

To ease this frequent use case, an injectable emitter is available in messaging. With lightweight single-thread implementation, configurable buffering strategies, and the ability to automatically connect to messaging channels, the emitter bridges the gaps from the first version of the Reactive Messaging specification.

Listing 13-47. Sending Messages from JAX-RS Endpoint

```
@Inject
@Channel("channel-1")
Emitter<String> emitter;

@POST
@Consumes("text/plain")
public void push(String payload) {
    emitter.send(payload);
}
```

Emitter sends messages asynchronously, backpressure from reactive stream is not propagated by blocking. Instead, overflow strategy can be configured with annotation @OnOverflow to indicate what should happen when downstream demand is lower than the number of sent messages.

Message

Reactive messaging is able to inject to your messaging methods either directly the payload, or a wrapper with metadata extending the org.eclipse.microprofile.reactive.messaging.Message. Every message has getPayload() and ack() methods for accessing payload and acknowledgment of successful reception in case of manual acknowledgment.

Listing 13-48. Consuming Message

```
@Incoming("channel-1")
public CompletionStage<Void> consume(Message<String> msg) {
    System.out.println(">" + msg.getPayload());
    return msg.ack();
}
```

A message wrapper can be extended and customized to carry more specific metadata. For example, when connecting to Kafka connector you can let messaging directly inject KafkaMessage to gain access to headers, partition, topic, offset and more.

Acknowledgment

Acknowledgment is an important feature for achieving resiliency in case of some catastrophic failure. Without the acknowledgment, if a consuming module crashes during processing of a consumed message, the producing side has no way to know if the crashed module was successful with message processing or not.

With the consuming side acknowledging successful consumption, the producing side can decide if the message needs to be resent to another consumer or not.

MicroProfile Reactive Messaging supports multiple acknowledge strategies for various messaging methods. Acknowledge strategy can be configured with @Acknowledgment annotation. There are multiple options to choose from.

- POST_PROCESSING is an automatic acknowledgment after the messaging method or supplied operator is invoked.

- PRE_PROCESSING is an automatic acknowledgment right before the method or operator is invoked.

- MANUAL means no automatic acknowledgment is performed.

- NONE means no automatic acknowledgment, and no manual acknowledgment is expected.

Caution   There are different default acknowledgment strategies for different messaging method signatures. Consult MicroProfile Reactive Messaging Specification for more information.

Manual acknowledgment makes the developer responsible for calling the Message.ack(), because the developer knows the best when business code processed the message successfully.

Listing 13-49 demonstrates monitoring an acknowledged callback.

Listing 13-49. Acknowledge Callbacks

```
@Outgoing("channel-1")
public PublisherBuilder<Message<String>> registerPublisher() {
    return ReactiveStreams.of("first", "second", "third")
            .map(payload -> Message.of(payload, () -> {
                return CompletableFuture.
                completedStage("Message " + payload + "
                acked!")
                        .thenAccept(System.out::println);
            }));
}

@Incoming("channel-1")
@Acknowledgment(Acknowledgment.Strategy.MANUAL)
public CompletionStage<Void> consume(Message<String> msg) {
    System.out.println(">" + msg.getPayload());
    return msg.ack();
}
```

```
>first
Message first acked!
>second
Message second acked!
>third
Message third acked!
```

Ack callback is observed manually in the example. If there would be Kafka connector configured as a publisher for channel-1, Kafka connector would commit offset. With the JMS connector the original JMS message would be acknowledged.

No Acknowledgment

For situations when it is already obvious the message can't be consumed or processed successfully, Message.nack(Throwable t) is available. The nack method triggers a callback for an explicit not-acknowledge, which can be supplied during message construction.

Listing 13-50. Ack and Nack Callbacks

```
Message<String> msg =
  Message.of("payload",
          () -> CompletableFuture
                  .completedFuture("Acked!")
                  .thenAccept(System.out::println),
          t -> CompletableFuture
                  .completedFuture("Not acked! Error " +
                  t.getMessage())
                  .thenAccept(System.out::println));
msg.nack(new Exception("BOOM!"));

> Not acked! Error BOOM!
```

Each connector has its own nacking strategies; usually, the channel is killed by default.

Messaging Health

When a messaging channel fails, and it can fail for many reasons, it can't be revived. A channel can fail for example because the connector lost connection to the messaging broker or because an exception was thrown in the messaging method. Since Helidon is a microservice framework, the obvious solution for reestablishing the connection is to restart the pod. To let K8s know that restarting of the pod is needed, you need a health probe. Reactive messaging has its own special health probe.

Listing 13-51. Messaging Health Dependency

```
<dependency>
    <groupId>io.helidon.microprofile.messaging</groupId>
    <artifactId>helidon-microprofile-messaging-health</
    artifactId>
</dependency>
```

Messaging health liveness check simply reports your channel DOWN if either of onError, onComplete or cancel signal has been detected in it.

Listing 13-52. Messaging Health Liveness Check

```
{
    "name": "messaging",
    "state": "UP",
    "status": "UP",
    "data": {
        "channel-1": "UP",
```

```
      "channel-2": "UP"
   }
}
```

Similarly, readiness check reports channel UP when onSubscribe signal has been detected.

Messaging Connectors

Helidon provides a variety of connectors for reactive messaging with the most used remote brokers. The connector is just an application scoped bean acting as a factory for creating publishers or subscribers from provided configuration.

Configuration is straightforward. The connector expects a global config under the property mp.messaging.connector.CONNECTOR_NAME. The global config can be overridden or extended with configuration of every specific channel. While incoming channels can reference connector as its publisher with property connector, outgoing channels use the same property for referencing connector as its subscriber.

Listing 13-53. Configure Helidon Messaging Connector

```
mp.messaging:
  incoming.from-jms:  ①
    connector: helidon-jms  ②
    destination: queue-1  ③
    type: queue

  outgoing.to-jms:  ④
    connector: helidon-jms
    destination: messaging-test-queue-1
    type: queue
```

```
connector:
  helidon-jms: ⑤
    user: frank
    password: secret1234
    jndi:
      jms-factory: ConnectionFactory
      env-properties:
        java.naming:
          factory.initial: org.apache.activemq.jndi.
          ActiveMQInitialContextFactory
          provider.url: tcp://localhost:61616
```

① Incoming channel configuration

② Connector is responsible for providing publisher
   to this channel

③ Channel-specific config for connector

④ Outgoing channel configuration

⑤ Connector's global config can be overridden or
   extended with channel-specific config

Figure 13-27 shows how the connector applies configuration to
construct the channel's publisher or subscriber. Notice how the channel's
config is enriched with global config; this way, you don't need to repeat
common properties for every channel. Global connector's config can be
overridden by channel property of the same name.

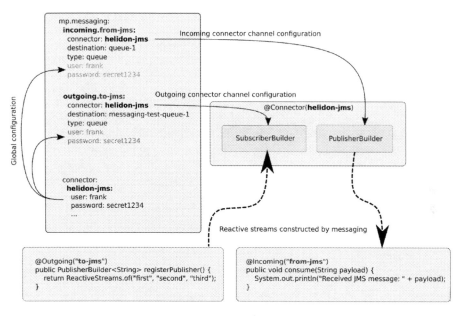

Figure 13-27. *Connector configuration structure*

When you know how to configure a connector as a publisher for an incoming channel or subscriber for an outgoing channel using connectors, it is only a matter of configuring connector-specific properties.

Kafka Connector

Kafka is a popular, distributed messaging system developed by the Apache Software Foundation. Designed to be highly scalable, fault-tolerant, and durable, Kafka can handle high volumes of data and is optimized for low-latency message delivery. In Kafka messaging, messages are organized into topics, which are partitioned across a cluster of servers called brokers. Each partition can be replicated across multiple brokers for redundancy and fault tolerance. Kafka is widely used in big data and streaming data applications for processing and analyzing large amounts of data in real-time.

For consuming and publishing messages from and to Kafka brokers, Helidon provides a connector for reactive messaging.

Listing 13-54. Kafka Connector Dependency

```
<dependency>
    <groupId>io.helidon.messaging.kafka</groupId>
    <artifactId>helidon-messaging-kafka</artifactId>
</dependency>
```

Kafka supports both point-to-point(queue) and publish-subscribe (topic) paradigms, by the same Kafka topic. Kafka topic is basically a partitioned queue, for which consumers share offset of the messages already read among groups. Each consumer can either subscribe as a part of an existing group (behaves like a queue) or a new group exclusive to a single consumer (works like a topic).

Listing 13-55. Kafka Connector Configuration

```
serializer.pkg: org.apache.kafka.common.serialization

mp.messaging:
 connector:
   helidon-kafka:
     bootstrap.servers: localhost:9092   ①
     key.serializer: ${serializer.pkg}.StringSerializer   ②
     value.serializer: ${serializer.pkg}.StringSerializer
     key.deserializer: ${serializer.pkg}.StringDeserializer   ③
     value.deserializer: ${serializer.pkg}.StringDeserializer
 incoming.from-kafka:
   connector: helidon-kafka
   topic: messaging-test-topic-1   ④
   auto.offset.reset: latest   ⑤
```

```
  enable.auto.commit: false   ⑥
  group.id: example-group-1   ⑦
outgoing.to-kafka:
  connector: helidon-kafka
  topic: messaging-test-topic-1
```

① Zookeeper or Kafka broker location

② Message serializers

③ Message deserializers

④ Topic name

⑤ When starting for the first time with current group ID, read only the new messages

⑥ Turn off auto commit, offset is committed by acknowledge mechanism

⑦ Group for which the topic behaves like a queue, index is shared

With disabled auto commit, reactive messaging acknowledgment effectively commits the partition offset for the current consumer group. This means that when a message is not acknowledged, an offset is not committed. When the messaging channel dies without acking a message and the microservice gets restarted, the message gets redelivered. This may not be always desirable so Kafka connection also supports reactive messaging nacking `Message.nack(Throwable t)`.

Nack Strategies

Kafka connector supports multiple nack strategies.

- **Kill channel** is the default strategy; when a message is nacked, the whole channel is killed.

- **DLQ** resends the message to pre-configured dead-letter queue, then ack.

- **Log** only means log error and ack the message.

By default, the channel is killed by a nack message. This is desirable when redelivery is required. A messaging health probe can detect a killed channel and K8s restarts the pod. The restarted pod resumes with the same message if it has no consumer group ID defined (topic) and `auto.offset.reset` is set to latest or is a single pod using the group ID. When multiple pods are using the same consumer group ID, the message is redelivered to one of the pods with the same group ID right after rebalance.

When sending the unprocessed message to the dead-letter queue is required, DLQ nack strategy is available.

Listing 13-56. DLQ Nack Strategy Configuration

```
mp.messaging:
  incoming:
    from-kafka:
      nack-dlq: my-dlq-topic   ①
```

> ① DLQ topic to send errored messages to on the same broker

When only the name of DLQ topic is configured, the same broker configuration including serializers is used as the one used for receiving the message. Serializers are derived from the incoming connection deserializers with following pattern, in the deserializer simple class name is replaced `Deserializer` by `Serializer`, when such class exists there is no need to configure serializer for DLQ.

Listing 13-57. DLQ Nack Strategy Advanced Configuration

```
serializer.pkg: org.apache.kafka.common.serialization

mp.messaging:
  incoming:
    from-kafka:
      nack-dlq:
        topic: my-dlq-topic-on-other-broker
        bootstrap.servers: localhost:9092  ①
        key.serializer: ${serializer.pkg}.StringSerializer  ②
        value.serializer: ${serializer.pkg}.StringSerializer
```

① Configuration for custom DLQ Kafka broker

② Custom serializer for DLQ

Log only nack strategy simply logs the exception and acks the nacked message. The nacked message is discarded, offset committed and the channel can continue consuming the subsequent messages.

Listing 13-58. Log Only Nack Strategy Configuration

```
mp.messaging:
  incoming:
    from-kafka:
      nack-log-only: true
```

JMS Connector

JMS stands for Java Message Service, a Java-based messaging API for creating, sending, and receiving messages. JMS provides a high-level abstraction of messaging allowing multiple vendors to provide messaging over the same API. JMS has become a widely adopted messaging standard

375

in the enterprise world, and many messaging products, including Oracle WebLogic, Oracle AQ, IBM MQ, Apache ActiveMQ, and JBoss Messaging, implement the JMS API. Over this versatility of JMS, the connector for reactive messaging opens the door to many messaging brokers at once.

Listing 13-59. JMS Connector Dependency

```
<dependency>
    <groupId>io.helidon.messaging.jms</groupId>
    <artifactId>helidon-messaging-jms</artifactId>
</dependency>
```

Injected ConnectionFactory

While JMS specification heavily relies on the JNDI, Helidon connector supports JNDI-less approach for supplying ConnectionFactory directly as a CDI bean. Helidon MP is a CDI 3.0 compliant injection framework. Creating a bean from an instantiated connection factory is simple with a CDI producer method or field.

Listing 13-60. Supplying JMS ConnectionFactory As a Bean

```
@Inject
@ConfigProperty(name = "jms.broker-url")
private String brokerUrl;  ①

@Produces  ②
@ApplicationScoped  ③
@Named("activemq-cf")  ④
public ConnectionFactory connectionFactory() {
    return new ActiveMQConnectionFactory(brokerUrl);
}
```

① Injecting custom configured broker URL

② Marking method as a bean producer

③ ConnectionFactory bean must be named to allow
   referencing from messaging configuration

When you have created a ConnectionFactory bean named `activemq-cf`,
you can simply reference it from messaging configuration.

Listing 13-61. Use ConnectionFactory Bean in JMS Connector

```
jms.broker-url: tcp://localhost:61616  ①

mp.messaging:
    connector:
      helidon-jms:
        named-factory: activemq-cf  ②
        user: frank  ③
        password: secret1234
```

① ConnectionFactory initialization needs to
   configured manually

② Use named bean `activemq-cf` as JMS
   ConnectionFactory

③ User name and password used for JMS connection
   creation

Lookup ConnectionFactory over JNDI

Supplying ConnectionFactory over JNDI lookup is possible, initial JNDI
environment properties can be configured with `jndi.env-properties`.
The JNDI name of the actual connection factory needs to be configured
with `jndi.jms-factory`.

Listing 13-62. Configure Helidon Messaging Connector

```
mp.messaging:
    connector:
      helidon-jms:
        user: frank   ①
        password: secret123
        jndi:
          jms-factory: ConnectionFactory   ②
          env-properties:   ③
            java.naming:
              factory.initial: org.apache.activemq.jndi.
              ActiveMQInitialContextFactory
              provider.url: tcp://localhost:61616
```

① User name and password used for JMS connection creation

② JNDI name of `ConnectionFactory`

③ Environment properties used for JNDI initial context creation

Destination

To select a queue or topic to publish or consume from, you must configure the vendor-specific destination name with `destination` configuration property or the JNDI destination identifier with `jndi.destination`. While vendor-specific destination works for both injected connection factory and JNDI looked up connection factory, JNDI destination configuration works only for JNDI looked up connection factory.

Vendor-specific destination name is a way of identifying destination over JMS API without JNDI usage. All JMS vendors provide their own syntax for selecting proper queue or topic, for example ArtemisMQ has its own address model with FQQN (Fully Qualified Queue Names), WebLogic JMS has CDI (Create Destination Identifier) and IBM MQ is using URI (Uniform Resource Identifier).

Listing 13-63. Configure Destination with or Without JNDI

```
activemq-cf: org.apache.activemq.jndi.
ActiveMQInitialContextFactory

mp.messaging:
  connector.helidon-jms:
    jndi:
      jms-factory: ConnectionFactory
      env-properties:
        java.naming.factory.initial: ${activemq-cf}
        java.naming.provider.url: tcp://127.0.0.1:61616
        queue.TestQueue1: TestQueue1   ①

  outgoing:
    toJms:
      connector: helidon-jms
      destination: TestQueue1   ②
      type: queue

  incoming:
    fromJms:
      connector: helidon-jms
      jndi.destination: queue.TestQueue1   ③
      type: queue
```

① ActiveMQ specific JNDI queue registration

② Vendor-specific destination identifier

③ JNDI destination identifier

Message

Reactive messages provided by JMSConnector are extended with special JMS-specific methods. For creation of the outgoing message, a handy JMS message builder is available.

Listing 13-64. Create New JMS Message from Incoming JMS Message

```
@Incoming("from-jms")
@Outgoing("to-jms")
public Message<String> process(JmsMessage<String>
incomingMsg) {  ①
    jakarta.jms.Message original = incomingMsg.
    getJmsMessage();  ②
    jakarta.jms.Session session = incomingMsg.getJmsSession();
    String propertyValue = incomingMsg.getProperty("my-jms-
    property");  ③
    return JmsMessage.builder(incomingMsg.getPayload())
            .property("my-jms-property", propertyValue.
            toUpperCase())
            .onAck(incomingMsg::ack)  ④
            .build();
}
```

① JMS connection produces an extension of standard reactive messaging Message

② `JmsMessage` provides JMS-specific features; you can access original `JMSMessage` object

③ JMS properties are generically typed

④ Chaining acknowledgment to ack incoming when outgoing message is acked

javax vs. jakarta JMS

In 2017, Oracle decided to transfer Java EE to Eclipse Foundation. A long transition process eventually progressed to the name change to Jakarta EE as it is known today. With the name change came a package name update in Jakarta EE 9 from `javax` to `jakarta`. This process, known as "jakartification," breaks the backward compatibility with older, `javax`-based implementations. Helidon 3 is fully "jakartified;" no `javax` namespaces are exposed anywhere.

For the JMS API, this means that instead of using `javax.jms.Message`, Helidon 3 works with `jakarta.jms.Message`.

But, no worries: older JMS clients implementing the `javax` API work with jakartified Helidon just fine. Helidon 3.0 has a special shim layer for legacy `javax`-based JMS implementations, which is implicitly used behind the scenes. You can even use it manually as an adapter between the two APIs.

Listing 13-65. Manual Usage of JMS Shim As an Adapter Between Javax and Jakarta APIs

```
jakarta.jms.ConnectionFactory cf =
    JakartaJms.create(new ActiveMQConnectionFactory
("tcp://127.0.0.1:61616"));
```

WebLogic JMS Connector

WebLogic Server has its own enterprise-class messaging system simply called WebLogic JMS. WebLogic cluster members can act as JMS brokers, implementing JMS specifications and providing various extension features like distributed destinations, load balancing, SAF (store and forward) service, and more.

JMS is needed in one of the specialized client libraries to connect to WebLogic. The most popular of those client libraries is `wlthint3client.jar`, distributed with WebLogic Server installation, usually in the `/u01/oracle/wlserver/server/lib` folder.

While it was possible to use any thin client JARs with Helidon 2, with the jakartification of Helidon 3, such a process became quite complicated with legacy javax-based thin clients from older WebLogic Server installations clashing with Helidon's already jakartified service loaders.

Helidon 3 has a special WebLogic JMS connector for simplified usage of any legacy thin client library operating within a custom classloader adapted by the jakarta shim layer.

Listing 13-66. WebLogic JMS Connector Dependency

```
<dependency>
    <groupId>io.helidon.messaging.wls-jms</groupId>
    <artifactId>helidon-messaging-wls-jms</artifactId>
</dependency>
```

WebLogic JMS connector can load `wlthint3client.jar` in specialized classloader. Instead of adding the thin client JAR as a dependency, the connector is configured with the location of the thin client JAR.

Warning   Don't add legacy javax-based *wlthint3client.jar* to the application classpath!

Listing 13-67. Configure Helidon WebLogic Messaging Connector

```
mp:
  messaging:
    connector:
      helidon-weblogic-jms:
        jms-factory: jms/TestConnectionFactory  ①
        thin-jar: /path/to/wlthint3client.jar  ②
        url: t3://localhost:7001  ③
        principal: weblogic
        credentials: Welcome1
    incoming:
      from-wls:
        connector: helidon-weblogic-jms
        destination: ./TestJMSModule!TestQueue  ④
    outgoing:
      to-wls:
        connector: helidon-weblogic-jms
        jndi.destination: jms/TestQueue  ⑤
```

① JMS factory configured in WebLogic

② Path to the WLS Thin T3 client JAR

③ Path to the WLS Thin T3 client JAR

④ WebLogic CDI syntax

⑤ JNDI destination identifier

Destination lookup is possible with the destination configuration key, which expects WebLogic-specific destination CDI syntax or with jndi. destination with a JNDI identifier.

WebLogic Destination CDI Syntax

When connecting to a WebLogic cluster with a Helidon JMS or WebLogic messaging connector, the destination can be configured with WebLogic CDI syntax supplied by the destination configuration property.

WebLogic CDI (Create Destination Identifier; don't confuse with context dependency injection), is WebLogic vendor-specific syntax for locating queues and topics over JMS API methods Session.createTopic(String name) and Session.createQueue(String name) with the actual MBean names (usually a name property in the WLS console).

Non-Distributed Destinations

When accessing a non-distributed queue/topic, you need to specify the JMS server name, the JMS module name, and the queue or topic name: jms-server-name/jms-module-name!destination-name. The syntax is as follows: the server name, a slash, the module name, an exclamation mark, and the destination name, which is the MBean name in WebLogic Server.

When you know that the queue or topic you want to access is located on the same server as the JMS Connection Factory you are using, an alias for the current server is possible with ./ instead of the full server name.

Listing 13-68. Non-Distributed Queue CDI Identifier

```
./jms-module-name!destination-name
```

Uniform Distributed Destinations (UDDs)

Distributed queues/topics are logical destinations acting as load balancers between physical queues/topics, usually residing on separated JMS servers/cluster nodes (UDD members). When accessing UDD, you can use jms-module-name!udd-name syntax on any server from the same cluster.

Warning   UDD destinations *must not* contain ./ or /, which can lead to intermittent issues.

To directly access a UDD member queue or topic, the syntax for a non-distributed destination is needed: jms-server-name/jms-module-name!member-name.

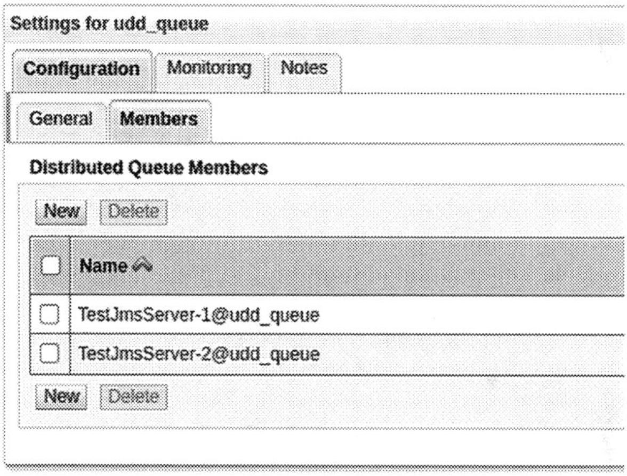

Figure 13-28. UDD member queues

To access the member queue *TestJmsServer-1@udd_queue* from Figure 13-28, the CDI syntax shown in Listing 13-69 is needed.

Listing 13-69. UDD Member Queue CDI Identifier

```
TestJmsServer-1/TestJMSModule!TestJmsServer-1@udd_queue
```

Warning   Directly accessing member queues is usually a bad practice.

JNDI Destination

Use jndi.destination instead of the destination configuration key for supplying JNDI (Java Naming and Directory Interface) identifiers. It is possible to look up JMS destinations over JNDI, which may be easier for destinations with more complicated subdeployment targets.

Oracle AQ Connector

Oracle Advance Queueing (AQ) allows you to use your Oracle database as a message broker with standard JMS API. This makes event sourcing over your relational data possible, leaving out a lot of indirect steps otherwise required.

Listing 13-70. Oracle AQ Connector Dependency

```
<dependency>
    <groupId>io.helidon.messaging.aq</groupId>
    <artifactId>helidon-messaging-aq</artifactId>
</dependency>
<!-- When using Oracle UCP for database connection -->
<dependency>
    <groupId>io.helidon.integrations.cdi</groupId>
    <artifactId>helidon-integrations-cdi-datasource-ucp</
    artifactId>
    <scope>runtime</scope>
</dependency>
```

Helidon AQ messaging connector uses Oracle AQ JMS API where JMS queue maps to an AQ single-consumer queue, and JMS topic maps to a multi-consumer queue.

Single Consumer Queue

A single consumer queue works exactly like a usual queue. It is a point-to-point model where one consumer can consume each message only once.

Listing 13-71. Create Oracle AQ Single Consumer Queue

```
DECLARE
    queue_name            VARCHAR2(32);
    queue_tab             VARCHAR2(32);
BEGIN
    queue_name := 'FRANK.SINGLE_CONSUMER_QUEUE';
    queue_tab :=  queue_name || '_TAB';
    DBMS_AQADM.CREATE_QUEUE_TABLE(queue_tab, 'SYS.AQ$_JMS_TEXT_
    MESSAGE');
    DBMS_AQADM.CREATE_QUEUE(queue_name, queue_tab);
    DBMS_AQADM.START_QUEUE(queue_name);
END;
```

Listing 13-72. Configure Helidon AQ Messaging Connector for Single Consumer Queue

```
javax.sql.DataSource:
  aq-test-ds:
    connectionFactoryClassName: oracle.jdbc.pool.
OracleDataSource
    URL: jdbc:oracle:thin:@localhost:1521:XE
    user: frank
    password: frank
mp.messaging:
  connector:
    helidon-aq:
      acknowledge-mode: CLIENT_ACKNOWLEDGE
```

```
    data-source: aq-test-ds  ①
  incoming:
    from-aq:
      connector: helidon-aq
      destination: SINGLE_CONSUMER_QUEUE
      type: queue  ②
```

> ① Reference to configured datasource
>
> ② AQ single consumer queue is mapped to
>   JMS queue

The AqMessage extension allows accessing the database connection used for the actual dequeue. Messaging acknowledgment commits this connection in CLIENT_ACKNOWLEDGE mode.

Listing 13-73. Consume AQ Message

```
@Incoming("from-aq")
@Acknowledgment(Acknowledgment.Strategy.MANUAL)
public CompletionStage<?> consumeAq(AqMessage<String> msg) {
    Connection dbConnection = msg.getDbConnection();  ①
    System.out.println("Oracle AQ says: " + msg.getPayload());
    return msg.ack();  ②
```

> ① Obtaining database connection used for
>   message dequeue
>
> ② Ack commits only in a non-transacted mode

Multi-Consumer Queue

Messages enqueued to an AQ multi-consumer queue behave as a JMS topic when dequeued with JMS non-durable consumer, which means a message is sent to all active subscribers. Any non-durable consumer who subscribes in the future won't receive previously published messages.

This behavior changes when a message is enqueued with the *recipient list*. Then each message remains in the queue until all consumers consume it.

Messages are treated as topics when enqueued to multi-consumer queue without recipient list, but with recipient list it behaves like multiple small queues for each recipient.

Listing 13-74. Create Oracle AQ Multi-Consumer Queue

```
DECLARE
    queue_name            VARCHAR2(32);
    queue_tab             VARCHAR2(32);
BEGIN
    queue_name := 'FRANK.MULTI_CONSUMER_QUEUE';
    queue_tab :=  queue_name || '_TAB';
    DBMS_AQADM.CREATE_QUEUE_TABLE(
            queue_table => queue_tab,
            multiple_consumers => TRUE,  ①
            queue_payload_type => 'SYS.AQ$_JMS_TEXT_MESSAGE');
    DBMS_AQADM.CREATE_QUEUE(queue_name, queue_tab);
    DBMS_AQADM.START_QUEUE(queue_name);
    DBMS_AQADM.ADD_SUBSCRIBER(queue_name, sys.aq$_agent('RED',
    NULL, NULL));  ②
    DBMS_AQADM.ADD_SUBSCRIBER(queue_name, sys.aq$_agent('BLUE',
    NULL, NULL));
END;
```

① Make this multi-consumer queue

② Register named subscribers in advance

Listing 13-75. Configure Helidon AQ Messaging Connector

```
mp.messaging:
  connector:
    helidon-aq:
      acknowledge-mode: CLIENT_ACKNOWLEDGE
      data-source: aq-test-ds
  incoming:
    from-multi-consumer-queue-red:
      connector: helidon-aq
      destination: MULTI_CONSUMER_QUEUE
      type: topic   ①
      subscriber-name: RED   ②
      durable: true   ③
    from-multi-consumer-queue-anonymous:
      connector: helidon-aq
      destination: MULTI_CONSUMER_QUEUE
      type: topic
```

① AQ multi-consumer queue is mapped to JMS topic

② AQ multi-consumer queue recipient name

③ Named consumer needs to be durable

When a message is enqueued without a recipient list, it acts as a topic to all non-durable subscribers but is queued for the existing RED and BLUE subscribers.

Listing 13-76. Enqueue to Oracle AQ Multi-Consumer Queue

```
DECLARE
    enqueue_options      DBMS_AQ.ENQUEUE_OPTIONS_T;
    message_properties DBMS_AQ.MESSAGE_PROPERTIES_T;
    recipients           DBMS_AQ.AQ$_RECIPIENT_LIST_T;
    message_handle       RAW(16);
    msg                  SYS.AQ$_JMS_TEXT_MESSAGE;
BEGIN
    msg := SYS.AQ$_JMS_TEXT_MESSAGE.construct;
    msg.set_text('for all ' || CURRENT_TIMESTAMP);
    DBMS_AQ.ENQUEUE(
            queue_name => 'FRANK.MULTI_CONSUMER_QUEUE',
            enqueue_options => enqueue_options,
            message_properties => message_properties,
            payload => msg,
            msgid => message_handle);
    COMMIT;
END;
```

Mock Connector

A mock connector is a testing tool designed to test reactive messaging methods without integration. By switching the configuration, reactive messaging methods can be connected to a mock connector that emits test data to the @Incoming method and asserts data reception when connected to the @Outgoing method.

Listing 13-77. Mock Connector Dependency

```
<dependency>
    <groupId>io.helidon.messaging.mock</groupId>
    <artifactId>helidon-messaging-mock</artifactId>
</dependency>
```

Warning   A mock connector is intended only for test usage and shouldn't be used in production.

A mock connector can be configured to automatically emit mock data right after subscription with mock-data configuration property.

Listing 13-78. Configure Mock Connector

```
mp.messaging:
  incoming:
    from-kafka:
      connector: helidon-mock
      mock-data: 9,10,11,12   ①
      mock-data-type: java.lang.Long   ②
```

> ① Mock data values for from-kafka
> @Incoming method
>
> ② Data type of mock data: java.lang.String is the
> default type

A mock connector is a standard reactive messaging connector bean that can be injected in @HelidonTest. For injecting, a mock connector is needed @TestConnector qualifier.

Listing 13-79. Mock Connector with @HelidonTest

```
@HelidonTest
@DisableDiscovery
@AddBean(MockConnector.class)  ①
@AddExtension(MessagingCdiExtension.class)  ②
@AddConfig(
    key = "mp.messaging.incoming.test-channel-in.connector",  ③
    value = MockConnector.CONNECTOR_NAME
)
@AddConfig(
    key = "mp.messaging.outgoing.test-channel-out.connector",
    value = MockConnector.CONNECTOR_NAME
)
public class MessagingTest {

    @Inject
    @TestConnector
    private MockConnector mockConnector;  ④

    @Incoming("test-channel-in")
    @Outgoing("test-channel-out")
    int multiply(int payload) {
        return payload * 2;
    }

    @Test
    void testMultiplyChannel() {
        mockConnector.incoming("test-channel-in", Integer.TYPE)
                .emit(1, 2, 3);  ⑤
        mockConnector.outgoing("test-channel-out",
        Integer.TYPE)
```

```
            .awaitPayloads(Duration.ofSeconds(5), 2,
            4, 6);  ⑥
   }
}
```

① Manually adds a `mockConnector` bean when bean discovery is disabled

② Adds messaging CDI extension when bean discovery is disabled

③ Connects mock connector to messaging channels

④ Injects mockConnector bean

⑤ Emits mock data to test-channel-in via mock connector

⑥ Asserts data coming from test-channel-out

Summary

- Reactive streams are a great combo with messaging.

- There are multiple reactive stream operator implementations to choose from in Helidon.

- Messaging channels can be tested with a mock connector.

CHAPTER 14

Long Running Actions (LRA)

This chapter covers the following topics.

- Introduction to SAGA based distributed transactions with MicroProfile

- Setting up JAX-RS resource as LRA transaction participant

- Understanding of participant state workflow

- Using MicroProfile LRA in an example cinema booking project

Distributed transactions are a very important tool for keeping consistency in all the complex systems molded together by various business requirements thrown at the developers. For years there was the two-phase commit (2PC) solving the problem. But with microservice architecture, a granular composition of many self-contained services which communicate with each other usually asynchronously, 2PC becomes a bottleneck. Due to the isolation requirement, resources got locked for too long, breaking all the achieved reactiveness as a result. It is a problem known for decades and has already been solved by the SAGA pattern. Saga is a series of local transactions with defined compensation actions. Instead of commits and rollbacks, you define general actions that need to be done to keep the system in a consistent state.

© Dmitry Kornilov, Daniel Kec, Dmitry Aleksandrov 2023
D. Kornilov et al., *Beginning Helidon*, https://doi.org/10.1007/978-1-4842-9473-4_14

Inspired by SAGA came MicroProfile Long Running Actions (LRA), which is a long-awaited specification that provides a lock-free, and consequently loosely-coupled, approach to achieve consistency in a microservice environment. Asynchronous compensations are used to maintain eventual data integrity without staging expensive isolation. And as LRA is an alternative to Java Transactions API (JTA), you can think about it similarly with few subtle differences. Instead of JTA transactional bean methods, you get transactional JAX-RS resources.

LRA Transaction

Multiple participants can join every LRA transaction. A participant is invoked by the JAX-RS method annotated with LRA-specific annotation. The @LRA annotation marks the JAX-RS method, which should join LRA when called. Whether a new LRA transaction is started or an existing transaction context is joined, it can be configured with a specific LRA type. It gets quite familiar for anyone who used JTA annotations before.

The following are LRA types.

- **REQUIRES_NEW**: Always create a new LRA transaction context, ignore any existing context

- **REQUIRED**: Create a new LRA transaction context or use existing

- **MANDATORY**: Return 412 Precondition Failed if called without LRA context

- **SUPPORTS**: When called without LRA context, execution continues as normal JAX-RS method

- **NOT_SUPPORTED**: Always executed without joining LRA

- **NEVER**: If called with LRA context, return 412
  `Precondition Failed HTTP`; otherwise, execute as
  normal JAX-RS method

- **NESTED**: Create new LRA transaction and use existing
  LRA context as parent

LRA participation isn't only the business method. Additional JAX-RS methods need to be defined for the compensation actions: `@Compensate` for failed transactions and `@Complete` for successful ones.

Listing 14-1. JAX-RS Resource with LRA

```
@Path("/example")
@ApplicationScoped
public class LRAExampleResource {

  @PUT
  @LRA(value = LRA.Type.REQUIRES_NEW, timeLimit = 500,
  timeUnit = ChronoUnit.MILLIS)
  @Path("start-example")
  public Response buyTicket(@HeaderParam(LRA_HTTP_CONTEXT_
  HEADER) URI lraId,

                                    String data) {
      ...   ①
      return Response.ok().build();
  }

  @PUT
  @Complete
  @Path("complete-example")   ②
  public Response success(@ HeaderParam(LRA_HTTP_CONTEXT_
  HEADER) URI lraId) {
      return LRAResponse.completed();
```

```
    }

    @PUT
    @Compensate
    @Path("compensate-example")   ③
    public Response failure(@HeaderParam(LRA_HTTP_CONTEXT_HEADER)
    URI lraId) {
        return LRAResponse.compensated();
    }
}
```

① Executed in the scope of new LRA transaction

② Called by LRA coordinator when buyTicket method successfully finishes

③ Called by LRA coordinator when buyTicket method throws exception or don't finish before time limit

Every participant joining the LRA transaction needs to provide its compensation links, those URLs leading to resources annotated with @Compensate, @Complete, @AfterLRA, and so on. The LRA coordinator tracks which resources to call when the LRA transaction state changes. When the JAX-RS resource method is annotated with @LRA(REQUIRES_NEW), every intercepted call starts a new LRA transaction within the coordinator and joins it as a new participant before the resource method body is executed. The ID of the created LRA transaction is accessible in the resource method through the Long-Running-Action header as a new LRA context. When the resource method invocation successfully finishes, the LRA transaction is reported to the coordinator as closed. If a participant has the @Complete method, the coordinator eventually invokes it again with the appropriate LRA ID header and the @Complete method of all the other participants joined within the same LRA transaction.

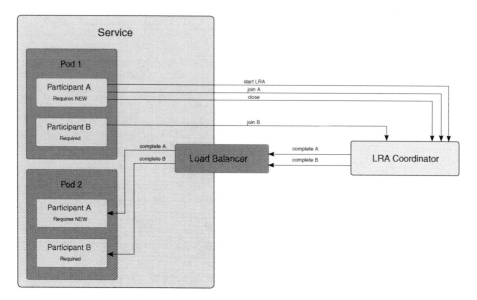

Figure 14-1. *Participants behind load balancer*

Warning   Compensation methods are JAX-RS methods that get load balanced as any other JAX-RS resource. Remember that the complete method doesn't have to be invoked on the same pod as LRA was started.

When a resource method finishes exceptionally, LRA is reported to the coordinator as canceled, and the coordinator calls the @Compensate method on all the participants registered under that transaction.

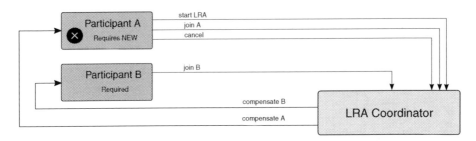

Figure 14-2. *Participant cancels*

When a transaction isn't closed before its timeout is reached, the coordinator cancels the transaction and calls the compensate endpoints for all participants of the timed-out transaction.

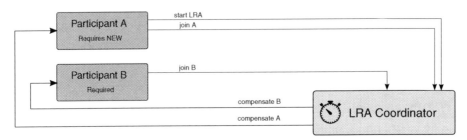

Figure 14-3. *Participant timeout*

Context Propagation

What better way to use for the context propagation between JAX-RS resources than the HTTP header? Every LRA is identified by the ID assigned by the coordinator when the new LRA is started. ID is distributed between resources over the HTTP header `Long-Running-Action`. When the header is present in the request, LRA enabled JAX-RS resource considers it part of the existing LRA context. This enables relaying the context even through the not LRA aware parties. MicroProfile LRA specification doesn't leverage only the server side JAX-RS but also the client side. JAX-RS client relays LRA ID automatically when a call is done within the LRA context.

Listing 14-2. JAX-RS Client, Context Propagation

```
@PUT
@Path("/payment")
@LRA(value = LRA.Type.MANDATORY, end = false)
public Response makePayment(@HeaderParam(LRA.LRA_HTTP_CONTEXT_
HEADER) URI lraId,
                               JsonObject jsonObject) {
        ClientBuilder.newClient()  ①
                .target("http://payment-service:7002")
                .path("/payment/confirm")
                .request()
                ...
```

① You don't need to propagate the LRA header using the JAX-RS client. The LRA header is propagated automatically.

Participant

When the JAX-RS method supporting LRA is called, it joins new or existing LRA transactions as a participant. A participant has a life cycle closely coupled with its transaction.

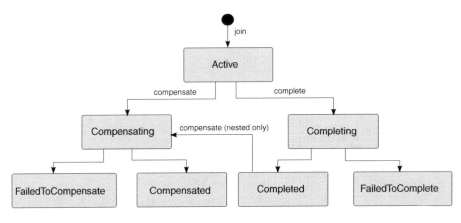

Figure 14-4. *Participant states*

Participant's state is very important for the LRA coordinator to know which compensation actions have been already called and which need to be yet called. Every LRA method needs to be accompanied by compensation methods and JAX-RS resources which can be called by the LRA coordinator when the LRA transaction is completed or canceled. Since compensation can be complicated, other methods for state keeping and additional resilience are available, as listed in Table 14-1.

Table 14-1. *Compensation Methods*

Annotation	Method
@Complete	PUT
@Compensate	PUT
@Status	GET
@Forget	DELETE
@AfterLRA	PUT

> **Caution**   Compensation methods are meant to be called only by the LRA coordinator.

@Leave is a special participant method to remove the participant from the LRA transaction. This is discussed later.

Complete

When the LRA transaction ends successfully, all the participants will be informed by the coordinator calling the participant's method annotated with @Complete. The complete method can answer either by success or by informing the coordinator that completion is being realized asynchronously, so the coordinator can attempt LRA state retrieval later.

Listing 14-3. JAX-RS Complete Resource, Called When LRA Successfully Completes

```
@PUT
@Complete
@Path("complete-example")
public Response success(@HeaderParam(LRA_HTTP_CONTEXT_HEADER)
URI lraId) {
    bookingRepository.confirmBooking(lraId);
    return LRAResponse.completed();
}
```

The following are expected responses.

- 200: Success

- 202: Still completing asynchronously

- 409: Failed to complete, payload must be actual participant status

- 410: Unknown LRA ID

Compensate

When the LRA transaction is canceled, all the participants are informed by the coordinator calling the participant's method annotated with @Complete.

Listing 14-4. JAX-RS Compensate Resource, Called When LRA Fails to Finish

```
@PUT
@Compensate
@Path("compensate-example")
public Response failure(@HeaderParam(LRA_HTTP_CONTEXT_HEADER)
URI lraId) {
    return LRAResponse.compensated();
}
```

The following are expected responses.

- 200: Success

- 202: Still compensating asynchronously

- 409: Failed to compensate, payload must be actual participant status

- 410: Unknown LRA ID

Status

The @Compensate and @Complete methods have been discussed, but you are probably wondering what happens in case of a network issue. What happens when a call to JAX-RS complete or compensate method fails? That could cause inconsistency, which we are carefully trying to avoid! Coordinators are well-prepared for that with numerous retry strategies. But is that enough? That depends on the fact if the method is reentrant or not. The coordinator doesn't know how the action changed the state of your participant. Did the compensation method manage to clear the seat booking from the database before it crashed or not?

You can use the @Status method, which is called by the coordinator to retrieve the status before the actual retry.

Listing 14-5. JAX-RS Status Resource, Called by Coordinator Whenever the State of the Participant Is Not Known

```
@GET
@Path("lra-status")
@Status
public Response status(@HeaderParam(LRA_HTTP_CONTEXT_HEADER)
URI lraId) {
    if(bookingRepository.isBookingCleared(lraId)){
        return Response.ok(ParticipantStatus.Compensated.
        name()).build();  ①
    } else {
        return Response.ok(ParticipantStatus.Active.name()).
        build();  ②
    }
}
```

① Compensation was successful. No need to call the
compensate method again.

② There was a call to compensate? Try again, please.

The following are expected responses.

- 200: Payload must be actual participant status.

- 202: Call me later. Getting status is in process.

- 410: Unknown LRA ID

The same logic can be applied to the complete action; only participant status names would differ.

The following are participant statuses.

- **Active**: Participant was not asked to complete or compensate yet

- **Compensating**: Async compensation in progress

- **Compensated**: Compensation is done

- **FailedToCompensate**: Compensation failed, and it shouldn't be reattempted; participant needs to report this status until @Forget is called

- **Completing**: Async completion in progress

- **Completed**: Completion is done

- **FailedToComplete**: Completion failed, and it shouldn't be reattempted; participant needs to report this status until @Forget is called

Forget

Compensation can also be a long-running asynchronous process.
In such cases, compensation methods return ParticipantStatus.
Compensating and status method needs to report the actual state when

asked. The coordinator checks the status regularly. The actual strategy is implementation specific. Participant needs to be able to report the state until the @Forget method is called.

Listing 14-6. JAX-RS Forget Resource, Called When the Participant State Is No Longer Needed

```
@DELETE
@Path("/lra-forget")
@Forget
public Response forget(@HeaderParam(LRA_HTTP_CONTEXT_HEADER)
URI lraId) {
    bookingRepository.clearLraMetadata(lraId)   ①
    return Response.ok().build();
}
```

> ① Let's clear up any metadata related to the state of this particular LRA transaction.

The following are expected responses.

- 200: Success

- 410: Unknown LRA ID

Coordinator lets you know through the @Forget method that a particular LRA transaction is considered finished, and no other compensation actions will be attempted.

AfterLRA

Complicated compensation logic can require action upon the final LRA outcome. After the compensation actions of all the LRA's participants are finished, AfterLRA methods are notified about the outcome of the LRA. Only the final LRA statuses can be reported to the AfterLRA method.

Listing 14-7. JAX-RS After LRA Resource, Called When All
Participants Are Completed or Compensated

```
@AfterLRA
@Path("/after")
@PUT
public Response after(@HeaderParam(LRA_HTTP_ENDED_CONTEXT_
HEADER) URI lraId,
                        LRAStatus status) {
    switch (status) {
        case Closed ->   ①
        case Cancelled ->   ②
        case FailedToClose ->   ③
        case FailedToCancel ->   ④
        default ->   ⑤
    }
    return Response.ok(ParticipantStatus.Completed.name()).
build();
}
```

① LRA finished, and all participants reported
   successful completion

② LRA is canceled, and all participants reported
   successful compensation

③ LRA finished, but one or more participants
   reported unsuccessful completion

④ LRA finished, but one or more participants
   reported unsuccessful compensation

⑤ Unexpected status

The following are expected responses.

- 200: Success

Leaving LRA

Finally, let's get to the special method @Leave. You can use this method for removing the participant from the LRA it's enrolled in. It is the only participant JAX-RS method aside from @LRA you are meant to call directly. When called with the LRA context header, the participant, if enrolled in the transaction, is removed from the transaction. Other compensation methods like @Complete won't be called in this transaction context as the participant is no longer tracked by the coordinator for this transaction.

Listing 14-8. JAX-RS Leave Resource, Used for Removing Participant from LRA Transaction

```
@Leave
@PUT
@Path("/leave")
public Response leave(@HeaderParam(LRA_HTTP_CONTEXT_HEADER) URI
lraId) {   ①
        return Response.ok();   ②
}
```

> ① ID of the LRA transaction participant needs to leave

> ② Method is executed after the coordinator has been asked to remove the participant from the LRA transaction

---

Note   The leave method is contrary to the other participant's methods, meant to be called directly.

Non-JAX-RS Participant Methods

You have already learned all the participant methods LRA JAX-RS resources can have. The spec strictly defines each method, so there is no need to define it as a JAX-RS method. When the method has LRA participant annotation and conforms to a specified signature, LRA Helidon implementation creates a surrogate JAX-RS endpoint and wires it together behind the scenes.

Let's look at the JAX-RS @Compensate method again.

Listing 14-9. JAX-RS Compensate Resource

```
@PUT
@Compensate
@Path("compensate-example")
public Response failure(@HeaderParam(LRA_HTTP_CONTEXT_HEADER)
URI lraId) {
    return LRAResponse.compensated();
}
```

Same participant method can be expressed with non-JAX-RS notation.

Listing 14-10. Non-JAX-RS Compensate Resource

```
@Compensate
public ParticipantStatus failure(URI lraId) {
    return ParticipantStatus.Compensated;
}
```

The only difference between the participant methods is that the compensation link sent to the coordinator will have a slightly different pattern because it targets the surrogate JAX-RS resource instead of our direct resource.

Asynchronous Compensation

Compensations can take a long time, and complicated clean-up jobs running for 5 minutes can be a reality. Blocking the @Compensate method for that long is not right, so you need to respond to the coordinator and continue asynchronously. What if an asynchronous compensation batch job fails? LRA has just the right API for such a situation. There are two options. The first option is to return ParticipantStatus.Compensating to inform the coordinator about the need to check the current compensation status via the @Status method later. Each coordinator has a retry strategy to retrieve the status eventually.

Listing 14-11. Asynchronous Compensation with Status Reporting

```
private Map<URI, ParticipantStatus> myStatusMap = new
ConcurrentHashMap<>();

@Compensate
public ParticipantStatus failure(URI lraId) {
    ourWizardService.compensateAsync(lraId)
        .whenComplete((u, t) -> {
            if (t != null) {
                myStatusMap.put(lraId, ParticipantStatus.
                FailedToCompensate);
            } else {
                myStatusMap.put(lraId, ParticipantStatus.
                Compensated);
            }
        });
    return ParticipantStatus.Compensating;
}

@Status
```

```
public ParticipantStatus status(URI lraId) {
    return myStatusMap.get(lraId);
}

@Forget
public void forget(URI lraId) {
    myStatusMap.remove(lraId);
}
```

You can leverage the @Forget method to clean up status references when the coordinator calls it to inform you it is not needed anymore.

The second option is even easier, as non-JAX-RS compensation methods support returning CompletionStage promises. The only setback is that the connection is kept open, but no thread is blocked.

Listing 14-12. Asynchronous Compensation with CompletionStage

```
@Compensate
public CompletionStage<ParticipantStatus> failure(URI lraId) {
    return ourWizardService.compensateAsync(lraId)
            .thenApply(s -> ParticipantStatus.Compensated)
            .exceptionally(t -> ParticipantStatus.
            FailedToCompensate);
}
```

LRA Coordinator

The Long Running Actions implementation in Helidon requires the LRA coordinator to orchestrate LRA across the cluster. This is an extra service you need to enable the LRA functionality in your cluster. The LRA coordinator tracks which participant joined which LRA transaction and calls the participant's LRA compensation resources when the LRA transaction is completed or canceled.

Compensation links always accompany requests from participants for joining existing LRA transactions. Compensation links are URLs pointing to the participant's compensation JAX-RS methods, annotated with @Complete, @Compensate, and so on, which is how the coordinator knows how to call participants. Compensation links are constructed from your JAX-RS resource context path and address configured with mp.lra,participant.url configuration key.

Listing 14-13. Configure Helidon to Use a Coordinator

```
mp.lra:
  coordinator.url: http://coordinator.service/lra-coordinator ①
  participant.url: http://participant.service  ②
```

① Used for the very first call to coordinator, use k8s service name or DNS name accessible from participant

② Used for construction of compensation links, use k8s service name or DNS name accessible from coordinator

Helidon supports the following.

- Narayana LRA coordinator

- MicroTx LRA coordinator

- Experimental Helidon LRA coordinator

Narayana LRA Coordinator

Narayana is a well-known transaction manager with a long history of reliability in distributed transactions built around the Arjuna core. The Narayana LRA coordinator supports Long Running Actions and was the first LRA coordinator on the market.

Listing 14-14. Narayana Local Installation

```
VER=5.13.0.Final && \
FILENAME=lra-coordinator-quarkus-$VER-runner.jar && \
FILEPATH=org/jboss/narayana/rts/lra-coordinator-
quarkus/$VER/$FILENAME && \
wget https://search.maven.org/remotecontent?filepath=$
FILEPATH \
-O narayana-coordinator.jar \
&& java -Dquarkus.http.port=8070 -jar narayana-coordinator.jar
```

Narayana LRA coordinator resources are accessible under the context /lra-coordinator. Helidon needs to be configured to know where to reach it when starting a new LRA.

Listing 14-15. Configure Helidon to Use Narayana

```
mp.lra:
  coordinator.url: http://127.0.0.1:8070/lra-coordinator  ①
  participant.url: http://127.0.0.1:7002  ②
  propagation.active: true
```

    ① Used for the very first call to coordinator, use k8s service name or DNS name accessible from participant

    ② Used for construction of compensation links, use k8s service name or DNS name accessible from coordinator

MicroTx

From the very same kitchen as the notoriously famous Tuxedo (Transactions for Unix, Extended for Distributed Operations) came the brand-new transaction manager MicroTx (Oracle Transaction Manager

414

for Microservices). MicroTx LRA coordinator offers additional features, such as bearer token-protected communication with the coordinator. You can obtain MicroTx from Oracle's image registry at container-registry. oracle.com.

Listing 14-16. MicroTx Coordinator Local Installation

```
docker pull container-registry.oracle.com/database/otmm:latest
```

MicroTx needs to be configured. Listing 14-17 is the minimal configuration needed for local development.

Listing 14-17. MicroTx Minimal Configuration File

```
tmmConfiguration:
  listenAddr: 0.0.0.0:8070
  internalAddr: http://127.0.0.1:8070
  externalUrl: http://127.0.0.1:8070  ①
  serveTLS:
    enabled: false
  storage:
    type: memory  ②
  narayanaLraCompatibilityMode:
    enabled: true  ③
```

① Used for LRA ID construction, use k8s service name or DNS name accessible from participant

② Where to store transaction log

③ Narayana compatibility mode is recommended for usage with Helidon

Don't forget to mount the configuration file to the /app/config folder when running the docker image. Remember that the coordinator needs to be able to reach participants' JAX-RS resources on compensation links provided during the LRA start request.

Listing 14-18. Run MicroTx in Docker

```
docker run --network="host" -it \
-v `pwd`:/app/config -w /app/config \
--env CONFIG_FILE=tcs.yaml \
container-registry.oracle.com/database/otmm:latest
```

MicroTx LRA coordinator resources are accessible under the context /api/v1/lra-coordinator. Helidon needs to be configured to know where to reach it when starting a new LRA.

Listing 14-19. Configure Helidon to Use MicroTx

```
mp.lra:
  coordinator.url: http://127.0.0.1:8070/api/v1/lra-
  coordinator  ①
  participant.url: http://127.0.0.1:7002  ②
  propagation.active: true
```

       ① Used for the very first call to coordinator, use k8s service name or DNS name accessible from participant

      ② Used for construction of compensation links, use k8s service name or DNS name accessible from coordinator

Experimental Helidon LRA Coordinator

Helidon now has its own experimental coordinator that is easy to set up for development and testing purposes. While it is not recommended in production environments, it is a great lightweight solution for testing your LRA resources.

Listing 14-20. Helidon Coordinator Local installation

```
docker build -t helidon/lra-coordinator https://github.com/
oracle/helidon.git#:lra/coordinator/server
docker run -dp 8070:8070 --name lra-coordinator --network=
"host" helidon/lra-coordinator
```

Online Cinema Booking System

Our hypothetical cinema needs an online reservation system. Let's split it into two scalable services: one for booking the seat and another for paying. Services are completely separated and integrated only through the REST API calls.

The booking service is going to reserve the seat first. The reservation service starts a new LRA transaction and joins it as a first transaction participant. All communication with the LRA coordinator is done behind the scenes and can be accessed through the LRA ID assigned to the new transaction in our JAX-RS method as a request header Long-Running-Action. Note that LRA stays active after the JAX-RS method finishes because Lra#end is set to false.

Listing 14-21. Create Booking with JAX-RS Resource Within LRA Transaction

```
@PUT
@Path("/create/{id}")
```

417

```
@LRA(value = LRA.Type.REQUIRES_NEW, end = false,
timeLimit = 30)  ① ②
public Response createBooking(@HeaderParam(LRA.LRA_HTTP_
CONTEXT_HEADER) URI lraId,
                                @PathParam("id") long id,
                                Booking booking) {

    booking.setLraId(lraId.toASCIIString());  ③

    if (repository.createBooking(booking, id)) {
        LOG.info("Creating booking for " + id);
        return Response.ok().build();
    } else {
        LOG.info("Seat " + id + " already booked!");
        return Response
                .status(Response.Status.CONFLICT)
                .entity(JSON.createObjectBuilder()
                        .add("error", "Seat " + id + " is
                        already reserved!")
                        .add("seat", id)
                        .build())
                .build();
    }
}
```

① Create new LRA transaction which won't end after
this JAX-RS method end

② Time limit for new LRA is 30 sec

③ LRA ID assigned by the coordinator is provided as
an artificial request header

Figure 14-5. *Create new seat booking*

Once a seat is successfully reserved, payment service will be called under the same LRA transaction. An artificial header, Long-Running-Action, is present in the response so the client can access it.

Listing 14-22. Call Create Booking JAX-RS Resource

```
reserveButton.click(function () {
    selectionView.hide();
    createBooking(selectedSeat.html())
        .then(res => {
            if (res.ok) {
                let lraId = res.headers.get("Long-Running-
                Action");  ①
                paymentView.attr("data-lraId", lraId);  ②
                paymentView.show();
            } else {
                res.json().then(json => {
```

```
                    showError(json.error);
            });
        }
    });
});
```

① Notice how you can access LRA ID even on the
   client side

② And save the LRA context for later

You can call other backend resources with the same LRA transaction
by setting the Long-Running-Action header again.

Listing 14-23. Call Payment JAX-RS Resource from Client

```
function makePayment(cardNumber, amount, lraId) {
    return fetch('/booking/payment', {
        method: 'PUT',
        headers: {
            'Content-Type': 'application/json',
            'Long-Running-Action': lraId   ①
        },
        body: JSON.stringify({"cardNumber": cardNumber,
        "amount": amount})
    })
}
```

① Using previously saved LRA ID to invoke JAX-RS
   resource under the right LRA context

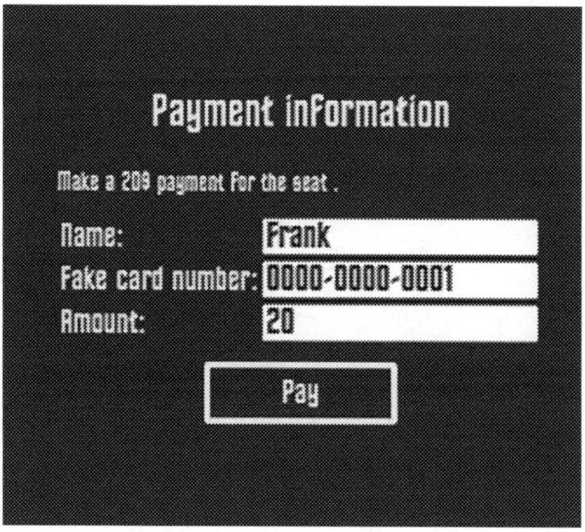

Figure 14-6. *Payment form*

The backend calls a different service over the JAX-RS client, so you don't need to set the Long-Running-Action header to propagate the LRA transaction. As with all JAX-RS clients, LRA implementation does that for you automatically.

Listing 14-24. Call Payment Service with Implicit LRA Context

```
@PUT
@Path("/payment")
@LRA(value = LRA.Type.MANDATORY, end = false)  ① ②
public Response makePayment(@HeaderParam(LRA.LRA_HTTP_CONTEXT_
HEADER) URI lraId,
                            JsonObject jsonObject) {
    LOG.info("Payment " + jsonObject.toString());
    ClientBuilder.newClient()  ③
            .target("http://payment-service:7002")
            .path("/payment/confirm")
            .request()
            .rx()
```

421

```
        .put(Entity.entity(jsonObject, MediaType.
        APPLICATION_JSON))
        .whenComplete((res, t) -> {
            if (res != null) {
                LOG.info(res.getStatus() + " " + res.
                getStatusInfo().getReasonPhrase());
                res.close();
            }
        });
    return Response.accepted().build();
}
```

① Needs to be called within LRA transaction context

② Doesn't end LRA transaction

③ No need to propagate LRA header when using
   JAX-RS client—LRA header is propagated
   automatically

The payment service joins this transaction as another participant. Any card number other than 0000-0000-0000 will cancel the LRA transaction. Finishing the resource method will complete the LRA transaction because Lra#end is set to true.

Listing 14-25. Payment Service Within LRA Context

```
@PUT
@Path("/confirm")
@LRA(value = LRA.Type.MANDATORY, end = true)  ①
public Response confirmPayment(@HeaderParam(LRA.LRA_HTTP_
CONTEXT_HEADER) URI lraId,
                            Payment p) {
    if (!p.cardNumber.equals("0000-0000-0000")) {
```

```
        LOG.warning("Payment " + p.cardNumber);
        throw new IllegalStateException("Card " +
        p.cardNumber + " is not valid! "+lraId);
    }
    LOG.info("Payment " + p.cardNumber+ " " +lraId);
    return Response.ok(JSON.createObjectBuilder().add("result",
    "success").build()).build();
}
```

① This resource method ends/commits LRA
transaction as successfully completed

If the payment operation fails or times out, the LRA transaction is going to be canceled, and all participants are going to be notified through the compensation links provided when they join. The LRA coordinator will call the method annotated with @Compensate with the LRA ID as a parameter. That is all that is needed in our booking service to clear the seat reservation and make it available for another customer.

Listing 14-26. Compensation if Payment Fails

```
@Compensate
public Response paymentFailed(URI lraId) {
    LOG.info("Payment failed! " + lraId);
    repository.clearBooking(lraId)  ①
            .ifPresent(booking -> {
                LOG.info("Booking for seat " + booking.
                getSeat().getId() + "cleared!");
                Optional.ofNullable(sseBroadcaster)  ②
                        .ifPresent(b -> b.broadcast(new
                        OutboundEvent.Builder()
                                .data(booking.getSeat())
```

```
                                    .mediaType(MediaType.
                                    APPLICATION_JSON_TYPE)
                                    .build())
                        );
            });
    return Response.ok(ParticipantStatus.Completed.name()).
    build();
}
```

① Compensate by clearing booked seat

② Notify clients over SSE that there is new seat
   available for booking

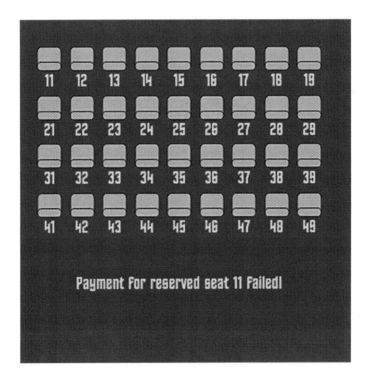

Figure 14-7. Payment failed notification

Maintaining integrity in distributed systems with compensation logic isn't a new idea, but it can be quite complicated to achieve without special tooling. LRA is tooling that hides the complexities, so you can focus on business logic.

Summary

- Distributed transactions need to sacrifice isolation to keep the microservice environment reactive.

- Compensation-based logic delegates responsibility for data consistency to the developer.

- LRA transactional context can be propagated through non-LRA-aware resources.

CHAPTER 15

Helidon SE

This chapter covers the following topics.

- Understanding Helidon SE and Helidon MP differences and similarities

- Creating a simple Helidon SE application

- Using routing, configuration, health checks, and metrics

- Other Helidon SE features not covered in this book

As you learned in Chapter 1, Helidon has two flavors: Helidon MP and Helidon SE. The entire book has been about Helidon MP, but we decided to dedicate the last chapter to Helidon SE. With it, the book is complete. Helidon SE is a big topic. It's challenging to fit it into one chapter. So, the information is less detailed and compressed but covers most Helidon SE features and provides recipes and best practices. Let's get started.

Helidon SE Basics

Helidon SE was compared with Helidon MP in Chapter 1. Let's quickly go over it to set up the context.

- Helidon SE is a reactive, non-blocking flavor of Helidon.

- It's built on top of Netty.

© Dmitry Kornilov, Daniel Kec, Dmitry Aleksandrov 2023
D. Kornilov et al., *Beginning Helidon*, https://doi.org/10.1007/978-1-4842-9473-4_15

- Helidon SE APIs are based on Java Flow APIs.

- Reflection API, annotations, and dependency injection are not used.

- Helidon SE is a natural fit for GraalVM Native Image.

- Helidon SE tries to fully leverage JDK functionality and minimize the usage of third-party dependencies.

Explaining the basics of reactive programming is out of this book's scope. We assume that you know the concepts of backpressure, publisher/consumer, schedulers, and so forth. It's required if you want to develop using Helidon SE.

Generating Helidon SE Application

Generating a Helidon SE application follows the same concepts as generating a Helidon MP application, explained in Chapter 2. This section guides you through this process, and you create the Helidon SE Quickstart application. The Quickstart application is a simple RESTful service ideal for demonstrating Helidon SE concepts. To generate it, you can use Project Starter or Helidon CLI.

Using Project Starter

Type `https://helidon.io/starter` in your browser address bar to open Helidon Project Starter (see Figure 15-1).

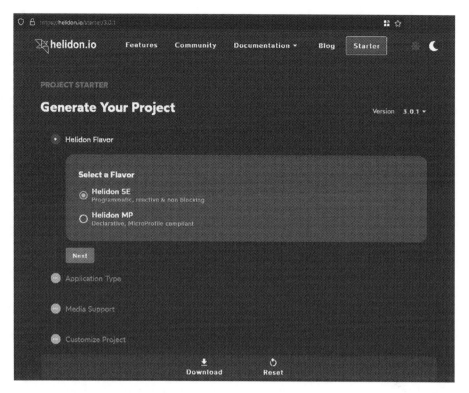

Figure 15-1. *Project Starter*

Helidon SE is the default choice for creating new applications. Quickstart application is also a default choice, so you can click Download to download a zip file with your Helidon SE project.

Note   Project Starter has many options and allows you to select features to add to your project. You can explore it by going through the application creating wizard. The *Custom* application type is a path containing all possible customizations.

Using CLI

Helidon CLI is another convenient way of generating Helidon SE applications. Installing CLI and its basic functionality was explained in Chapter 2.

To generate the Helidon SE Quickstart application, use the CLI `init` command.

```
$ helidon init
```

On the first Helidon Flavor screen, type **1** to select Helidon SE, or press Enter because it's a default choice.

```
| Helidon Flavor

Select a Flavor
  (1) se | Helidon SE
  (2) mp | Helidon MP
Enter selection (default: 1):
```

CLI and Project Starter designed how the Helidon SE Quickstart application is generated if you follow defaults. There is no way to skip CLI steps as you can in Project Starter. So, press Enter at all the steps to generate your application.

Analyzing the Generated Project

The generated Helidon SE Quickstart application is very similar to the Helidon MP Quickstart application described in Chapter 2. It contains a Maven project, Dockerfiles to build a jar, a jlink image, a GraalVM native image, and Kubernetes app.yaml. It implements the same greeting service, but the source code and concepts significantly differ from Helidon MP. This chapter discusses the differences while explaining how the Helidon SE application works.

Now, let's see what's been generated.

Listing 15-1. Helidon SE Generated Quickstart Application Source Code Tree

```
$ tree quickstart-se/
quickstart-se
        app.yaml                                            ①
        Dockerfile                                          ②
        Dockerfile.jlink                                    ③
        Dockerfile.native                                   ④
        pom.xml                                             ⑤
        README.md
        src
            main
                java
                    com
                        example
                            myproject
                                GreetService.java           ⑥
                                Main.java                   ⑦
                                package-info.java
                                SimpleGreetService.java
                resources
                    application.yaml                        ⑧
                    logging.properties
            test
                java
                    com
```

```
        example
            myproject
            MainTest.java                    ⑨
    resources
        application.yaml                     ⑩
```

① Kubernetes deployment descriptor

② Dockerfile to build a docker image with your
   application running on standard Java runtime

③ Dockerfile to build a Docker image with your
   application running on custom Java runtime
   (jlink image)

④ Dockerfile to build a Docker image with your
   application's native image

⑤ Maven project

⑥ Greet RESTful service

⑦ Main class with `main` method and web server
   initialization code

⑧ Application configuration

⑨ Example JUnit test

⑩ Configuration for testing

Main Method

Helidon SE application is a standard Java application. It must have a
`public static void main(String[] args)`, an application entry point.
Note that there is no requirement to write the `main` method in Helidon MP.
The framework provides it.

In the Quickstart application, the `main` method is implemented in `Main.java`.

```
public static void main(String[] args) {
    startServer();
}
```

The `main` method creates and starts the web server. It differs from Helidon MP, where the same web server automatically starts under the hood. It's convenient but gives users less control over how the web server starts and gets configured.

To properly run your application, specify your class containing the `main` method in Maven `pom.xml`.

```
<properties>
    <mainClass>com.example.myproject.Main</mainClass>
</properties>
```

Creating and Starting a Web Server

Before creating a server, you need to create and initialize the resources it uses. It includes creating a configuration, initializing logging, creating routing, instantiating internal services you plan to use, such as health checks or metrics, and creating and initializing user services, such as `GreetService`. And here comes another difference from Helidon MP, where all of these are done automatically by the framework.

Now let's see how the web server is created and started in the Quickstart application (see Listing 15-2).

Listing 15-2. Initializing and Starting the Web Server

```
static Single<WebServer> startServer() {
    LogConfig.configureRuntime();                    ①
    Config config = Config.create();                 ②
```

```
WebServer server = WebServer.builder(          ③
        createRouting(config))                 ④
    .config(config.get("server"))              ⑤
    .addMediaSupport(JsonpSupport.create())    ⑥
    .build();

Single<WebServer> webserver = server.start();  ⑦
...
return webserver;
}
```

① Initializing logging

② Loading configuration (By default, it loads application.yaml from the classpath.)

③ Creating a web server using WebServer.builder

④ Creating routing and passing it to the web server

⑤ Passing server configuration section to the web server

⑥ Adding Json Processing (JSON-P) support

⑦ Starting the server

Configuration

Helidon SE configuration is a core Helidon SE component. The following briefly describes its features and the differences between it and Helidon MP configuration.

- No annotations are used, only programmatic APIs (By comparison, Helidon MP uses MicroProfile Config, which contains annotations and programmatic APIs)

- Uses a tree structure (By comparison, Helidon MP uses a flat structure)

- Immutable by design but supports change listeners

- Supports configuration sources such as environment variables, system properties, directory, property files, YAML, JSON, and HOCON (extensible with custom configuration sources)

- Filters, references, and substitutions

- Configuration profiles (e.g., dev/test/prod)

- Conversion to simple and complex types, custom converters

Quickstart application configuration sits in the `application.yaml` file and contains server host, port, and default greeting properties.

```
server:
  port: 8080
  host: 0.0.0.0

app:
  greeting: "Hello"
```

Routing

The next step of the application initialization is creating routing. It's done in the `createRouting` method. It uses a builder to register pairs of the path and the corresponding service instance, which handles requests coming to this path. Note that in Helidon MP, routes are managed by JAX-RS `@Path` annotation.

- Helidon SE routing is configured programmatically in the Routing class instance.

- For convenience, the Routing class provides a builder (Routing.builder()), which supports several ways of creating mappings.

- Mappings can be defined using HTTP methods, routing, path matching, and request predicates.

- Users can organize code into services to logically separate routes related to specific parts of your application functionality.

- Routing is immutable. It's not possible to change routes after the web server has started.

There are two user services in the Quickstart application: SimpleGreetService and GreetService. Requests coming to /simple-greet are handled by SimpleGreetService, and requests coming to /greet are handled by GreedService.

```
private static Routing createRouting(Config config) {
    ...

    Routing.Builder builder = Routing.builder()
        .register("/simple-greet", new
        SimpleGreetService(config))
        .register("/greet",  new GreetService(config));

    return builder.build();
}
```

RESTful Services

User services implement the `Service` interface to manage route mappings and encapsulate handlers in one class. It's done by implementing `update(Routing.Rules)`.

```
public class SimpleGreetService implements Service {        ①
    ...
    @Override
    public void update(Routing.Rules rules) {               ②
        rules.get("/", this::getDefaultMessageHandler);     ③
        ...
    }

    private void getDefaultMessageHandler(ServerRequest
    request,                                                ④
            ServerResponse response) {
        String msg = String.format("%s %s!", greeting,
        "World");
        JsonObject returnObject = JSON.createObjectBuilder()
                                  .add("message", msg)
                                  .build();
        response.send(returnObject);
    }
}
```

   ① `SimpleGreetService` must implement the
      `Service` interface

   ② `update(⋯)` method updates global routing rules

③ Register the `getDefaultMessageHandler()`
method to be called when a GET request comes to
the / path

④ `getDefaultMessageHandler()` returns the default
greeting message

Health Checks

Due to different design concepts, Helidon SE cannot implement
MicroProfile Metrics specifications (see Chapter 4). However, it contains
health check support, which provides the same functionality as Helidon
MP but uses the Helidon SE programming model.

You need to add the `helidon-health` dependency to your Maven
project to use health checks.

```
<dependency>
    <groupId>io.helidon.health</groupId>
    <artifactId>helidon-health</artifactId>
</dependency>
```

You may also add a dependency to the `helidon-health-checks`
module, which contains optional built-in checks such as deadlock
detection, available disk space, and available heap memory.

```
<dependency>
    <groupId>io.helidon.health</groupId>
    <artifactId>helidon-health-checks</artifactId>
</dependency>
```

To use health checks, you need to create the `HealthSupport` class
instance and register the built-in checks and your custom health checks.
The following shows how it's done in the Quickstart application (the
snippet is taken from the `createRouting` method).

```
HealthSupport health = HealthSupport.builder()
    .addLiveness(HealthChecks.healthChecks())
    .build();
```

To expose your service health on the /health endpoint, register your HealthSupport in the web server routings.

```
Routing.Builder builder = Routing.builder()
    .register(health)
    ...
```

Now you can request your service health status using this command.

```
curl http://localhost:8080/health
```

Metrics

Helidon SE provides a way to collect and expose metrics. As with health checks, functionality is very similar to Helidon MP. The difference is that Helidon SE has only programmatic API, which differs from what Helidon MP provides.

You must add the helidon-metrics dependency to your project's pom. xml file to use metrics.

```
<dependency>
    <groupId>io.helidon.metrics</groupId>
    <artifactId>helidon-metrics</artifactId>
</dependency>
```

When added, you can use the MetricRegistry class instance to register the metrics you want to track. Helidon SE supports the same metric types as Helidon MP: counter, concurrent gauge, gauge, histogram, meter, timer, and simple timer.

The Quickstart application contains a sample of using a counter in the SimpleGreetService class.

```
private final MetricRegistry registry = RegistryFactory.
getInstance()
        .getRegistry(MetricRegistry.Type.APPLICATION);
```

```
private final Counter accessCtr = registry.
counter("accessctr");
```

After registering a counter, you can use its inc() method to increase its value. The Quickstart application counts how many requests were received by the /greet-count endpoint. To do it, a chain of request handlers is registered to process this path.

```
public void update(Routing.Rules rules) {
    ...
    rules.get("/greet-count", this::countAccess, this::getDefault
    MessageHandler);
}
```

The handler increases the counter, and calls request.next() to continue processing on the next registered handler.

```
private void countAccess(ServerRequest request, ServerResponse
response) {
    accessCtr.inc();
    request.next();
}
```

To expose your metrics on the /metrics endpoint, create the MetricsSupport class instance and add it to your routes. In the Quickstart application, it's done in the Main.createRouting method.

```
Routing.Builder builder = Routing.builder()
    .register(MetricsSupport.create())
    ...
```

Now users can access metrics data at the following endpoints.

- /metrics/base means base metrics.

- /metrics/vendor means vendor-specific metrics.

- /metrics/application means application metrics. It's where accessctr is located.

Like Helidon MP, users can get metrics data in OpenMetrics and JSON formats. For example, use the following command to get the accessctr metric in OpenMetrics format.

```
curl http://localhost:8080/metrics/application/accessctr
```

You get a response similar to the following.

```
# TYPE application_accessctr_total counter
# HELP application_accessctr_total
application_accessctr_total 42
# EOF
```

To get it in JSON format, add the Accept: application/json header, as follows.

```
curl -H 'Accept: application/json' -X GET http://
localhost:8080/metrics/application/accessctr
```

RESTful API is the same as in Helidon MP. Please refer to Chapter 4 for more details.

Building and Packaging

Build and packaging commands are identical for Helidon SE and Helidon MP applications.

To build your project, use the following Maven command.

```
mvn package
```

To run your application, use the following.

```
java -jar target/myproject.jar
```

You see an output similar to Listing 15-3 if your application has been started successfully and is ready to serve requests. You also see enabled features (Config, Fault Tolerance, Health, Metrics, Tracing, and WebServer).

Listing 15-3. Running Your Project

```
$ java -jar .\target\myproject.jar
2022.12.28 08:42:51 INFO io.helidon.common.LogConfig
Thread[#1,main,5,main]: Logging at initialization configured
using classpath: /logging.properties
2022.12.28 08:42:52 INFO io.helidon.common.HelidonFeatures
Thread[#38,features-thread,5,main]: Helidon SE 3.1.0 features:
[Config, Fault Tolerance, Health, Metrics, Tracing, WebServer]
2022.12.28 08:42:52 INFO io.helidon.webserver.NettyWebServer
Thread[#39,nioEventLoopGroup-2-1,10,main]: Channel '@default'
started: [id: 0x02e402f0, L:/[0:0:0:0:0:0:0:0]:8080]
WEB server is up! http://localhost:8080/greet
```

You can also build a jlink image and a GraalVM native image. The commands are the same as in Helidon MP. See Chapter 2 for a detailed description.

Other Helidon SE Features

The Quickstart application is only a small application demonstrating basic Helidon SE functionality. Helidon SE provides a much more comprehensive set of features not covered in this book. The following lists the complete set of Helidon SE features.

- Reactive Web Server

- RESTful web services

- Configuration

- Security

- Observability: health checks, metrics, tracing, logging

- Fault Tolerance

- gRPC

- WebClient

- DBClient

- Reactive Stream Operators

- Reactive Messaging

- CORS

- GraphQL

- OpenAPI

- WebSockets

- Integrations with OCI, Neo4j, HashiCorp Vault

For more information, please refer to Helidon documentation on the official website at `https://helidon.io`.

Summary

- Helidon SE is a reactive, non-blocking flavor of Helidon.

- Helidon SE programming model differs from the Helidon MP programming model.

- Helidon SE doesn't support dependency injection.

- You must implement the `main` method in your Helidon SE application.

Index

C

Y, Z

Printed in the United States
by Baker & Taylor Publisher Services